FRAGRANT HARBOURS
DISTANT RIVERS

SHAPING OF MODERN AFRICA

J. T. DOWNES. I.S.O

Edited by Jonathan Downes
Cover Photograph taken by Chris Moiser
Cover and internal design by Mark North for CFZ Communications
Using Microsoft Word 2000, Microsoft , Publisher 2000, Adobe Photoshop CS.

First published in Great Britain by CFZ Press

CFZ Press is a division of:

CFZ Communications
15 Holne Court,
Exwick,
Exeter.
EX4 2NA

CFZ PRESS

ISBN: 0-9512872-5-7

For Mary,

Who had heard this story - so many times!

- CONTENTS -

⸗ INTRODUCTION ⸗

This is a little known and even less reported historical account of the extraordinary inter-relationship between - and parallel lives - of the major characters so central in Britain's involvement in both Africa and China. But it is not a dull history book of 19th century Imperial history. In many respects, it reads like a deliberately structured novel of intrigue, romance and adventure. However, these extraordinary actualities were stumbled upon, quite by accident, by the present author who inadvertently followed in the footsteps of one of the characters through Northern Nigeria to Hong Kong. It might even be said that here is one chronicle where truth is indeed stranger than fiction.

Two of the central characters - David Livingstone and Henry Stanley - are already ascribed adventure book status in British culture because of the single claim: *"Doctor Livingstone, I presume?"* But how many know of Stanley's illegitimate birth to a Welsh butcher's daughter, or his adoption by an American cotton broker in New Orleans after he ran away to sea? Who can say they know that Livingstone started life as a humble millworker so inspired by a missionary's reports from China that he decided there and then to qualify as a doctor in order to join him?

Another major character - British Army officer Frederick Lugard - had become suicidal following a disastrous love affair in India. Obtaining indefinite leave, he travelled to East Africa hoping to meet an honourable death and the end to his misery. Instead he created a concrete link between Africa and China already begun by Livingstone and Stanley and completing a connection between the continents that they never managed.

The author discovered strange, if sometimes tenuous, connections between the activities of each character and their individual stories are interwoven throughout the book. The reader is led from China to Africa and back again in a series of incidents and events, echoes of which still resound around the world despite the fact that, for the most part, the world has forgotten or has never known, how it all started.

Briefly, the chronology is as follows. David Livingstone, inspired by reports on the activities of Karl Gutzlaff - a medical missionary in China - also wanted to go there to help. However, the 'Opium Wars' which led to the acquisition of Hong Kong by Britain and to the temporary cessation of missionary endeavour in China resulted in Livingstone travelling reluctantly to Africa instead where he arrived in Cape Town in 1841. In Africa, he gained fame and notoriety as much for his intrepid exploration as for his missionary activities. Whilst still searching for the source of the Nile, he met journalist Henry Stanley who had been searching for him after reporting on the opening of the Suez Canal.

After Livingstone's death, Stanley went back to Africa in an attempt to confirm Livingstone's theories about the River Nile. Whilst in Buganda, he wrote to the British and American press appealing for Christian missionaries to save the country from Islam. Catholic and Protestant missionaries flocked to Buganda and tensions soon grew between their respective supporters. The young Frederick Lugard was sent to sort out the problems caused by Stanley's call for missionaries. War between England and France was only narrowly averted and Lugard returned to England in disgrace, never to return to Buganda. He subsequently went to West Africa eventually becoming High Commissioner of the Protectorate of Northern Nigeria. When he fell out with the Colonial Office, he resigned his post and was sent to Hong Kong as Governor thus completing a circular chain of events which had begun many years earlier with David Livingstone's original desire to spread Christianity to the peoples of China.

Between them, Gutzlaff, Livingstone, Stanley and Lugard altered the shape of Africa and, to some extent, the future of China. If it had not been for Gutzlaff, the Opium Wars might have had a very different outcome and Livingstone might never have become a missionary. Had it not been for Livingstone, Stanley would never have gone to Buganda. Had it not been for Stanley's efforts to bring Christianity to that part of Africa, Lugard would not have become involved and might never have gone on to West Africa or to Hong Kong.........
and the face of Africa might have been very different today.

John Tweedle Downes, I.S.O
(Companion of the Imperial Service Order)
2005

I'll love you, dear, I'll love you
Till China and Africa meet,
And the river jumps over the mountain
And the salmon sing in the street.

W.H.Auden

CHAPTER ONE

But for the events about which I write, Hong Kong might never have become a British Crown Colony, Uganda and Kenya would probably never have existed as we know them today, and the huge country which we call 'Nigeria' - if it had been created at all - would certainly never have been called 'Nigeria'!

Many national boundaries within Africa would have been very different, and even the balance of power in Europe, in Africa, and in the Far East, might have changed, if a Scottish crofter had not been dispossessed of his farm, if a German missionary doctor had not become involved in the drug trade, if a Welsh butcher's daughter had not so willingly surrendered her virginity to a drunken farmer, and if a shy young English army officer had not fallen in love with the wrong sort of woman.

Because these events, and the extraordinary 'knock-on' effect each had on the next, touched - and still touch - the lives of millions of people. I think that the story must be told before the waves of time wash it all away, leaving the world to wonder how it all began.

So how and where did it all begin? Perhaps in the year 1792 on the small island of Ulva off the coast of the Isle of Mull, which itself lies off the wild, wet and windy west coast of Scotland?

Here a number of crofters scratched a meagre living from the unforgiving soil until their landlord, the `Laird`, decided that sheep would be more profitable than the crofters' rents. Since the Act of Parliament which was to give crofters security of tenure was not to become law for another ninety four years, in those days, tenants were entirely at the mercy of their landlord, and this particular Laird, like many others at the time, evicted his crofters, allowed their cottages to fall down, and imported sheep to graze on the remains of their pathetic little fields, which lay amongst the heather, the bracken, and the boulders.

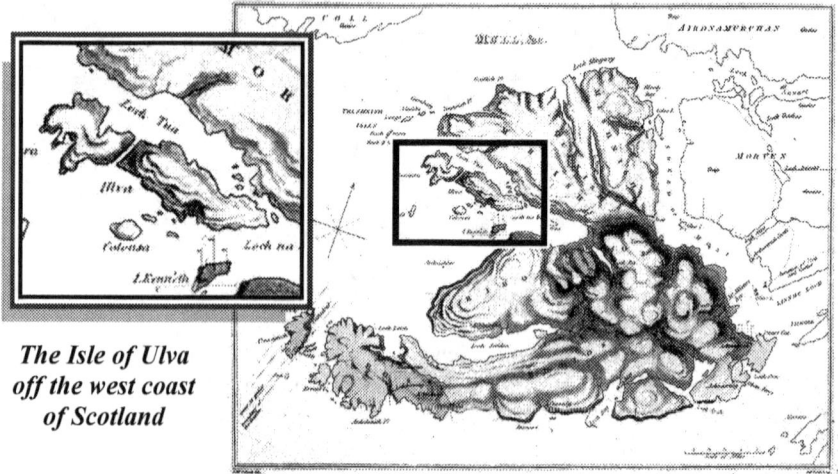

The Isle of Ulva
off the west coast
of Scotland

Some of the crofters emigrated to Canada, but the majority went to the mainland in search of work, despite the fact that Britain itself was in a state of turmoil. The whole nation still reeled from the effects of the 1789 French Revolution, and many in power were shocked, because events in France had been widely welcomed by many political radicals - particularly by those in Scotland who still bitterly resented the 1707 Union with England.

In Britain, there was much talk of revolution, and only a year before the eviction of the crofters from Ulva, Thomas Paine - a journalist who had made his name in America and had helped to inspire the Declaration of Independence - had published a book called *The Rights of Man*. In this he had set out his belief that men had equal rights in nature and therefore equal rights of representation. He claimed that all men had a right to liberty, property, security, and freedom from oppression. He was charged with treason, and fled to France, but his writings caused considerable controversy and, as a result of them, there were riots in a number of places - including Birmingham.

Thomas Paine

Some wealthy Scots were in the forefront of a reform movement, since many had been disenfranchised by the system of electing MPs to the House of Commons in far-off London. Because of this, there were riots in Edinburgh and Glasgow. Crowds in Perth had burnt an effigy of the British Home Secretary, and in Dundee, riots lasted for two weeks before being put down by the army.

It was not an auspicious time for anyone to come to the mainland in search of a living, because in addition to political unrest, there was growing resentment amongst the labouring classes against the increased use of machinery in the weaving industry. In Manchester, weavers had even attacked and burnt down a factory in protest! Nevertheless, the crofter in whom we are interested, found work in the cotton spinning mills, and with his wife and their four-year-old son Neil, settled in a small town some eight miles south-east of Glasgow.

Having been used to hard graft all his life, work in the mills, though not to his liking, represented no particular hardship to the crofter, and he and his wife settled down to their new existence, bringing up their small son Neil on strict Calvinistic principles. The little boy was taught to fear his father and God, (most probably in that order), and was destined to live in an age of tumult and change. Less than a year after the family's arrival on the mainland, revolutionary France declared war on Britain, and British troops moved to capture French colonies in the West Indies and in India.

The war with France rumbled on, and in September 1795, when Neil was just turned seven years old, British troops occupied Capetown in southern Africa where the settlers, mainly Dutch, had declared a 'revolutionary republic' on French lines. All British ships sailing to India had to pass around the Cape of Good Hope, and *had* Capetown fallen into the hands of the enemy, the consequences would have been severe, so Britain had no option but to occupy it.

Neil was nine years old when a young commodore called Nelson defeated a Spanish convoy off Cape St. Vincent, and he was old enough in 1797 to appreciate the triumphs of his fellow countryman, Mungo Park, when he returned to Scotland after having become the first white man to see the great river Niger in West Africa. Neil and his family rejoiced in 1798 at Nelson's victory over the French fleet in Aboukir Bay in Egypt, and it was at about this time that his father, determined that Neil should not follow him into the mills, saved enough money to apprentice him to a local tailor.

He was thus a fourteen year old apprentice tailor in 1802 when Britain and France signed a peace treaty at Amiens, which resulted in many of the overseas territories, including Capetown in southern Africa, being handed back by the British to their former owners. The peace was not to last very long, and in 1803

Napoleon violated the terms of the treaty, and Britain declared war on France. Neil's father, although naturally interested in the outcome of the new war, was far more interested in the activities of a man called Wilberforce, who was pressing for the abolition of the slave trade, for the former crofter was a compassionate man and knew just a little of what it felt like to be a slave.

David Livingstone's birthplace

With the rest of Britain, Neil's family mourned the death of Nelson in 1805 during the Battle of Trafalgar and, as good Christians, rejoiced when, in 1807, the slave trade was made illegal. As the war with France continued Neil worked out his apprenticeship, and fell in love with Mary, the tailor's daughter. When his apprenticeship ended, he married her, gave up tailoring, moved into Glasgow and became a travelling tea salesman. He and his wife did not stay in Glasgow for long and soon returned to the family 'home' where, on 19th March 1813, their second son, David was born.

Neil, who was a strict teetotaller, abhorred novels as things of the devil and never used bad language, was a very good father. He taught his sons to read, bringing them up, as he himself had been brought up, in the manner of a strict Calvinist, telling them that men were either born to be 'saved' or to be 'damned' and that the 'damned' would certainly go to hell. David suspected that he was one of the 'damned' - a feeling that was to stay with him all his life.

In 1819, when David was only six years old, the Factories Act was passed through Parliament restricting working hours of children under the age of sixteen to a mere twelve hours a day! This was regarded as being a revolutionary idea, and a move to extend controls to all working children was opposed by the Upper House in which their Lordships objected to anything that would 'interfere' with the manufacturing industry which was of such importance to Great Britain. At the age of ten, David went to work in the cotton mills as a 'piecer', his task being to 'piece' together threads of cotton as spools became empty. His working day started at six o'clock in the morning, and ended at eight o'clock at night with time off for breakfast and lunch, but when the working day was over, David and some of the other boys went to a night school run by the mill owner, where they studied until ten o'clock.

Most boys then staggered off home to bed, but not so David, who lived with his father and mother in a single room in a three-storey tenement with his six brothers and sisters. He often continued to read by candlelight until well after midnight when his mother had to insist that he got a little sleep. David was not naturally gregarious, and was unpopular with the other boys because he could already read, and instead of sitting with them with their English 'primers', he had already started to learn Latin! He was a very lonely little boy, and wandered off by himself when he could, collecting plants and flowers and bringing them back to the tenement to classify them. This activity did not please Neil who distrusted any form of 'science', until one day he read a book by Doctor Thomas Dick, a Scottish nonconformist minister, who said that interest in science need not conflict with Christian beliefs and thereafter Neil actively encouraged David in his scientific researches. But here we must leave young David for the time being and look at something that was happening on the other side of the world which would affect not only *his* life, but the lives of millions.

CHAPTER TWO

In 1486, Bartolomeu Diaz, a Portuguese mariner in command of three ships, had sailed down the West African coast, and rounded its southernmost cape dominated by a huge mountain whose top was as flat as that of a table. He named it the 'Cape of Storms', but despite the fearful weather, he sailed on to what is now called Algoa Bay. He would have continued northward, up the eastern coast of Africa to see what lay ahead, had his crews not been frightened and threatened mutiny thus forcing him to return to Portugal.

The news of his discoveries excited the rest of Europe, where traders were anxious to find a sea route to the 'Spice Islands', and shortly after his return another Portuguese adventurer, Vasco da Gama, rounded the Cape of Storms and sailed up the east coast of the continent to a land called 'Zinj' - a Persian word meaning the 'land of the Black People'. He found that Arab traders from Oman, and seafarers from India and China, had long been trading there, but da Gama, with typical European arrogance, immediately seized the territory for Portugal before sailing onwards across the Ocean to India where he fell foul of the 'Zamorin', at that time the richest King in the sub-continent. The Zamorin, denied him a foothold, but his arch-rival, the Rajah of Kolatiri, whose territories lay some way to the north, saw the arrival of the Europeans as a means of getting even with the Zamorin so he gave them a trading base. When Vasco da Gama returned to Portugal, Pedro Alvarez Gabral was sent to India to consolidate the position, and obtained continuing permission for Portugal to trade. Gabral could never have dreamed of what would happen as a result of his venture!

The English and Dutch were not prepared to allow Portugal to have a monopoly

Sir Tho.ˢ Stamford Raffles. Knt FRS A.S.

of trade with India, and in 1591 three of Queen Elizabeth's ships, under the overall command of Sir James Lancaster, sailed into the Indian Ocean to compete with the Portuguese and Dutch. Nine years later in 1600 the `Honourable East India Company`, was granted a Royal Charter by the Queen.

In 1602, the Dutch formed a rival Company called the 'Vereenigde Oostindische Compagnie', but the British rapidly established themselves as the principal European power on the Indian coast, leaving the Dutch to concentrate their efforts on the Island of Java.

In 1639 a treaty was signed between the East India Company and the local ruler of the Coromandel Coast, and a trading base was established at Madras called 'Fort St. George'. From here the East India Company sent its ships still further eastwards, and by 1699 it was importing the first tea to Britain from China itself. Company bases were soon established in the Malaysian peninsula at Penang and Malacca, and rivalry between Britain and Holland continued, turning into open hostility when the Dutch allied themselves with Napoleon at the end of the eighteenth century.

In 1805 the East India Company decided to increase its establishment in Penang, and Thomas Stamford Raffles was sent there as an Assistant Secretary. Since the fresh outbreak of war, French Privateers were taking refuge in Dutch controlled harbours and attacking British shipping, so the Governor General of India decided to occupy Batavia on the Island of Java to put a stop to this. Mr

The East India Company flag

Raffles went with the expedition, and after the occupation was left behind in Java as Lieutenant Governor, where, he stayed until 1816.

Raffles returned to England in 1817, where he was duly knighted for his efforts, and in 1818 he urged the Company to establish a base at the southernmost tip of the Malaysian peninsula in order to maintain British trading rights in the region. He recommended the island of Singapore, which had a population of only about one hundred and fifty souls, of whom the majority were Malayan, and only thirty were Chinese. Raffles got his way, and on 6th February 1819 a treaty was signed between the Honourable East India Company and the '...*ruler of Singapore...and all the islands which are under the government of Singapore in his own name and in the name of Sree Sultan Hussein Mahummud Sha, Rajah of Johore.....*'

Within a very short time, Company ships styled 'H.C.S' (Honourable Company Ships), or 'H.C.C' (Honourable Company Cruisers), started calling at Singapore , and the island began to thrive. In June 1819 Raffles wrote:

"...*my new colony thrives most rapidly. We have been established four months, and it has received an accession of population exceeding 5,000 - principally Chinese, and their number is daily increasing......*"

With the Chinese came the Christian missionaries and in the early 1820's, at just about the time when young David was starting work in the mill, a Pomeranian missionary called Karl Gutzlaff started handing out Chinese translations of the Christian Gospel to boat people in Singapore harbour. He was no ordinary missionary. Not only was he a qualified medical doctor, but he was a talented linguist who, whilst in Malaysia, had learned a number of Chinese dialects and could even read and write Chinese characters.

In 1828 he and a fellow missionary left Singapore and went up the coast to Siam taking with them no fewer than twenty-seven crates full of Chinese translations of the scriptures. They were not exactly welcomed in Siam, until Gutzlaff combined his Christian mission with his medical expertise and soon many people came to him to be cured of what Gutzlaff described as:

"...*blindness and the maladies produced by opium smoking...*"

In the light of what was to happen, this was perhaps a trifle ironic.

He left Siam in 1831 and made for Macao, a Portuguese enclave on the southern China coast, where he met William Jardine, a part-

Karl Gutzlaff

Asia in the mid-nineteenth century showing:
A - Singapore, B - Siam, C - Macao.
in relationship to India and mainland China

ner in one of the major trading concerns affiliated to the Honourable East India Company. Jardine explained to Gutzlaff that for many years the balance of trade between China and Britain had been in China's favour because the Emperor distrusted all 'foreign devils' and refused to let them inside to pollute his Kingdom. An attempt had been made in 1793 by the Honourable East India Company to open up the China trade, but it failed. Britain tried again in 1816, but when Lord Amherst refused to 'kowtow' (to kneel three times and to knock his head on the floor as a mark of respect), his mission failed, and trading conditions were made almost impossibly difficult by the Chinese authorities. The only port of access was Canton on the Pearl River.

Then, Jardine explained, the Honourable East India Company had found a solution to the adverse balance of trade. For many years Portugal had been importing opium from India to Macao and from thence to China, and Jardine and others argued, that since there was a demand for it, the East India Company should take over the Portuguese trade. The Company had long had the monopoly of opium growing in India but had begun to note the deleterious effect that the drug was having on addicts there and was looking for a suitable outlet for its produce, even though the Chinese had declared it to be illegal to buy or sell opium. Jardine's justification for this illegal trade was that it was all the Chinese Emperor's fault anyway because, if he would only be reasonable and allow free trade, there would be no need to become involved in drug-running. A specious argument but one which seems to have salved consciences all round.

Jardine persuaded Gutzlaff that although engaged in smuggling opium into China, the company was genuinely interested in missionary work, and Jardine offered him passage on Company ships in exchange for his services as an interpreter. Jardine cannot be accused of subterfuge for when he wrote to Gutzlaff offering him a passage on one of the Company ships, the *Sylph* which was to carry some four thousand pounds worth of legitimate trade goods, he said:

".....as the expense of the voyage cannot be defrayed from this source we have no hesitation in stating to you openly that our principal reliance is on opium. Though it is our earnest wish that you should not in any way injure the grand object you have in view by appearing interested in what by many is considered to be an immoral traffic, yet such traffic is absolutely necessary to give a vessel a reasonable chance of defraying her expenses, that we trust you will have no objection to interpret on every occasion when your services may be requested....."

Jardine added, persuasively,

"....the more profitable the expedition, the better we shall be able to place at your disposal a sum that may hereafter be employed in furthering your mission,

and for your success in which we feel deeply interested....."

After careful consideration and, what Gutzlaff described in a letter to his missionary society as, "*..... conflict in my own mind.....*" , he duly embarked on the *Sylph* and sailed from Macao on 20th October 1832. It was to be a tumultuous voyage and the ship nearly foundered, but, Gutzlaff wrote:

"*...God who dwelleth on high did not forsake us, His Almighty hand upheld our sinking vessel.....*"

and although he never seems to have made direct reference to the illegal part of the cargo, he did say:

Karl Gutzlaff

"*....our commercial relations are at the present moment on such a basis as to warrant a continuation of the trade along the coast. We hope that this may tend ultimately to the introduction of the Gospel, for which many doors are opened.....*"

Gutzlaff seems to have accepted that legitimate trade with China was not possible unless it was financed by the illegal sale of opium, but argued that God Himself must approve of what he was doing, for had He not saved the *Sylph* which was carrying opium in her hold?

Gutzlaff's missionary society published a number of his reports, at least one of which sounded like an extract from the *Acts of the Apostles*, saying that Gutzlaff was:

"*...harrassed by the police, stoned by the mob, hauled before magistrates.....*"

Some of these reports reached Britain and one day in 1834 - the year after slavery had been abolished throughout the British Empire - David's father, Neil, read one of these and passed it on to his son. David was fascinated by what he read and immediately decided, that he would not spend the rest of his life working in the mills but that he too would become a medical missionary and go to help Gutzlaff in his mission to the heathen Chinese.

It was not particularly difficult for him to gain access to a medical school, the only major problem being the question of fees of twelve pounds per session; an enormous sum to find for someone whose total wage was around four shillings (twenty pence) a week. However, with his father's encouragement he saved much of his wages for the next eighteen months, and with the help of his

brother, managed to raise twelve pounds for the first session at Anderson's College in Glasgow in the autumn of 1836. As he had already learned enough Latin at night school, he was able to pursue his studies. Medical knowledge was limited. Chloroform was not yet in use, antiseptics had not been discovered and little was known about the origins of disease. Students learned about the human anatomy by dissecting corpses of executed criminals, or from bodies purchased secretly from grave robbers, but David learned fast. In addition to his medical studies, he attended lectures on Greek and Theology at Glasgow University and obtained an interview with the London Missionary Society on 13th August, 1838. The interviewers were not impressed by what one of them described as his "....heaviness of manner united ....with a rusticity...." and they were inclined to reject him as a candidate for the Ministry. Nevertheless, after careful consideration they decided to 'apprentice' David to a clergyman at Chipping Ongar in Essex, and the Reverend Richard Cecil taught him and six other students - Greek, Hebrew, Latin and Theology.

CHAPTER THREE

In 1834, the year when the Tolpuddle 'martyrs' were deported to Australia for forming a branch of the 'Friendly Society of Agricultural Labourers' and trying to join up with the 'Grand National Consolidated Trades Union', and the year when Britain had no less than four different Prime Ministers - Earl Grey, Lord Melbourne, the Duke of Wellington and finally Sir Robert Peel - Britain's monopoly of trade with China, for so long enjoyed by the Honourable East India Company, came to an end.

With the abolition of this monopoly, the British Government wanted to open up trade with China to all comers, and - without consultation with the Chinese authorities - appointed Lord Napier with the extraordinary title of 'Chief Superintendent of Trade in China'. It was extraordinary because there was little trade in China for him to 'superintend' except that which came to Canton; for the Chinese refused to discuss anything at all, let alone expansion of trade with foreign Governments.

Lord Napier and his staff duly went to Canton, but the Chinese refused to deal with him, and after a very difficult and frustrating time, he fell ill, retired to Macao and died. But trade, both legal and illegal prospered, with British traders buying tea, silk and rhubarb[1], and selling small quantities of trade goods in return, supplemented by huge sales of opium.

His successor made another effort to negotiate with the Chinese Viceroy, but still with no success. Then he retired and was succeeded by Captain Charles Elliot, of the Royal Navy.

---

[1] Much in demand in Britain for medical purposes, but not at that time cultivated outside China.

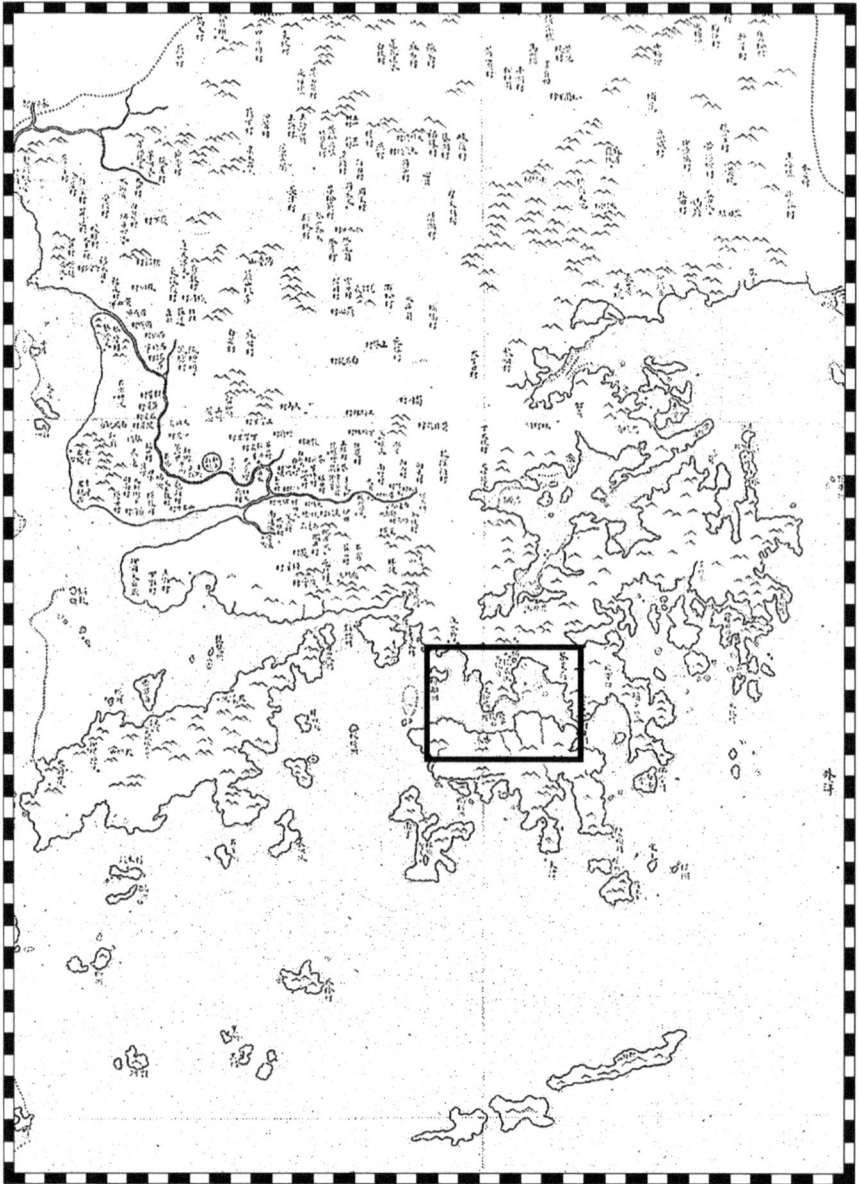

*Chinese map of Hong Kong at the time of the British arrival
(the 'Fragrant Harbour' in the highlighted area)*

In December 1838 the Chinese Emperor issued an edict saying that the illegal opium trade must be stopped, and he appointed a commissioner to go to Canton to stop it. The commissioner arrived in Canton in March 1839 and issued an order, commanding the 'barbarians' to surrender all opium contained in their store ships alongside the wharves at Canton. If, he said, it was not surrendered within three days, it would be removed by force. Merchants tried to bargain their way out of their dilemma offering to surrender one thousand and thirty seven 'chests' of opium (each 'chest' weighing one hundred and fifty pounds), but this was not acceptable, and the Commissioner's order stood.

Captain Elliot was visiting Macao at the time and did not hear of these events until the end of March. When he realised what was happening, he ordered all incoming British ships not to proceed up the Pearl River towards Canton, but to anchor a little way up the coast in a natural harbour between the peninsula of the 'Nine Dragons' and a small island immediately to the south of it; an anchorage which the Chinese called the 'Fragrant Harbour'.

Then Elliot returned to Canton where the Commissioner had forbidden all Chinese servants to go to European households, and had cut off all supplies of food and water to the traders. This was too much for Elliot, and, on 27th March, he decided to order British merchants to surrender all their opium, assuring them that they would be compensated for their loss by the British Government. By now there were no less than twenty thousand, two hundred and eighty three chests of opium (over one thousand, three hundred and fifty tons) in store, and Elliot wrote to the commissioner saying that he would surrender it. The Commissioner agreed, and said that he would permit the resumption of legitimate trade, provided that all British traders signed a bond, promising never again to deal in opium. The Merchants agreed to these terms, some of them with fingers crossed, for they were already planning to open up an alternative trade along the China coast, shipping in opium from Manila.

Elliot then decided to evacuate all British citizens from Canton until he received instructions from London, and he said that all British ships should stay either at Macao or at anchor in the 'Fragrant Harbour' to await developments. Meanwhile some merchants, bypassing Elliot, had written to Lord Palmerston, the British Foreign Secretary, seeking compensation for the loss of their opium and demanding military action against China.

In July 1839 a party of British and American sailors from ships at anchor in the 'Fragrant Harbour' went ashore, got roaring drunk, had a fight with some of the locals and killed one of them. Elliot put the seamen responsible on trial, but there was insufficient evidence and they were acquitted. The Chinese demanded that one man be handed over to them for trial and almost certain execution, but Elliot refused. He then heard that the Chinese were going to Macao to force the

surrender of the seaman, so he ordered all British shipping in Macao to move to the 'Fragrant Harbour', which now contained over fifty ships. As a reprisal, the Chinese stopped all supplies of food and water to ships in the harbour and Elliot was forced to go ashore, to try to obtain supplies, taking the Reverend Doctor Karl Gutzlaff with him as an interpreter. Having tried - without success for six hours, the two men withdrew.

Hong Kong in 1838

HMS Volage then arrived on the scene from India, in response to Elliot's request for assistance. On 5th September 1839 Elliot ordered that the *Volage* should open fire on the Chinese junks in the harbour which were preventing the sale of food and water to the British ships. The Chinese were astonished by this action , and allowed supplies to be delivered.

Elliot restarted negotiations with the Chinese Commissioner and all was going quite well until a British Captain, ignoring Elliot's instructions, sailed up to Canton. His ship was immediately seized by the Chinese, and holding the ship and its crew as hostage, the Commissioner demanded that all British captains should sign a penalty bond promising never again to smuggle opium, on pain of death. Elliot refused to agree and sent *HMS Volage* and *HMS Hyacinth* up river towards Chuenpee, where a fleet of fifteen Chinese war junks and fourteen fireboats awaited them. After a somewhat one-sided battle on 3rd November 1839 the Chinese were defeated.

In February 1840, unaware of what was now going on in China, Palmerston, in response to the traders demands, instructed the Government of India to dispatch sixteen men-of-war, four armed steamers, and four thousand troops to go to Elliot's aid. This fleet, under the command of Elliot's cousin, Rear Admiral the Hon. George Elliot, arrived in the 'Fragrant Harbour' at the end of June 1840 and sailed up the Chinese coast where Admiral Elliot, under a flag of truce, tried to deliver a letter to the Emperor. The Chinese, who knew nothing of European conventions concerning flags of truce, refused to allow the Admiral's men ashore, so he took his fleet further north to Chusan island and placed it under British administration, giving the Reverend Doctor Karl Gutzlaff the post of Resident Magistrate.

Palmerston's letter was finally delivered to the Emperor who sent his 'Grand-Secretary', Qishan (Ke-shen) to negotiate with the Admiral. Sadly the Admiral fell ill, retired to England, and left his cousin, Captain Elliot in charge. Negotiations failed and Captain Elliot, again resorted to force and occupied two Chinese forts on the Pearl river. After an engagement in which five hundred Chinese were killed and a great many wounded, Qishan gave in. In January 1841 he entered into an agreement known to history as the 'Convention of Chuenpi', the agreement involving the cession to Britain of the island to the south of the peninsula of the 'Nine Dragons'. A Naval landing party formally occupied the island on 26th January 1841 where they raised the British flag. In June, Elliot began to sell plots of land on the island to interested merchants. The Cantonese words for 'Fragrant Harbour' are romanised as 'Heung Kong' but the British, unable to pronounce this outlandish phrase, called it 'Hong Kong'.

Neither Palmerston nor the Chinese Emperor accepted the terms of the Chuenpi agreement. Palmerston was furious with Elliot who was dismissed and replaced by Sir Henry Pottinger. Hostilities recommenced. A year later the war ended with the Treaty of Nanking, signed on 29th August 1842, under which the island, now called 'Hong Kong' was ceded to Britain in perpetuity and five more ports on the Chinese coast were opened to international trade. The Chinese were also required to pay full compensation for the opium which had been handed over to them by Captain Elliot and that was the end of the opium wars. The new British base at Hong Kong became the springboard for Christian missionary endeavour in China, and no further missionaries were sent directly from London. David Livingstone's dream of working in China with Gutzlaff, was shattered!

Robert Moffat

Because of these events, David was told that he would either be sent to the West Indies, to the South Seas or perhaps to southern Africa. He was bitterly disappointed until he met Robert Moffat, a gardener turned missionary who had made a name for himself in southern Africa, not only by establishing a mission at a place called Kuruman but having also made contact, and become friends with the dreaded

Mzilikazi, king of the Matabele. David was impressed by Moffat and decided that if he couldn't go to China to work with Gutzlaff, then he would go to southern Africa and work with Robert Moffat.

He continued his medical studies at the British and Foreign medical school at Charing Cross before returning to Scotland, where he took, and passed, the relevant examinations qualifying as a Doctor with a licence from the Faculty of Physicians and Surgeons (Glasgow).

In June 1840, he attended a public meeting of the 'Society for the Extinction of the Slave Trade and the Civilisation of Africa' in London. The meeting, which was also attended by the recently married Prince Albert, was told that Africans could only be saved from the internal slave trade, if they could be shown how to raise money for trade goods by selling surplus produce instead of selling their unwanted brothers, sisters and children. Only a combination of 'Commerce and Christianity' could rid Africa of the scourge of slavery and David was forcibly reminded of Karl Gutzlaff's approach to evangelism via trade on the China coast. He was now determined to go to Africa.

He was ordained as a Minister of the Church on 20th November 1840, and thereby became Doctor the Reverend David Livingstone; a man whose name will long be connected with the African Continent, and who was to inspire millions. He sailed for southern Africa on the 8th December 1840.

His great adventure had begun.

CHAPTER FOUR

W hen David Livingstone first went to Africa some one hundred and fifty years ago, the majority of African countries which we take for granted today, simply did not exist. To many people in Britain in 1840, with the possible exception of Egypt and the Mediterranean coast of North Africa, Africa was still very much a *terra incognita*. Indeed, it was still often called the 'Dark Continent' and was popularly believed to be inhabited solely by naked savages and strange beasts.

The northern coastline didn't come into this category of course, because this was seen as being the southern 'fringe' of European civilisation only separated from the rest of Europe by the Mediterranean Sea. There was some justification for this view. The territory now known as Morocco had been part of the Roman province of Mauretania, Algeria too had been a Roman province, and Tunisia had been the administrative 'capital' of Roman North Africa. Libya, also once part of the Roman Empire, had come under Turkish domination in the 16th Century and Egypt had a history which was better known to many European scholars than the history of Europe itself, but little was known of the rest of the continent. In order to put this story into its historical perspective, it is necessary record what was - and what was not - known about Africa in 1840.

Egypt was part of the Ottoman Empire, and, in theory, was governed by a Turkish Viceroy but in practice - until 1805 - the real power had rested in the hands of the 'Mamelukes'. (This name, which means 'male slave', referred to young boys, purchased by the Turks from families in Southern Russia. These children were converted to Islam, and on reaching manhood had been imported into Egypt to help the Turks maintain control over the native Egyptians). Mamelukes were not permitted by their Turkish 'masters', to marry, and as a result many became homosexuals, and over the years. Homosexuality had become one of their 'hallmarks'. Gradually they had become more powerful than the Turks and by the end of the 18th Century, there were some one hundred thousand of them in Egypt, many living in great state in Cairo.

Egypt had long been seen as the 'gateway' to the 'East', and the shortest route to India was via the Mediterranean and across the Sinai Peninsula, to the Red Sea.

The Napoleonic Campaign in Egypt

In 1798, after Britain had captured Cape Colony in order to keep it out of his hands, Napoleon had invaded Egypt.

Although Nelson had defeated the French fleet in the Battle of the Nile, and had effectively cut off communications between the French expeditionary force and mainland France, Napoleon had personally stayed in Egypt until August 1799, when he returned to France, leaving one of his Generals in charge.

In March 1801, a combined Anglo-Turkish force had landed at Alexandria and the last French troops had been driven out of Egypt by the end of that year. Britain had then remained in nominal control until 1803 when she withdrew her troops. War broke out between the Mamelukes and the Turks, and arising from this turmoil, a Turk - Mohammed Ali - had raised a 'private army' of ten thousand Albanians, and had overthrown the Turkish Governor, and established himself as 'Pasha'.

In 1807, Turkey had become an ally of France, and Britain - intending to rally surviving Mamelukes against the Turks - had invaded Egypt. Sadly, the British had been savagely defeated; one thousand were killed or captured and the heads of four hundred and fifty dead British troops were stuck on poles and exhibited in central Cairo. The surviving British forces sailed away, leaving Mohammed Ali in control. In March 1811, he called all surviving Mamelukes to a celebration, and having invited them to ride in a procession, blocked off their route and slaughtered them all. This was the end of Mameluke power, and, when Livingstone sailed for Capetown, Mohammed Ali was still in control of Egypt.

In western Africa, the first recorded English trading voyage was in 1530 when William Hawkins went there, *en route* for Brazil and brought back a profitable cargo of ivory from Africa. His venture was followed in 1540 by some merchants from Southampton. In 1553 a syndicate of London merchants which had been trading along the Barbary Coast extended their operations to the 'Guinea Coast'[1] of west Africa where the Portuguese, who had traded there for some time, claimed a monopoly and English shipping was not welcomed.

When Queen Elizabeth came to the throne in 1558, although forbidding English ships to visit territory physically occupied by the Portuguese, she personally financed some ships for trading expeditions to western Africa on her behalf. Gold and ivory had been the principal commodities traded until 1562, when William Hawkins' son John discovered that negro slaves shipped across the Atlantic to America by the Spanish and Portuguese were much in demand, and as a result he carried out the first slave raid led by an Englishman.

By 1569, Queen Elizabeth was pursuing a policy of friendship towards Portugal, and she forbade any further trading on the Guinea Coast by English ships and trade of all kinds stopped for some years. However, in 1580, Portugal came under Spanish rule, and Elizabeth's attitude changed. She was openly hostile to

---

[1] The North African coast from Egypt to the Atlantic, named after its principal inhabitants - the Berbers. The coast of West Africa from the Gambia River to Cape Lopez in Gabon. The word "Guinea" was originally coined by the Portuguese from the Moroccan Berber's word Akal n-Iguinawen meaning "land of the Negros".

Spain, and no longer objected to reviving trade on the Guinea Coast. In 1588 some West Country merchants were granted a patent which gave them a ten year monopoly of trade between Senegal and the Gambia river, leaving the coast south of the Gambia open to all-comers.

Merchant adventurers from London went as far south as Benin, where they bought pepper, ivory and palm oil, from the local chieftains. Then in 1618 some other London merchants were granted a charter by the Crown in the cumbersome name of 'The Governor and Company of Adventurers of London trading into the ports of Africa', but this company was not successful, and petered out during the Commonwealth.

At about the same time, a Sir Nicholas Crispe built what is claimed to have been the first permanent English foothold in west Africa - a 'fort' on what came to be called the Gold Coast (now Ghana), and in 1631 the Crown gave him and his partners a monopoly of trade on the west coast of Africa, prohibiting any other English trader from importing west African produce into England.

The company's monopoly was renewed in 1651, but its finances deteriorated, and in 1657 it sold the remaining grant of this monopoly to the East India Company, which was glad to have stopping-off ports on the west coast of Africa for their ships bound to and from India.

The grandson of King James I, known as Prince Rupert of the Rhine had fought bravely for the Royalist cause during the Civil War, but after King Charles I had surrendered, Rupert had been banished from England. Soon after the restoration of the Monarchy in 1660, he had returned to England, and turned his interests from war to trade.

Although he was later to play an important role in the war at sea against the Dutch, the Prince became interested in the possibility of gold mining in western Africa. He readily obtained a Royal Charter, and founded the 'Company of Royal Adventures into Africa'. This company surrendered its charter in 1663, and a fresh charter was issued by the Crown to 'The Company of Royal Adventurers of England Trading into Africa'. These Royal Adventurers were granted a monopoly for buying and selling slaves and merchandise in West Africa, and took over the forts on the Gold Coast.

Here the Adventurers found themselves in competition with the Dutch, but they also had difficulty in getting paid for slaves shipped to the West Indies where sugar prices had slumped. In 1667 they abandoned direct trading either in slaves or in merchandise, and concentrated on issuing licences to individual traders on the west coast. By the end of the 1660's the company had been wound up and a fresh charter was issued to yet another company, this one with the more reason-

able name of 'The Royal African Company of England' which, despite many financial difficulties, continued to trade until 1752 when it was dissolved.

In 1772 after a law case had been brought against a British slave-owner who had recaptured a runaway slave in England, the Lord Chief Justice ruled that the slave be released, and, as a result, some fourteen thousand negro slaves in England were immediately given their freedom. This gave rise to problems and many former slaves were destitute. In 1783 it was proposed that such destitute former slaves from Britain and former slaves who had fought for the British during the American War of Independence should be returned to west Africa and a plan for a settlement at Sierra Leone was prepared. The 'Sierra Leone Company' received a charter from the Crown, and, despite many difficulties, which included attacks by the French and raids by neighbouring hostile tribes the Company maintained the settlement until 1st January 1808 when Sierra Leone became a Crown Colony.

In addition to these British trading and slaving activities the Portuguese and Dutch also had bases at points along the west African coast, but the interior of western Africa remained unknown until 1795, when Livingstone's fellow Scot, Mungo Park, visited 'Hausaland' in the north of what is now known as 'Nigeria', and reached the great Niger river. In 1840 it was not yet known that the huge and powerful empires of Ghana, Songhay, and Kanem Bornu, had been flourishing in western Africa long before the Norman Conquest of Britain, or that for almost a thousand years - unknown to Britain - Muslim pilgrims from west Africa had been crossing the continent to go to Mecca!

Mr. M. Park.

In the 1820's Clapperton, Oudney, and Denham had crossed the Sahara, reached the kingdom of Kanem-Bornu, and had seen for the first time the huge Lake Chad which they believed must be the vast 'sink' into which the River Niger flowed. It was only ten years before Livingstone sailed for Africa, that Lander had discovered that the Niger did, after all, run into the sea. Even as Livingstone's ship was on its way down the coast, the lower reaches of the Niger were still being explored.

Arab traders and others had long known about the land of Zinj on the east coast of Africa.

The Portuguese had started to build 'Fort Jesus' in 1593, but they had been driven out by the Omanis in 1729, and Zinj had been governed on behalf of Oman by a powerful family called the 'Mazuri', who, rather like the Mamelukes in Egypt, had become more powerful than their masters in Oman.

In 1799, Napoleon tried to get a message to the Omanis telling them that, after he had control of Egypt, the French would 'protect' Oman and her overseas territories - including Zinj - from the `wicked and rapacious` British. But British Government agents had somehow intercepted this message, and had passed it to the Governor General of India, (who was responsible for British activities in the Indian Ocean area). The Governor General responded by inviting the Omanis to sign a treaty with Britain, who would undertake to protect them from the `wicked and rapacious` French!

The Omanis agreed, and Zinj had thus come within the British sphere of influence. Despite this, slaving had continued, and, when Livingstone was on his way to Capetown in 1840, the number of African slaves bought and sold in Zanzibar - all having been captured, or purchased, in the interior of Africa by the Arabs - was estimated to be between forty thousand and forty-five thousand annually.

At the southern end of the continent, the Dutch East India Company had established a foothold at the Cape of Good Hope in 1602 with the intention of growing fruit and vegetables to supply ships going to and from Java. When Louis XIV of France revoked the Treaty of Nantes in 1685, many French Huguenot families had fled to Protestant Holland, and many went to the Cape of Good Hope where they started to colonise and create a new nation of 'Afrikaners'. By the 1720's these people, many known by then as the 'Boers' (the Dutch word for 'farmer'), had begun to move inland to escape from the control of the `Dutch East India Company` which ruled the small colony from far away Holland. In 1776 on the banks of the 'Fish' river, the Boers had encountered black peoples of the Xhosa tribe; people of Bantu origin who had been slowly moving southward for many generations in search of fresh grazing for their cattle.

In 1795, Britain had occupied Cape Colony to stop it from falling into the hands of the French, and British missionaries had hurried to get there to save the souls of its native inhabitants from falling into the hands of the devil. By 1811, some missionaries had initiated legal action against certain Boers for their maltreatment of non-whites, and, as a result, missionaries were generally unpopular. In 1814, Cape Colony had become a British possession, and Britain 'inherited' a large number of rebellious and difficult colonial 'citizens',who had long wanted independence from their masters in Holland, and felt no better about their new masters in Britain.

In 1816, in what is now called 'Natal', but then well outside the sphere of British influence, an extraordinary man called Shaka had become King of the small and relatively unknown Zulu clan, and had set about absorbing all neighbouring clans into what had rapidly become known as the 'Zulu Nation'.

Shaka Zulu

One of Shaka's 'generals', called Mzilikase, had rebelled against Shaka and had moved northward into what is now called the 'Transvaal', and from there into what is now modern Zimbabwe. Here he had created the Matabele nation which soon came into conflict with the indigenous Mashona tribe.

In 1828 Shaka had been killed by his two half-brothers, Mhlangana, and Dingane. Then Dingane had killed Mhlangana and had become King of the now large Zulu nation. In the same year, Britain resolved that all citizens of Cape Colony should have the same freedoms and protection - what we should call today 'civic rights' - a concept which horrified and puzzled the 'Boers' who had always regarded non-whites as being 'inferior' in the eyes of God.

Boers from Cape Colony began to move northwards in search of freedom from the British, and when in 1833, only seven years before Livingstone sailed for Capetown, slavery became illegal throughout the British Empire, more and more Boers moved north away from Cape Colony to escape British jurisdiction.

In 1837, one hundred and twenty Boers and their families reached the borders of Dingane's kingdom, and one of their leaders called Piet Retief tried to negotiate with the King for permission to settle there. On February 4th 1838, Dingane had put his mark on a document giving the Boers rights to settle, but he killed Retief, and his warriors went on the rampage killing forty one Boer farmers, together with fifty six of their women, and one hundred and eighty five of their children, who were waiting for Piet's return.

The surviving Boers had been rallied by Andries Pretorius, and on December 9th 1838, the Boers promised God that if they won a battle with the Zulus, they would build Him a church and evermore remember the day. They were attacked by twelve thousand Zulus, of whom three thousand were slaughtered without a single Boer casualty, and this encounter, which is still remembered, came to be known as the 'Battle of Blood River'.

After their victory the Boers found Retief's remains and in his pocket the document signed by Dingane which gave them rights to settle on the fringe of Zululand. Soon they were joined by other northward trekking Boers and they founded a Republic which they called 'Free Province of New Holland in South East Africa', and named its capital town 'Pietermaritzburg'.

In broad terms, most of the rest of Africa was virtually unknown when Doctor the Reverend David Livingstone landed at Capetown in 1841.

CHAPTER FIVE

The year when David Livingstone finished his medical and theological training saw a number of other events, including the conception of the second main character in this story.

In February 1840, the young Queen Victoria who had come to the throne only three years previously, was married to Albert of Saxe-Coburg-Gotha, and in May the world's first adhesive post-age stamp, the 'Penny Black' bearing a picture of the young Queen's head, had been introduced. Industrialisation was boom-ing, and railways were spreading out across the land; metal arter-ies of trade giving rise to much urban development.

The Penny Black

In South Wales in particular, there was a near total transformation. Steam had come to the foundries and coke ovens, and pig-iron production had more than doubled in some cases. Steam was also being used to pump flood water from the mines, and coal exports from the new heavy duty loading dock in Cardiff were growing rapidly as the demand for coal for the railways and industry grew.

A new rail link between Cardiff and Merthyr Tydfil was being planned, al-though there had been industrial unrest. Troops in Newport had even fired on workers as they marched in protest against the arrest of one of the leaders of a movement which demanded better conditions for the labouring classes, but the economy continued to boom, turning Welsh valleys, once so green, into black and forlorn eyesores.

It was a different story in rural North Wales, where the pace of life was much the same as it had been for generations, but there, as everywhere else, there was a drift of population from the countryside to the growing industrial towns of northern England and southern Wales. As a result, in Denbeigh, a sleepy little town not far inside the Welsh border with England, and only about sixteen miles from Chester, Butcher - Moses Parry - had lost many of his customers and no longer had a thriving shop. Now he was forced to live in the upstairs rooms of a cottage occupied by one of his sons, and he spent much of his time worrying about the behaviour of his daughter - Elizabeth - whose morals were not all that they should have been. Sadly, neither he nor his neighbours could claim to have been particularly surprised when, in the spring of 1841, she had given birth to an illegitimate baby boy.

Nobody, least of all Elizabeth, seemed to know which of her many admirers was the father, until a farmer by name of John Rowlands from the village of Llan-rhaidr, about three miles down the road, got drunk one night and claimed that the child was his. The neighbours were not so sure and it was rumoured that the real father was a highly respectable local solicitor called James Vaughn Horne, who also lived in Llanrhaidr. When Emma, the second of Elizabeth's string of four illegitimate babies - was born, eyebrows were again raised, and tongues began to wag, when yet another farmer, John Evans, also from Llanrhaidr, claimed responsibility. (Maybe both men were bribed to cover up on behalf of the solicitor - the world will never know).

Whatever the truth of the matter, Elizabeth's first baby was named 'John', and christened at St Hilary's Church in Denbeigh when he was given the drunken farmer's surname of 'Rowlands'. This seemingly unimportant little drama took place as David Livingstone's ship the 'George' sailed slowly towards Capetown; a voyage which took three months to complete, and, if anyone at the time had suggested to him that these events in far off Denbeigh would have been of the slightest interest to him, he would surely have thought them mad!

During the long voyage, David had persuaded the Captain to teach him how to use a quadrant - a forerunner of the sextant - and to fix his position from the stars and by the time the 'George' arrived at Capetown on 15th March 1841 he was a moderately efficient astral navigator. The twenty-eight year old mission-ary doctor stayed in Capetown for a few weeks before following in the wake of Bartolomeu Diaz; sailing on to Alagoa Bay where he hired a wagon and a 'span' of oxen for the long journey to Moffat's mission station at Kuruman (between Upington and Vryburg in the Transvaal). David was in no hurry. It was good to be on dry land after so many months at sea; good to be away from the hustle and bustle of industrial Britain and - best of all - it was good, for the first time in years, not to be under the pressure of medical and religious studies. He was still interested in botany, and he delighted in the strange plants and trees which grew along the way.

Map of the Transvaal showing the location of
Moffat's station at Kuruman

He was fascinated also by the African landscape with it's strange flat-topped hills, which in the Afrikaans language were called 'Kopjes', and by the vast herds of antelope and the other wild animals which he saw daily, roaming without restraint across the sunbaked land.

The average day's - journey with a team of oxen - was less than ten miles - since the animals had to be allowed to graze during daylight hours. This meant that David did not reach Kuruman until the end of July 1841, but when at last he got there, he was astonished! Moffat had led him to believe that Kuruman was a thriving mission, but he found that it was in reality only the equivalent of a small village containing less than forty nominally 'Christian' - natives. David was astonished and disappointed. How, he asked himself, could such a famous missionary as Moffat have achieved so little in over twenty years endeavour? He was soon to find out!

It appeared that nobody at Kuruman knew anything about David, still less about what plans Moffat had for him, and nobody at the station was prepared to take any decisions on his future, until Moffat returned from England.

Livingstone was given lodgings in the house of Rogers Edwards, an artisan missioner, and had only been at Kuruman for about a month when Edwards was given permission to make a journey of several hundred miles to the north to look for a suitable site for a satellite mission station. Edwards asked David if he would like to accompany him. The young doctor readily agreed, and the two men - accompanied by a few native servants - were away from Kuruman from September to December 1841.

They returned to Kuruman without having achieved much. Robert Moffat had still not returned, and David was still unemployed, so the following spring he decided to go off again - this time by himself - deliberately cutting himself off from his fellow missionaries, in order - he claimed - to concentrate on learning the native language. In fact, he had never been very happy in the company of others, and he simply wanted to be alone. He also enjoyed being away from the restraints of the mission at Kuruman, and he found that although he was ill-at-ease with his fellow white men, he could rapidly establish a rapport with the natives. As he became fluent in their language, he began to realise that orthodox Christian teachings and Victorian morality could be a threat to the social pattern of their lives. He - like most other missionaries - had considerable difficulty in explaining the benefits of industrial 'civilisation' to peoples who had never even seen a European-type house or a factory, who could not begin to envisage a steam engine or a railway train, and to whom in any case, 'work' was a woman's activity and not something to be undertaken by a warrior.

He soon discovered that there were no words in their language which he could

use to describe what he wanted to talk about, and his problems were not there-fore confined to preaching the Gospel - which in all conscience was difficult enough - but in preaching the allied concept of legitimate forms of trade which were, he hoped, to replace the sale of brothers, sisters, parents, and unwanted children, to the highest bidding slave trader as a means of economic prosperity. Nevertheless, he became sympathetic towards un-converted natives and did not automatically condemn their age old customs and - what his fellow missionaries would call - their 'heathen' practices. His understanding and affection for the native peoples of Africa grew, and was to last for the rest of his life.

His unorthodox attitudes towards native law and custom made him unpopular with his fellow missionaries, and - when he started to write critical letters to the London Missionary Society about them this did not increase his popularity. He went, again alone, off into the bush to escape his fellow whites, and eventually found what he considered to be an admirable site for a new mission station at a village known as Mabotsa, but when he returned to Kuruman, he was told that he could not start building without Moffat's specific approval. This was not good enough for the impetuous doctor who decided to ignore this instruction, and go ahead and start building anyway. He somehow persuaded Edwards to go with him, and together they started to build a hut, and to lay down a watercourse for the future mission.

After three months of hard work, they heard that - at last - Moffat was back in Africa, and was even then on his way to Kuruman. This meant that the day of reckoning was at hand, and Edwards was clearly alarmed at the prospect of hav-ing to confess to Moffat. Not so David! He went to meet Moffat and rode south of the Vaal river (south east of Kuruman) to intercept him, and when they met, it seems that they talked and talked and that somehow Moffat was persuaded to give his retrospective blessing on the new outpost.

When David was still in England he had declared that he would only marry if his usefulness as a missionary would be *'augmented by getting a wife'*. In prac-tice, however, in the loneliness of the African bush he had discovered that, mis-sionary activities apart, he needed companionship, so he decided to marry one of Moffat's two daughters. Neither was good looking but they were both good girls, used to the rigours of bush life, and well aware of the difficulties and re-sponsibilities of a missionary's wife. David had no particular preference for ei-ther, but was determined to marry one of them on his next visit to Kuruman.

His next visit was to be considerably delayed however, because one day when he was working on the new watercourse for the mission, some natives came to him and begged him to hunt and kill a lion which had been attacking their sheep. David, who was terrified of snakes, but not a bit afraid of lions, took a double-barrelled gun, found the lion, fired both barrels at it, but failed to kill it.

The lion, maddened by pain turned on David and grabbed him by the left arm and shook him - as he reported later - *"...as a terrier dog does a rat...".*

Mebalwe, an elderly native teacher, one of Moffat's earliest converts who had gone to Mabotsa to help Livingstone, hurried to load another gun, but it misfired, which was just as well since he was more likely to have killed the doctor than the lion! Nevertheless the sound of the misfire distracted the lion which dropped Livingstone and turned on Mebalwe and badly mauled him. A second native who tried to rescue David was also badly bitten and mauled, but before the beast could do any more damage, suddenly it dropped dead; presumably from the wounds originally inflicted by David's gun.

"As a terrier dog does a rat"

The missionary's injuries were frightful. His left arm was shattered, and he had to supervise the setting of the bones - this done, of course, without any anaesthetic - and he must have been in dreadful pain. The wounds suppurated for many months, but gradually he recovered, and by July 1844 returned to Kuruman where he was nursed back to health by Mary Moffat. Having recovered sufficiently, he asked Mary to marry him, but although she accepted the proposal, the wedding did not take place until January 1845. He and his wife then spent two months at Kuruman before returning to Livingstone's new mission site at Mabotsa.

While they were at Mabotsa, David met William Cotton Oswell, a big-game hunter, who chanced to call at the mission one day. Oswell, who had been educated at the famous public school Rugby, and the army public school Haileybury, had entered the Indian Civil Service, but had retired after only ten years to travel and hunt big-game. Coming from a very different class of society, he was an unlikely companion for Livingstone, the mill boy turned missionary doctor. But he was a kindly soul without any personal ambition, and if he had any views on any subject, he was too well bred and polite to allow them to conflict with those of his host. The two men took a liking to each other, and discussed what might lie beyond the far horizon.

The Livingstones were not happy at Mabotsa, because Edwards claimed that Mary was her father's 'spy'. Using as an excuse that they were moving to avoid further unpleasantness, David and Mary packed up and went to live in Chonuane, forty miles to the north of Mabotsa the home of Sechele, Chief of half of the Bakwain tribe. The Sechele had already told Livingstone that he would be welcome, so they moved first, and asked permission from Moffat later. This Chief responded to Livingstone's teaching, showed a facility for learning and soon could read and write and eventually becoming Livingstone's one and only convert. It was at Chonuane, early in 1846, that their first baby was born. They called him 'Robert', and Mary Livingstone acquired a new name. She was now known to all the natives as 'MaRobert'.

Mebalwe, who had saved his life when he was being mauled by the lion, had gone with him together with another of Moffat's early converts, appropriately called 'Paul'. Livingstone had some thoughts of sending these two men off into the surrounding villages and kraals to preach the gospel by themselves, but the Boers who had settled in farms in the area indicated only too clearly that they didn't want natives entering their territory preaching the Christian message of 'equality' to their native African staff. This was not so much a question of religion but of politics because the Boers, who had trekked north to escape from the rules of the British Colony at the cape - the hated *'roineks'* (rednecks; British) - feared that Livingstone's native assistant teachers would report adversely on the Boers' treatment of natives, that Livingstone would in turn report to the governor of Cape Colony and that the British might use this as an excuse of trying to incorporate the Boers' land into the British colony.

Livingstone was soon brought to realise that the use of native convert teachers was never going to be acceptable in 'Boer country' but he took Paul with him when he ventured into unknown territory. In 1847 the springs around Chonuane began to dry up as a result of a prolonged drought, and Livingstone decided to move yet again, this time to Kolobeng, forty miles to the north west of Chonuane. Their second child, Agnes, was three months old when the family left for their new home, but despite this move to fresh country, Livingstone was restless, and late in 1847 he wrote to Oswell to persuade him to come with him to find a lake which the natives called 'Ngami'. There was no reply.

Mary Livingstone neé Moffat

CHAPTER SIX

I n Wales - at about the same time as the Livingstone family was moving to Kolobeng - the four-year old John Rowlands was sent to a small school which was held in the crypt of the church in which he had been christened. He continued to live with his grandfather. Elizabeth, by now the mother of another bastard child, wanted nothing to do with him - and when old Moses died, John was boarded out with relatives until February 1847, when he was sent to the workhouse at St. Asaph; a village some six miles north of Denbeigh. The Government of the day had created a 'Poor Law Board' to supervise the activities of local 'Boards of Guardians' which had come in for much criticism for the way they ran their institutions for the poor, and perhaps John's relatives hoped that conditions in workhouses would soon improve. Despite the new Board, conditions and discipline in the workhouse were harsh, and John, not the easiest or most amenable of children, was frequently flogged by the workhouse 'Master'.

His childhood was thus unhappy. He never received love or affection from anyone and he had to learn to defend himself against all-comers, and this background affected him for the rest of his remarkable life.

Early in 1849, Livingstone at last received a reply from Oswell. He explained that he had not answered earlier because he had been in India, but that he and a friend, Mungo Murray - would come to Kolobeng by the end of May, and together they would go with Livingstone to help him find the mysterious lake. This timing suited Livingstone very well, because Mary was expecting her third baby in March and it would have been delivered before Oswell arrived.

Oswell brought with him twenty horses, eighty oxen, and two wagons, with

enough supplies to keep the expedition going for a year, so Livingstone sent his wife and three children to Kuruman to await his return. He left Kolobeng on the 1st June with Oswell and Murray and J.H. Wilson - a trader from Kuruman - who was interested in the ivory trade.

Five weeks later they reached the river Zouga. They and followed it north-wards, finding that another river (the Thamalakane, a tributary of the Okavango), flowed into the Zouga, suggesting that perhaps the land to the north of the lake might contain a major river network. When eventually they reached the lake, they were disappointed because it was very shallow, surrounded by swamps and was not above seventy miles long (it will be found on the map to the south of the Okovango swamps in the north west of the territory now called 'Botswana').

Livingstone wanted to cross the river Zouga and go further north to see what lay beyond, but the local chief refused permission because he suspected that if the white men got over the Zouga, they would march on and reach the land of the Makololo people, whose chief, Sebitoane, would take revenge on him for allowing the foreigners into his territory.

Reluctantly, Livingstone returned to Kolobeng from whence he wrote to the Missionary Society about 'his' discovery. (He insisted that it was he who had discovered the lake, and implied that Oswell and the others would never have reached Ngami without his assistance.) He claimed that he had to return to Ngami, to cross the Zouga, and find the river network which - he was convinced, lay beyond and said that there was a possibility of a 'highway' which could be traversed by boats, which could be used to 'plant the seed' of the Gospel where others had not planted. In the meantime, Oswell went to Capetown to buy a collapsible boat in which they could cross the Zouga without seeking permission of the Ngami people.

The Foreign Secretary of the Society decided that Livingstone's 'discovery' of Lake Ngami should be given publicity; for the Victorian public loved to read about geographical explorations particularly if they were made in the name of religion. Therefore, although the Society had no intention of establishing further mission stations in the area explored by Livingstone, it decided that his 'discovery' - if given the right publicity - might attract subscriptions which would help finance their more orthodox missionary work elsewhere. As a result, the account of the journey to Lake Ngami was published in the missionary magazine in March 1850, and the Royal Geographical Society awarded Livingstone the sum of twenty-five pounds, which the Missionary Society collected and pocketed on his behalf!

Livingstone didn't wait for Oswell to return but set off again in April 1850, tak-

Victoria Falls and Lake Nyami

ing his wife - who was five months pregnant - and his three children with him. Robert was aged four, Agnes was three, and Thomas barely a year old.

They got to the river Zouga without any trouble, but here their oxen were bitten by tsetse fly and they began to die. Then the children got malaria (and it must be remembered that it was not until 1898 that the connection between malaria and mosquitoes was established - until then it was thought that the fever came from breathing 'bad air' [Italian: *mala aria*] from swampy ground). However, it was known that quinine was an effective remedy for it and Livingstone was able to treat the children. But despite this they suffered terribly, and Livingstone was forced to turn back on his tracks, and head for home. They were back at Kolobeng by mid-August, and a week later Mary gave birth to her fourth baby, which fell ill and soon died. Livingstone briefly recorded this sad event in his journal, saying that one of their number was now in heaven!

Mary was also ill - with half of her face paralysed - and her mother insisted that the entire family went back to Kuruman to recuperate. They were there from November 1850 until the following February. Despite these misfortunes, eight months later, in April 1851, (with Mary yet again pregnant), the whole family set out northwards, travelling along the Zouga river to avoid the unhelpful natives on the shores of Lake Ngami. This time they were joined by Oswell, who went on ahead at times to dig wells in the semi-desert to ensure that the expedition had sufficient water. After crossing the Zouga they struck north- east in order to reach the lands of the Makololo without having to deal first with the Ngami peoples, but here there were few wells - and what water existed was stagnant and polluted by animal dung. Once more, Mary and the children suffered dreadfully, but at last the expedition reached the river Chobe (to the north east of the Okavango swamps), where they left Mary with the children - whilst Oswell and Livingstone trekked onwards to find Sebitoane, the chief of the Makololo, a tribe that had been driven from their former home by the Zulus.

The Makololo had settled along the Zambesi, but were still under threat from the Matabele, the breakaway Zulu sub-tribe that was now led by the fearsome Mzilikazi. They found Sebitoane in a temporary encampment, and he gave them a warm welcome - because he thought that they had come to sell him guns with which to fight the Matabele! - but shortly after Livingstone's arrival, Sebitoane died of pneumonia. This much delayed Livingstone and Oswell but eventually the chief's successor gave permission for them to continue their journey northward, and on the 4th August 1851 they reached the great Zambesi River, which was almost a quarter of a mile wide, flowing fast despite the drought. The sight of the great river inspired Livingstone to think it could be used as 'God's Highway' for missionaries travelling into the heart of Africa to plant the seeds of the Gospel and encourage legitimate trading enterprises which would replace the trade in human lives.

He was astonished and alarmed to see that many of the natives were wearing what was obviously cast-off European clothing, and that others were draped in cloth of European origin. He was told that these clothes were obtained in exchange for slaves sold to Portuguese or half-cast Arab traders who came from the distant east - or west - coasts to trade. The discovery that, despite the embargo on slave trading in Europe, the trade was still flourishing within Africa,

with blacks selling their fellow blacks to traders in exchange for cloth or beads, made him determined to establish a Christian mission amongst these degenerate peoples.

He was told that there was a great waterfall some miles downstream, but he decided that missioners could at least come up river as far as the waterfall, and then have a much shorter and easier trek overland to their new mission field.

As he camped by the Zambesi, he decided that he must find a suitable site for his new mission and then go upstream towards the west coast and downstream to the east coast to see which route gave the better access to the missioners whom he felt sure - must be sent to this area. But first he decided that he must send his family home to England - they were becoming too much of a liability. So he returned to the Chobe river, collected his children and his, by now *very* pregnant wife, and began the long and dangerous trek southward towards Capetown.

When they reached the Zouga river they followed it upstream and made camp on its bank; a camp site which Livingstone named 'Belle Vue', and here on 15th September 1851, another son was born. He was christened William Oswell, but his family always called him 'Zouga'.

The family reached Capetown on 16th March 1852, and on 23rd April, Livingstone put them on a homeward-bound ship and that was the last he saw of them for over four years. Having said goodbye to them, Livingstone began getting ready to go north again. First he took lessons from the Astronomer-Royal in Capetown. He taught him how to use a sextant and chronometer, to enable him more accurately to fix his position during his wanderings, than he had been able to with the old fashioned quadrant which he had learned to use on his original outward sea journey to the Cape.

It seems that the London Missionary Society had by this time more or less accepted Livingstone's self-imposed role as a peripatetic spreader of the Gospel, probably hoping that his further explorations and discoveries would bring it *kudos*. The directors made a half-hearted suggestion that Livingstone should take another man with him on his travels, but he refused. He wasn't going to share his triumphs - or dangers - with anyone.

He left Capetown - alone - on 8th June 1852,

reaching Kuruman in mid August where his parents-in-law told him that Sechele had been attacked by angry Boers, that the mission house which Livingstone had built had been ransacked, that sixty natives and thirty six Boers had been killed, that Sechele had lost three thousand cattle, eleven horses, and forty eight guns, and that the retreating Boers had taken two hundred women and children into slavery. The Moffats were quick to point out that placing the mission station so far to the north had been a total disaster.

Livingstone dismissed the whole affair as justified punishment upon those natives who had refused to receive the Gospel of Christ, and he made no attempt to go to Sechele's rescue. Instead, he stayed with his parents-in-law for three unhappy months. Mr and Mrs Moffat strongly disapproved of what they called his 'wanderings', and were sad to know that their beloved daughter and their grandchildren had been sent back to Scotland, and that they might never see them again. There were many harsh exchanges, and they simply could not understand why Livingstone could not settle down - as they had - and become a real missionary.

Livingstone left Kuruman in mid-December, and went north, back towards the Zambesi reaching the town of Linyanti on the river Chobe, towards the end of May 1853. He was greeted by a large gathering of natives, and by Sekeletu, their new eighteen years old chief, who seemed pleased to see him, and was inclined to be helpful. Livingstone established his base camp at Linyanti, and then, at the end of June, he and Sekeletu together with two hundred of his warriors, set out for the Zambesi, which lay about one hundred miles to the north. Having reached the river, they assembled a fleet of thirty-three canoes and went some three hundred miles upstream, looking for a suitable site for a mission station, but without success. He returned to Linyanti, and spent some time planning his next journey. He intended to go upstream again, still in the hopes of finding a site, but principally with the intention of reaching the west coast of Africa, to see how easy - or how difficult - it would be for missionaries to disembark there, to trek to the headwaters of the Zambesi, and to travel down the river to the mission station which Livingstone was determined to build.

Dr. David Livingstone

CHAPTER SEVEN

Because events in Europe were ultimately to have a profound effect on what happened in Africa, it is necessary briefly to examine events on the world stage at the time that Livingstone was about to set out on his hazardous journey to the west coast.

The Ottoman Empire, which had dominated Eastern Europe since capturing Constantinople in 1453, was crumbling. Greece, a mainly Orthodox Christian country, was the first to gain independence from the Turks after a struggle which had ended in 1832 when the Ottoman Empire gave in, and reluctantly recognised the new Greek monarchy.

Since then, tension had been growing between the Greek Orthodox and the Roman Catholic Churches, as to which of them had the right to guard the holy places in Jerusalem.

Russia supported the Orthodox Church, but France supported the Catholics. The Tsar of Russia was being urged by the Orthodox Church to have himself recognised as the 'Protector' of all Christians within the Ottoman Empire, but Britain - and her old enemy France were afraid of Russia becoming too powerful, and decided instead to support the Muslim Turks.

In 1853 ships of the Royal Navy were sent to the Dardanelles to join a French squadron there as a warning to Russia against interfering with Turkish affairs, but Russia had ignored these gestures, and had declared war on Turkey anyway!

THE OTTOMAN EMPIRE IN 1801.

A Contemporary Map of the Ottoman Empire

In these days of 'instant' news by radio and satellite television, it is sometimes difficult to remember that Livingstone knew little or nothing of current events. Mail and newspapers, which came first to Capetown, were taken to Kuruman by ox wagon, and sent on to Livingstone by "runners", who - if they were not killed by hostile natives or eaten by a lion - eventually caught up with the missionary. As a result information about the outside world was always in arrears - and when he set out on 11th November 1853, heading northwestwards up the Zambesi, he almost certainly didn't know that war with Russia was imminent.

As he journeyed, he was frequently ill with malaria, but drove himself onwards with fanatic determination, and by December had reached the point at which he and Sekeletu had turned back earlier in the year.

By the end of January 1854, the Zambesi River had become so narrow that Livingstone had to abandon it and fight his way onwards through thick rainforest. As he travelled, he saw much evidence of the slave trade, and many of the native peoples he encountered, having rapidly learned that Arab slave raiding parties were prepared to pay for the privilege of proceeding without opposition, demanded payment before they would allow him and his small caravan to pass.

By the end of February, most of his porters were ill, and Livingstone himself was too weak to sit for long on the back of an ox which he rode like a horse. Some of his porters threatened to mutiny, and Livingstone, (who for all his gruff manner and his inability to get on with his fellow whites, was a gentle and kindly man, who abhorred violence of any kind), had to threaten to shoot them if they did not continue to go along with him.

By early April he was on the edge of 'Angola' - a territory claimed by the Portuguese in the 1500's from whence they had shipped slaves across the south Atlantic to their other colony of Brazil in South America. In 1839 Britain, poacher turned gamekeeper, had begun to use force to prevent the trade in slaves from all territories, no matter to whom they belonged, but *despite* this Portugal still managed to ship out something like twenty thousand slaves each year. By 1850 the Royal Navy had begun to seize and search ships outward bound from Angola for Brazil, and by 1854, when Livingstone reached the borders of their territory, the Portuguese slave trade had more or less ceased.

When he was about four hundred miles east of Luanda, he met a party of Portuguese militia under the command of a young sergeant, who - despite suspecting that Livingstone was not a missionary at all but a spy of the wretched and interfering British anti-slavers - took pity on his condition, gave him and his porters some much needed food, and treated them with extraordinary kindness.

Strengthened by the food and assistance given to him, Livingstone, ill though he was, pushed forward but had to be carried into Luanda by his porters on 31st May 1854. By this time he was far too weak even to make up his journal, let alone write to the London Missionary Society, but he dictated some letters to the only Englishman in Luanda; Edmund Gabriel, who had the imposing title of 'Her Majesty's Commissioner for the Suppression of the Slave Trade'.

Livingstone stayed in Luanda for four months and was offered, but refused, a passage to England on *HMS Polyphemus* which called there whilst on anti-slaving patrol. A doctor on the ship gave him quinine, and suppositories made from opium and gradually his health improved. When he was well enough, he took his remaining Makololo porters on board another British ship - *HMS Pluto* - whose guns were fired in his honour. The porters were so impressed by this, that they begged to be given one of the guns, so that they could take it back with them to their village and use it against the Matabele when next they raided. The ship's captain, Lieutenant Norman Bedingfield, to whom Livingstone immediately took a great liking, declined to help!

One can only imagine that Livingstone caught up with news of the outside world when he met the officers of the Royal Navy, but he left Luanda on his return journey on 20th September 1854, and was deep in the rainforest before

the six hundred and seventy three men of the Light Brigade charged the Russian guns at Balaclava. He was still only some two hundred miles east of Luanda when, in mid-December, a runner sent by Mr Gabriel, brought him news that all the letters and reports which he had dispatched from Luanda had been lost in a shipwreck, so he stopped his trek for two weeks, whilst he re-wrote every letter, and sent them back by the same runner.

Despite the loss of his letters, news of his exploits had somehow reached England, and whilst he was busily re-writing his reports, another runner arrived from Mr Gabriel bearing a copy of a letter from Lord Clarendon, the British Foreign Secretary, and a cutting from the London Times in which his westward journey was hailed as 'one of the greatest geographical explorations of the age'.

As he marched westward, he suffered from recurrent bouts of malaria, and by mid-March 1855 his fever was seriously affecting him. Furthermore he had walked into an overhanging branch and damaged one of his eyes, and his hearing was affected by the quantity of quinine he was taking. In short, he was in a very bad way indeed, and his daily trek was frequently less than seven miles. But he plodded on, finally reaching the Zambesi, and followed it down-stream to the place from which he had started. He then returned to Linyanti, arriving there on 10th September 1855.

Although tired and ill, Livingstone didn't waste any time and on 3rd November 1855 he set off for the east coast with one hundred and fourteen porters to carry his loads. He had discovered that it was difficult to approach the headwaters of the Zambesi from the west coast of Africa and he was desperately hoping that, by following the river downstream, he would find an easier route from the distant east coast of the continent. Soon he reached the great waterfall which the native peoples called 'Mosioatunya' - the smoke that thunders - and which Livingstone decided to name the 'Victoria Falls'. Here the Zambesi is almost a mile wide and it drops over an abrupt rock edge, thundering into a narrow gorge, now known as the 'Boiling Pot'. Livingstone could see that this was going to have to be the end of 'God's Highway', and that from here onwards, missionaries and traders would have to go on foot. But - he argued - at least they would have come most of the way by boat.

The local people told him that the land to the north of the river and to the east of the falls was high, fertile, and healthy and, deciding that this would probably be the ideal site for his new mission, despite his hurry to get to the coast, he made a detour on to the Batoka Plateau, and found that the reports were true. It was well watered without being swampy, and seemed to be suitable for cattle. It was an answer to a prayer - here was the ideal site for a mission station, accessible from the great river and not too far from native habitation above the falls.

Victoria Falls

Picture courtesy of C. M. Moiser

Early in 1856 he rejoined the river, and went - quite swiftly - downstream. He reached the confluence with the River Luangwa, which joins the Zambesi from the north (now on the border between Zambia and Mozambique), where the natives were far from friendly and resisted his crossing the stream. He eventually got across by keeping them 'amused' by showing them his watch and compass, and by indicating that he was not a slave raider nor hostile to them.

Having reached the south bank of the Zambesi river, impatient to reach the coast, Livingstone decided to 'cut' a corner and go overland to the Portuguese settlement at Tete, and in doing so he did not see the rapids in a gorge called Kebrabasa. The town of Tete had been established by the Portuguese in the 16th century, when they hoped to find gold or silver in the area, but since there were no precious minerals, the town had depended largely on the slave trade for its survival, and in March 1856, the town had a population of around four thousand souls, of whom all but three hundred and fifty were slaves. Of the remainder, thirty were pure Portuguese, and the *rest*, the result of liaisons between the Portuguese and the native population. Livingstone was disgusted, but he was treated with great kindness by the Portuguese commandant of the garrison, Major Secard, who brought him up to date with European news, and told him that a conference had been convened in Paris to bring an end to the hostilities in the Crimea.

Secard allocated him a house, and promised him a canoe in which to go down-stream to Quilimane, the largest port on the east African coast to the north of the Zambesi delta. After two months rest, Livingstone went on his way. He decided to 'travel light', and left all but eight of his porters in Tete, where Major Secard promised to allocate them land, and to see that they did not starve. Livingstone told these men that he would return within a year to lead them back to their homes upstream of the great waterfall. With his eight remaining Makololo porters for company, Livingstone then headed for Quilimane, and although desperately ill and thinking that he was about to die, he reached there on 25th May, 1856, after a canoe journey of two hundred and seventy miles.

The Ephratah,
sister ship to the **Frolic.**

In Quilimane, Livingstone received a letter from Dr. Tidman of the London Missionary Society in which, after having praised his achievements, Tidman told him that the 'Board' felt financially unable to aid plans connected, *"....only remotely with the spread of the gospel...."*. The Society foresaw in his scheme (for missions on the Zambezi) *"very formidable obstacles"* and saw no likeli-hood of being able to enter *"untried, remote and difficult fields of labour"*. Livingstone was astonished and angry.

He then discovered that Mr Gabriel in Luanda had written to the British Foreign Secretary, giving him approximate dates on which to expect Livingstone's arrival at the coast, and that a succession of H.M. ships had been calling at the mouth of the Zambesi, looking for him. HM brig *Frolic* had even sent a boat across one of the sand bars at the mouth of the river to enquire after him, but the boat had capsized and the crew drowned.

The *Frolic* remained in the area, and kept coming back to the delta to look for him, and when Livingstone at last appeared, the Captain took him on board on the first leg of his journey back to England. In a letter dated 5th August 1856 - written on board he wrote to Sir Roderick Impey Murchison; the President of the Royal Geographical Society in which he said inter alia:

"As I concieve (sic), [Livingstone's spelling was not always of the best], that the future of the African Continent will be one of great importance to England.....I feel anxious to give a few hints which your influential position may enable you to turn to good account...."

In view of what eventually happened, one cannot help wondering if Livingstone already had thoughts of obtaining Murchison's assistance. He went on:

"I may venture to tell you, though I never enjoyed the honour of your acquaint-ance, that the London Missionary Society has thrown a cloud on my further pro-gress by the intimation, in a letter I received at Quilimane, that the Directors are restricted in their power of aiding plans connected only remotely with the spread of the gospel....I suspect I am to be sent somewhere else, but will prefer dissolving my connection with Society and follow out my plans as a private Christian...."

Livingstone eventually reached England and was re-united with his family in December 1856, having been out of Britain for sixteen years.

It was a very different Britain from the one which he had left in 1840. The re-peal of the Corn Laws, abolishing the duty on imported maize, and reducing tax on imported wheat, oats, and barley was good for the urban population, but bad for the farmer and the countryman. Towns had continued to grow in size as in-creasing numbers of farm workers and their families pulled up their rural roots and went in search of a better life. Everything pointed towards industrialisation at the expense of the rural economy, and a national census taken in 1851 had shown that whilst there were still one million four hundred and sixty thousand people involved in agriculture, the number employed in textile mills, and iron foundries, was one million one hundred and eighty thousand, and growing. The end of the Crimean War had released men from the army and navy, most of whom were seeking work in the towns. Attempts had been made to improve the lot of the growing urban 'working class' population and legislation had been in-troduced to limit the working day for women and children in factories (they had already been banned from working underground in the coal mines).
The Great Exhibition of 1851, designed to promote Britain's industrial power,

The Crystal Palace

had been housed in a huge greenhouse-like structure of iron and glass, which was immediately known as the 'Crystal Palace', and as Britain became an industrial power, more and more railways criss-crossed the land on over seven thousand miles of track, and a further three thousand miles had been approved by Parliament. A bridge had been built to carry trains across the Menai straits, and railway travel had ceased to be a 'nine day wonder'.

David Livingstone stayed in Britain from December 1856 until March 1858, during which time he was treated - for the most part - as a 'hero'. The Royal Geographical Society was to give him a Gold Medal, and he received an Honorary Degree from Oxford University. He was made a freeman of a number of British cities, and had a personal interview with Queen Victoria. This was all rather 'heady' stuff for a lad born in a Blantyre tenement. While it is probably unfair to suggest that the fame went to his head, it made him very unsure of what to do with the rest of his life, for both the London Missionary Society and the Royal Geographical Society, were interested in him and his exploits.

Despite the fact that he was - to say the least - an unorthodox missionary, the Missionary Society saw his activities as a potential source of future income for them, because the Victorian public was very ready to donate funds to the Society on his behalf - and saw his wanderings as a wonderful 'spreading of the Gospel'. The Geographical Society on the other hand, wanted him for themselves, as it bathed in his reflected glory.

Livingstone just didn't know what to do! His final decision was to affect many more lives than just his own.

CHAPTER EIGHT

The next part of this story might have been very different had Mary Jane got on well with her Mama. In these days we tend to think that all 'Victorian' children were obedient, dutiful, and loving towards their parents, and it comes as a bit of a surprise to know that they weren't - not all of them anyway.

To be strictly accurate, Mary Jane was not a 'Victorian' child at all, for she had been born in 1818, the daughter of an impoverished clergyman in northern England. We do not know a lot about her childhood, but we do know that, at a time when all young ladies of good birth were content to sit at home, sew their seams and wait for a husband, young Mary Jane Howard, probably unable to bear the thought of remaining at home with her mother until the right man turned up to marry her, packed up her bags, and went to India to work for the Church Missionary Society.

After many years of exhausting work amongst the Indians in Madras, at the age of thirty six she met and married the Reverend Frederick Grueber Lugard who was a Chaplain to the Madras establishment of the Honourable East India Company.

Born in 1808, the son of an army officer, Frederick Grueber had been ordained in 1831, and at the age of twenty-six, shortly after his ordination, he had married a beautiful young girl, who presented him with three daughters in quick succession before deserting him, and leaving him with a burden of debt from the divorce proceedings, and the three motherless children. He had gone to India in 1837, and in 1848 he had married again, this time to a female missionary in Madras by whom he had two more daughters before she died of cholera.

It might be claimed that his third marriage to Mary Jane Howard was one of convenience, for although the daughters of the first marriage had more or less grown up, little Lucy and Emma, the children of his second marriage, still badly needed the care and love of a mother. Perhaps it was a marriage of convenience on *his* part, but there can be no doubt that Mary Jane was deeply in love with Frederick Grueber, so she happily accepted her step-children and soon began to provide her husband with a third young family. The first child, Agnes, was born in 1856, closely followed in 1857 by Ellen Christiana who died shortly after birth. Then, in 1858, the next character in this story, Frederick John Dealtry Lugard, was born.

This event in India, of which David Livingstone would have been completely unaware, takes us a little ahead of ourselves, so we must briefly go back to England in 1857.

The Royal Geographical Society arranged a meeting at the Mansion House in London, to inaugurate a testimonial fund for Livingstone as an individual, but the Directors of the Missionary Society believed that any monies raised should go to them, and not to David. Accordingly, the Directors launched a 'counter attack' and held a meeting in Livingstone's honour during which he embarrassed them by repeating his claim that a new mission must be established on the pleasant plateau which he had 'discovered' to the north of the river Zambesi. Here the native peoples could be moved from the malarial swamps on the banks of the river to enjoy both Christianity and a better climate. He said that the Zambesi should be opened up for commerce as well as for Christianity, claimed that cotton could be grown on the Batoka plateau and argued that the Portuguese should be encouraged to engage in 'legitimate' trade to replace their dreadful dependence on slavery. He went even further - he stated that a second mission station should be established to the south of the Zambesi to be used to convert the ferocious Matebele to Christianity and to prevent them from raiding the Makololo neighbours to the north. It has been suggested that he implied that he would take charge of the northern station whilst his father-in-law, Moffat, already friendly with Mzilikazi, the king of the Matabele, should have the mission to the south of the river. Whatever the truth of the matter, there is little doubt that this is what the Missionary Society believed.

The directors realised that if they didn't agree with Livingstone, they were in danger of losing the benefits of his great public popularity so, after some deliberation, they agreed that two new mission stations were to be built - the one 'among the Makololo' to which a missionary would be appointed to assist Doctor Livingstone and the other to be run by David Moffat, or a member of his family, in Matabeleland.

Meanwhile, the Secretary of the Royal Geographical Society (with Livingstone's knowledge, but without that of the Missionary Society), had written to the Foreign Secretary suggesting that Her Majesty's Government should make use of Livingstone's talents, and suggested that if he were to be given an official 'consulship' to the native peoples of central Africa, he would be not only able to continue his missionary activities, but could also work in England's interests in the region.

Meanwhile Livingstone toured the British Isles lecturing on his journeys and spreading the gospel about Christianity and Trade working hand in hand to 'civilise' Africa. He was an enormous success, and did nothing to dispel the public image of him as a 'simple' missionary facing fearful odds whilst preaching the word of God to the grateful heathen.

In May 1857 the Royal Geographical Society managed to persuade the government to offer Livingstone an appointment as a British Consul for Mozambique and all areas to the west of this Portuguese Colony, and offered him a salary of five hundred pounds a year. The government, preoccupied with the bloody uprising of native troops in India, hadn't much time to consider Livingstone's future until the October of that year, when - with the re-capture of Delhi - the mutiny in India showed signs of coming under control. Perhaps matters were re-awakened by the publication of Livingstone's book *Missionary Travels and Researches in South Africa*, which sold seventy thousand copies, and which made him rich as well as famous.

Then Livingstone astonished the Directors of the Missionary Society, by writing to them to say that he would no longer accept 'pecuniary support' from them, but would 'probably' work for the British Government instead. He added that he would continue to give the Missionary Society every support in establishing a mission north of the Zambesi, but made it clear that he would not take charge of it. The Directors were appalled! The public had already donated generously towards the foundation of the mission stations and they had no alternative, Livingstone or no Livingstone, but to go ahead with the project. They appointed a Mr Holloway Helmore, who had been one of their missionaries in South Africa since 1839, to lead the mission north of the river. Helmore was to be assisted by a Mr Roger Price, and despite the fact that Livingstone had made it clear that he would only help if he could, both these men were given the impression that Livingstone would meet them on the Zambesi, and help them get established.

On December 11th 1857, the Chancellor of the Exchequer told the House of Commons that the Government intended to vote the sum of five thousand pounds to Doctor Livingstone to enable him to embark on a voyage of discovery on the Zambesi river, and the following day the Prime Minister invited Livingstone to a reception at 10, Downing Street, and told him that preparations should

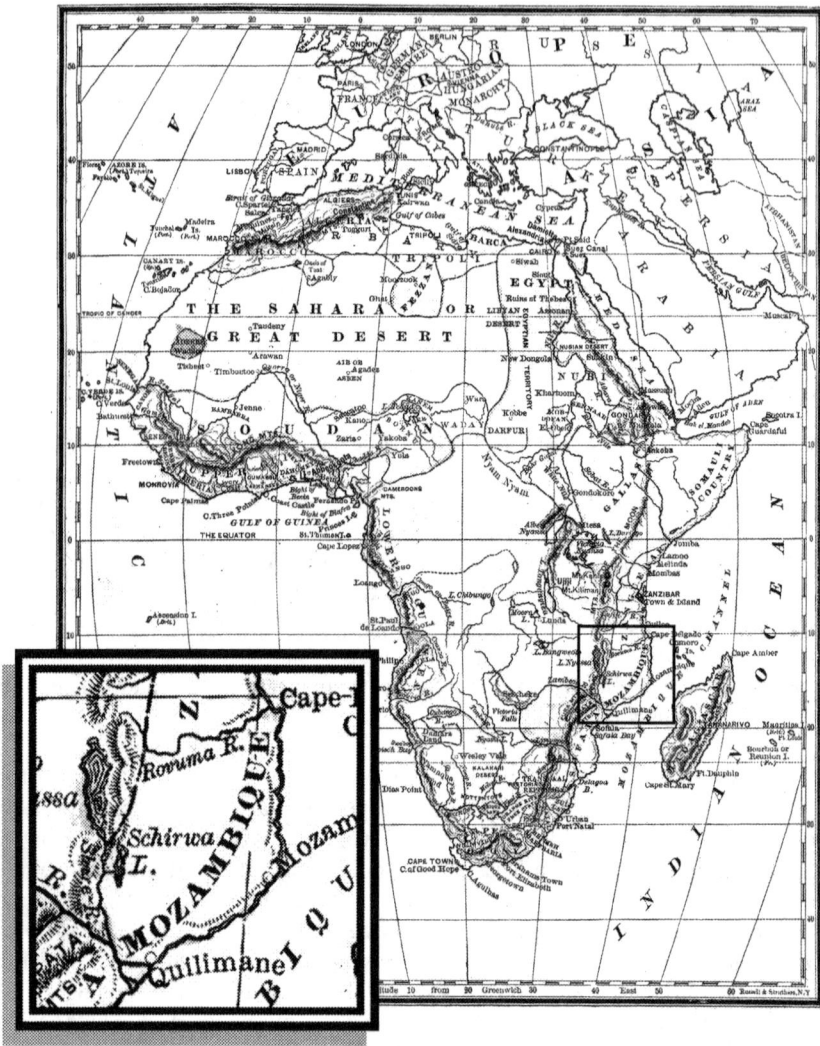

"In May 1857 the Royal Geographical Society managed to per-suade the government to offer Livingstone an appointment as a British Consul for Mozambique and all areas to the west of this Portuguese Colony, and offered him a salary of five hundred pounds a year". (page 63)

be put in hand at once for an expedition which was to last for two years.

Livingstone selected six men to go with on what soon came to be called the 'Zambesi Expedition'. His second-in-command was to be none other than Commander (formerly Lieutenant) Bedingfield of the Royal Navy, with whom Livingstone had become friendly in Luanda. One can only assume that no detailed check was made on this officer's service record which showed that he had twice been court-martialled and once dismissed his ship on charges of being contemptuous and quarrelsome towards his superiors. Failure to check on Bedingfield's record was to have unfortunate results.

Richard Thornton, a student in his early twenties at the School of Mines who had been recommended personally by Murchison, was engaged as geologist, and the expedition's 'botanist' was to be Doctor John Kirk. Although only twenty-six years of age, Kirk had gained valuable experience in the Royal Infirmary in Edinburgh working under Joseph Lister, and had also had 'field' experience in a hospital during the Crimean War.

The next appointment was surprising to say the least - Livingstone's brother Charles who was to be the 'Moral Agent' of the expedition. Charles was eight years his junior, a non-ordained preacher in America, who had left his wife in New York State to join the expedition. Charles seems to have been recruited principally because he claimed that he understood cotton and the machinery used to process it, and was to act as photographer and keep magnetic records. But his inclusion in the team was to have dire consequences for some of his fellow members.

The expedition was to be provided with a steam driven launch, built by Macgregor-Laird of Birkenhead on the pattern of launches used on explorations of the River Niger. She was - in effect - nothing much more than a seventy-five foot long, flat-bottomed 'canoe' with an eight foot beam, and a draught of only two feet. She was to be driven by paddles, powered by a twelve horsepower steam engine whose boiler was designed to burn wood. She was supposed to carry up to thirty-six men, and up to twelve tons of cargo, and the engineer who was to operate the engine was Gordon Rae, a merchant seaman of considerable experience.

The final member, the 'Artist' and 'Storekeeper', was Thomas Baines, a man in his thirty-eighth year who had travelled extensively in Southern Africa. He had been a 'war artist' from 1851 and 1853, and had al-

John Laird:
Founder of the Laird,
Son & Co Shipbuilders

ready participated in an exploration of Northern Australia.

Bedingfield who had been present at the launch's trials on the River Mersey, reported that she was capable of nine knots, and that her performance was satisfactory, so the little ship was therefore dismantled and loaded on board the steamer *Pearl*, which had been loaned by the Colonial Office to carry the expedition and its gear up the Zambesi as far as Tete, before proceeding on her own business to Ceylon.

Livingstone named the little vessel the *MaRobert* (the name given to Mary Livingstone at Chonuane when her first son had been born). He planned to steam up river as far as the Victoria Falls carrying a portable 'iron' storehouse, and sundry agricultural implements which would enable the expedition to start sugar and cotton growing experiments on the plateau.

The **MaRobert** *- a painting by Thomas Baines*

The expedition sailed in the *Pearl* from Liverpool on the 10th March, 1858, and in addition to the six members of the expedition, Livingstone took his wife and his six year old son, Oswell. The remainder of the children were left behind in Blantyre to be looked after by their grandmother.

The *Pearl* reached Sierra Leone on the 25th March where the expedition stayed until the 31st, having recruited twelve men and a headman from Kroo Town, that part of Sierra Leone where the majority of the native population lived. Livingstone refers to these men in his journal as 'Kroomen'[1] and to the headman as 'Tom Jumbo'. Their task seems to have been to provide a pool of labour for the expedition, and 'deckhands' for the *MaRobert*. They were to be used for manual

---

[1] The term 'Kroomen' was widely used of natives of Sierra Leone a territory ceded to Britain in 1787, as a settlement for freed slaves. Many Kroomen had a reputation for being skilful seamen.

work such as cutting wood for the launch's boilers.

By the time the *Pearl* steamed into Table Bay on 21st April ,1858, Mary Livingstone was again pregnant and it was decided to send her and little Oswell to Kuruman, where the latest baby could be born in peace and relative comfort and safety. The *Pearl* then continued her voyage northwards to the mouth of the Zambesi, where they dropped anchor on 14th May. The mouth of the Zambesi river forms a delta through which there are numerous channels and the expedition experienced great difficulty in finding one deep enough to take the *Pearl*.

The situation was not helped by a clash of personalities between Commander Bedingfield and the Master of the *Pearl*. Bedingfield, like many officers of the Royal Navy, had little time for Merchant seamen, however competent they might be, and he openly criticised the Master's handling of the *Pearl*. Livingstone in turn rebuked Bedingfield, unwisely in front of his subordinates, and the Doctor's journals include copies of several angry letters which were exchanged between the two men. In one such letter, Livingstone said:

"....With the change of climate there is often a peculiar condition of the bowels which makes the individual imagine all manner of things in others. Now I earnestly and most respectfully recommend you try a little aperient medicine....you will find it much more soothing than writing official letters."

Bedingfield was furious, and after a further exchange of letters, he tendered his resignation which was accepted. Before he left the expedition it was decided that the *Pearl*, which was one hundred and sixty feet long and had a draft of nine feet seven inches, could go no further, and after off loading the 'iron house' and stores, the *Pearl* left for Ceylon towards the end of June, 1858.

Commander Bedingfield finally left for England in mid August, and the expedition was reduced to Livingstone and five others, none of whom had any boat-handling experience. Nevertheless, Livingstone personally assumed command of the *MaRobert,* and they steamed up and down the river ferrying stores and equipment which were to have been carried by the *Pearl*, had navigation of such a large vessel not proved to be so difficult.

Livingstone and his team reached Tete on the 8th September 1858 where he was reunited with the Makololo porters whom he had left on his first journey to the coast in 1856. He records that he was:

"....at once surrounded by my faithful Makololo. They grasped my hands all at once and some began to clasp me round the body...."

Throughout September the expedition continued to ferry stores up to Tete in the

much overworked *MaRobert* and towards the end of the month an officer from *HMS Lynx* arrived with the news that his ship had brought some items of stores which Livingstone had requested, and the *MaRobert* went back down to the mouth of the river to collect these

The expedition appears to have had a lot of help from the Royal Navy, despite Livingstone's fracas with Bedingfield. Indeed, three officers of the *Lynx* volunteered to go with him to undertake the work intended for Bedingfield. However, it seems that the Doctor was not willing to add another commissioned naval officer to his expedition and instead accepted the services of two petty officers, one as a quartermaster and the other as leading stoker. The quartermaster was to take charge of the Kroomen and the stoker would be Rae's deputy in case of illness.

In November Livingstone set out for Kebrabasa which he had not visited on his journey downstream to the coast in 1856. He records:

"....The scenery presented to our view is quite remarkable and totally unlike anything that has ever been said of the rapids of Kebrabasa...."

He went on to say, optimistically,

"I believe that, when the river rises about six feet, the cascades may be safely passed...."

but a week later he wrote:

"....Things look dark for our enterprise. This Kebrabasa is what I never expected. No hint of its nature ever reached my ears.......what shall we do it this is to be the end of the navigation I cannot now divine, but here I am, and I am trusting Him who never made ashamed those who did so...."

He and his companions continued to explore, hoping to find an easier way through the rapids and Livingstone continued to believe that a more powerful steamer might pass when the river was in flood but he recorded:

"....to make it permanently available for commerce the assistance of a powerful Government is necessary, and a company of sappers would soon clear the channel...."

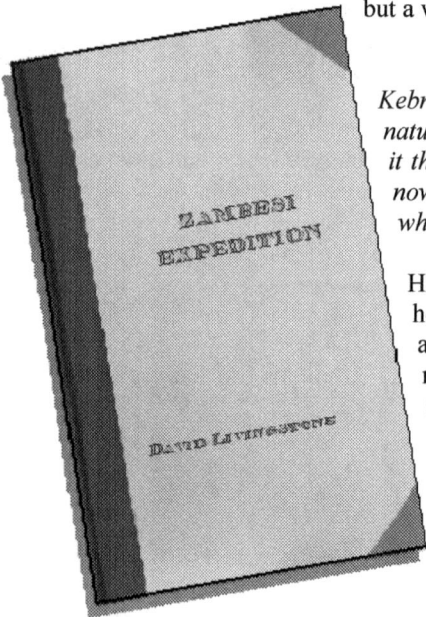

ZAMBESI EXPEDITION

DAVID LIVINGSTONE

By the 5th December, 1858, with provisions running low they returned to Tete, and on the 20th December abandoned any attempt to go further upstream in the *MaRobert*. Livingstone seems to have begun to think that God had deliberately placed the Kebrabasa rapids across the river, because He didn't want a mission on the Zambesi after all, but on the River Shiré instead!

Whatever the thinking, they steamed back to the junction of the River Shiré and the Zambesi and - early in January 1859, entered the River Shiré, where - Livingstone recorded - the adjoining land was 'amazingly fertile', and that it could be drained and irrigated. His journal for the period ends with the words:

"When will this fertile valley resound with the church-going bell? The Lord, the Good Lord, grant that our entrance may be the precursor to that happy time".

CHAPTER NINE

When John Rowlands was fifteen years old, he ran away from the workhouse at St. Asaph - no attempt seems to have been made to recapture him, but this was perhaps because the 'Master' was glad to be rid of him!

John had a cousin who owned a small private school at Brynford, some ten miles away from St. Asaph, and he sought refuge there. Despite his own meagre education, he was employed as a 'pupil teacher', but his cousin's mother, John's Aunt Mary, had little sympathy for her loose-living sister Elizabeth, and still less for her young bastard son, and she soon sent him packing off to Liverpool. There he stayed with other relatives, who promised to try and get him a job in an Insurance Company Office, but the Insurance Company was unimpressed with him, and instead, John found himself a job as an Errand Boy.

One cold winter's day in December 1858 when he was delivering some groceries to the *Windermere*, a ship commanded by a Captain David Hardinge, John met the Captain who persuaded him to sign-on as a Cabin Boy and without bothering to say 'goodbye' to his relatives, John sailed out into the muddy waters of the River Mersey on his way to New Orleans. Nobody in Liverpool or Wales either knew - or seemed to have cared - where he had gone. It was 'goodbye and good riddance' to an unloved and unwanted nuisance.

Captain Hardinge seems deliberately to have ill-treated the boy during the westward voyage, with the intention of making him 'jump ship' in America without collecting any wages due to him; John duly obliged and went ashore in New Orleans, entering America as an illegal immigrant. He wandered about New Orleans, doing odd jobs in exchange for food, until - by chance - he met a wealthy cotton broker, a strange man who had once been ordained, but had left the Church in favour of trade. This man took an interest in this homeless and friend-less young Welshman, and helped him to get a job in a merchant's office at a wage of twenty five dollars a month, and invited him to his home to meet his wife.

The couple, who were childless, became very attached to the boy, and - for the first time in his life - John was loved and cared for. Eventually the broker, whose name was Henry Hope Stanley, decided to 'adopt' him and they went through a strange 'Christening' ceremony in which John Rowlands was re-named "Henry Stanley Jr".

Henry Stanley, as we must call him from now onwards, was fitted out with new clothes, and was made to study for several hours a day in order to 'improve' him-self, but young Henry didn't entirely enjoy all this attention. He much preferred the freedom which he had won when he ran away to sea, and despite their kind-ness, he rebelled and relationships between him and his newly found 'parents' were not happy.

Henry Stanley senior and his wife were soon to discover that their newly adopted son was wilful, and hard to control, and when he began to run away from home he gave rise to much unhappiness and bewilderment. In an attempt to improve the situation, they sent Henry to work on a friend's plantation, but in the autumn of 1860 - only nine months after his adoption - Henry Stanley Jr. broke off relations with his 'parents', and was never to see or contact them again. Nevertheless, he retained his new name, and John Rowlands, the illegal immi-grant from Wales had disappeared for ever.

Meanwhile, back in Africa, by the 8th January 1859, the *MaRobert* had steamed up the River Shiré and was within the sound of rapids where the river fell twelve feet in one hundred and fifty six yards, and was littered with large rocks. Living-stone soon had to admit that the rapids were impassable by launch, but - unde-terred - he named them after Sir Roderick Murchison, and decided to return soon and cross them on foot, to see what lay beyond.

He and his team then went back downstream and, leaving the *MaRobert* in the care of the two naval Petty Officer volunteers from *HMS Lynx* and placing his brother Charles in overall charge, Livingstone went with Kirk on foot beyond the Murchison Falls.

They were soon to discover that the territory was dominated by tribes who seemed to be acting as 'agents' for the Arab slavers. They were not at all friendly towards the two white men, but nevertheless provided guides (who proved to be useless), but Livingstone and Kirk eventually reached Lake Shirwa on the 18th

The Livingstone Memorial at Victoria Falls

Photo: C.M.Moiser

April.

They then returned to Tete, where Charles Livingstone reported that he was having problems with two of the expedition members, Thornton and Baines.

He claimed that young Thornton was doing nothing, was inveterately lazy, and wanted good sense, and that Baines had been 'heady' for three weeks, and had stolen expedition goods while so affected.

Without any investigation, Livingstone accepted his brother's word. He delivered a stern written warning to Thornton and stopped his pay and gave Baines an equally severe rebuke[1].

[1]Thornton eventually left the expedition in May 1860, trekked overland to Zanzibar and joined another expedition to climb Mount Kilimanjaro. He later returned to the Zambesi where he was permitted to rejoin Livingstone's team. During his absence, he wrote a letter to Livingstone which probably persuaded the Doctor to re-employ him. He said: "....I wrote to Sir Roderick Murchison....laying before him the main points of the case ....and concluded with the following two charges against you - First, that you condemned mainly on the evidence of your brother C. Livingstone, without making a proper enquiry into the truth of that evidence, and without giving me an opportunity to. To this day you do not know what geology I did or did not whilst a member of the Expedition...."

It was not a happy time for anyone, and on 1st August 1859, Livingstone wrote a scathing report on the condition of the *MaRobert*. His journal records that the plates on the hull were rusted through in several places, and that he had been obliged to plug the holes in the hull with clay in canvas bags covered with India rubber. The funnel, he says, was also full of holes. The 'bridge' of the boiler had broken for the fourth time, and the hull was taking in "a good deal of water".

There is then a gap in Livingstone's journals until 17th September, when he records that he had *"....reached Lake Nyassa from which the Shiré emerges"*. He was beginning to find out that his 'promised land' was a hot bed of slavery, and warring tribes each trying to out-do the other to escape from the unwelcome attentions of the Arab slavers, and even the optimistic Livingstone had to admit that there would be 'political' problems before the area could be opened up to Christianity and commerce. Apart from anything else that would have to be overcome - including the Murchison rapids - the area could only be approached by water from the Zambesi and Shiré rivers, both of which ran through Portuguese areas of influence. Since the Portuguese were Catholics, he realised that they might resent a stream of Protestant missionaries, traders, and settlers passing through 'their' territory on their way to the 'Shiré Highlands'. It was indeed remarkable that the Portuguese had allowed him and his expedition to enter the territory at all, for despite the kindness shown to him in Angola and Tete, Livingstone had spoken out against the Portuguese on many occasions, and had publicly described their morality - or the lack of it - as being: *"worse than Sodom!"*

Although Livingstone must have realised that any missionaries or traders, let alone settlers, would have a very rough time, he wrote to his wife (who by then had been safely delivered of her latest baby, and had returned to Scotland from Kuruman), telling her that she should join him as soon as possible. He also wrote to the Foreign Secretary appealing for Government assistance and sponsorship for settlers from Britain willing to come and assist in the grand scheme of civilising the environs of Lake Nyassa. He told neither his wife nor the Foreign Secretary of the difficulties and dangers which he had already experienced, and one can only assume that this was because he badly wanted to found a mission in the Shiré Highlands in order to provide an alternative to the Batoka Mission, and to justify the Zambesi expedition. He seems to have convinced himself that once a mission had been established, and settlers settled, the wicked slave traders would go away, but even he realised that something positive would have to be done to curb the slave trade before all this could happen. He wrote to the Foreign Secretary saying that he must have an armed anti-slave-trade gun boat to patrol Lake Nyassa. Such a vessel, he said, would have to be sent to Africa in sections, so that these could be carried over the Murchison cataract, and assembled on the other side of the Lake.

All Livingstone's letters had to be taken to the mouth of the Zambesi and left at a pre-arranged place to be picked up by the next Royal Naval vessel which happened to pass by - which was roughly every three months. As a result of this rather haphazard means of communication, the Foreign Secretary did not get any of Livingstone's letters until early 1860. When he did at last get them, he showed them to the Prime Minister - who wanted nothing more to do with settlements in Africa, particularly if they involved building a collapsible gunboat in which to chase Arab slavers. The Foreign Secretary accordingly wrote to Livingstone, saying 'No', but his letter didn't arrive until 1861.

Meanwhile there was another problem looming on the horizon. When Livingstone had been in England, he had appealed to young men from Oxford and Cambridge Universities to dedicate their lives to the 'salvation' of Africa. As a direct result of this appeal, a 'Joint Universities Mission' had been established by graduates of Oxford, Cambridge, Durham, and Dublin Universities. In March 1859 the Bishop of Capetown had written to Livingstone, telling him of the formation of the mission, and seeking his advice as to where it should start work. Livingstone had replied, seemingly without hesitation, that the Shiré Highlands would be an ideal starting point, telling the Bishop nothing of the difficulties and dangers which he had himself encountered, except for saying that the mission could expect 'some' opposition from the native population.

CHAPTER TEN

W hen he got to the *MaRobert* on the 8th October Livingstone found that the leak did not let in much water, *"unless canoes or boats come alongside and shake her...."* when, he said, *"funnel, furnace, deck and bottom all become shaky simultaneously...."*

Clearly the launch was in a hopeless condition, useless for further exploration of the Shiré, and by the 8th November the crew had to pump her out and plug holes with mud. Two days later they discovered that there were large leaks in all compartments, and that the steel plating was so rusted and thin that it could easily be bent by hand.

Problems with his fellow explorers continued, and on 23rd November 1859 Livingstone sent for Baines and questioned him about the disappearance of stores. He then banished him from the company, and the poor fellow had to live in a whaler (on loan from the Navy) under an awning moored in the vicinity of the rusting *MaRobert*. Baines protested his innocence to the last, but was finally dismissed, and sent back to England on *HMS Lynx* on 12th December 1859.

The first entry in a new journal started on the 1st December; he summarised his views on the members of the expedition. He said:

"....I took a botanist (Kirk), a mining geologist (Thornton), an artist (Baines), a naval officer (Bedingfield), besides a general assistant (his brother Charles). The naval officer was intended to give accurate information of the capabilities of the rivers....His views however turned out to be different. He came to exalt himself, and began to scheme his own promotion by my fall. He tampered with

*the Kroomen and told all manner of lies to the other members against myself....
The geologist became so insufferably lazy that after eight month's idleness....I
was obliged to cut off his salary and himself from the expedition....The artist and
storekeeper ....took the opportunity....of secretly disposing of quantities of public
goods, painting portraits for Portuguese and going off skylarking with certain
low characters. I have been obliged to cut him off in consequence....The botanist
and my own assistant have fully answered my expectations.........."*

On the 7th March 1860 he recorded that the holes in the launch were

"....so large it is almost impossible...."

and on 10th he said:

*"....Mr Rae still mending steamer - 35 patches each covering not 2 but on aver-
age 4 holes...."*

On 17th March a leak occurred in fore compartment and they went to the bank
and stuffed a flannel jacket and fat into the hole. Despite this deterioration they
took the *MaRobert* up to Tete from whence Livingstone intended to trek on foot
to Linyanti to return the remaining Makololo porters, as promised. There is a
very curious entry in his journal for the 13th May 1860 in which he says that his
brother (Charles) told him that members of the expedition were

"always at a loss how to act...."

and that he, Livingstone, was to blame for having rejected a vessel called the
Bann[1]. Livingstone was beginning to wonder if the recruitment of his brother
had been such a good idea after all, for the entry continues,

*"....As he seems to let out in a moment of irritation a long pent up ill-feeling, I
am at a loss to know how to treat him. As an assistant he has been of no value.
Photography very unsatisfactory. Magnetism still more so. Meteorological observations not creditable, and writing in the journal in arrears. In going up with
us now he is useless, as he knows nothing of Portuguese or the native languages. He often expected me to be his assistant instead of acting as mine...."*

---

[1] *This seems to be the first time that Livingstone mentions this vessel in his journals and one has to turn to a Post
Script of his letter dated 6th August 1858, to Lord Malmesbury at the foreign Office in London (who was nominally
responsible for the activities of the Expedition) to find out what he is talking about. In it he complains at length
about Commander Bedingfield, and says, inter alia:* "A vessel named the Ban (sic), now or lately lying unemployed at Woolwich, was offered for the use of this expedition. I paid so much deference to Cr.B's (Bedingfield's)
judgement that, though it only draws three feet and would navigate this river during at least ten months in the year,
I allowed its rejection...."

*The implication was that it was all Bedingfield's fault that the MaRobert was such a disaster and that they would
have been better off with the other vessel!*

CHAPTER ELEVEN

Although Britain had abolished slavery throughout her Empire in 1833, the United States of America, as a whole, had not. Some states had done away with the system or had no need for it, but it was claimed - probably with justification, that the entire economy of the southern states of America depended upon Negro slave labour imported at such an appalling cost in human lives from the continent of Africa. Plantation owners defended slavery as being *'so necessary that it ceased to appear evil'*.

In the Northern States of America, most people were indifferent to slavery principally because it did not affect them personally, until the publication in 1852 of Harriet Beecher Stowe's novel *Uncle Tom's Cabin* aroused public outrage.

There was also a great deal of controversy as new territories were admitted to the Union. In Kansas, this controversy turned to violence when a pro-slavery group sacked the town of Lawrence. As a reprisal, John Brown, a fanatic abolitionist from Ohio, helped by his four sons dragged five pro-slavery men from their beds and killed them. In October 1859 John Brown, with his four sons and a handful of followers, seized the Federal arsenal at Harpers Ferry, declared war on the United States and freed a number of very confused slaves. Brown's small force was defeated by Federal marines, he was captured, tried and hanged. Southerners rejoiced, but Anti-slavery Northerners regarded John Brown as a martyr - John Brown's body was a-mouldering in the grave, but his soul went marching on!

During the American Presidential election of 1860, a Southern Senator demanded that Northern States should repeal their Personal Liberty laws and stop interfering in the business of Southern States. He claimed that the Federal Government had no right to prohibit slavery and indeed that it should protect those States in which slavery was still legal. Then, in December 1860 the State of South Carolina, in order to retain its right to its own destiny - and its slaves - declared that the Union of 1788 between South Carolina and all other States, was dissolved. South Carolina's example was soon followed by Mississippi, Florida, Alabama, Georgia, Louisiana and Texas, and delegates from these States met in Alabama in February 1861, and formed a `Confederacy` under Jefferson Davis as President.

The Union was in turmoil. Many regular troops joined the Southern cause, and all Federal military posts in the south passed into the hands of the new Confederation, except the forts of Charleston Harbour which continued to fly the Stars and Stripes. The Commandant, when called upon to surrender, refused to do so and withdrew to Fort Sumter which stood on an island. Here food began to run out and when a relief ship arrived from the North, it was driven off by cannon fire from Confederate troops.

Many in the North were prepared to give in to the Southerners, and let them have their own way, but the newly-elected President of the Federation, Abraham Lincoln, sworn in on 4th March 1861, stood firm despite the fact that all around him the Federal Government was falling to bits. He appealed for patience and conciliation, but said that he intended to hold on to all forts and property of the United States and in April he told the Governor of South Carolina that he would re-victual Fort Sumter. President Davis ordered his officers at Charleston to demand the immediate surrender of the fort, but the Commander declined. On April 12th Confederate batteries opened fire on the fort, and the American Civil War had begun.

Abraham Lincoln

None of these events was of particular interest to young Henry Stanley, who had not stayed for long on the plantation to which his adoptive parents had sent him, but who had got himself a job with a German Jewish trader at a place called Cypress Bend in Arkansas. In 1860, in Arkansas, almost everybody carried a gun so he bought a Smith and Wesson pistol, practised daily and soon became an excellent shot - an achievement which stood him in good stead in later years -

but when the Civil War broke out and Arkansas joined the Confederacy, Stanley claimed that he was a Welsh national, and had nothing to do with American politics.

When volunteers were called for to join the Confederate army, he again argued that it was nothing to do with him and that he wanted no part in the argument, but one morning he received a parcel from a girl-friend. It contained a woman's petticoat - the equivalent of the more conventional 'white feather' and this was too much for Stanley. He was furiously angry and went straight out and joined the 'Dixie Greys', which marched to war from Little Rock, Arkansas in August 1861.

Livingstone had heard nothing more about the University's mission, and had decided that he could do nothing more on the Shiré until he had his 'gunboat', so he decided to return to Tete, to collect the few remaining porters from his 1855 east-bound journey, and take them back to their home on the upper Zambesi. Before setting out on his journey, however, he took the rapidly decaying *MaRobert* down to the delta again to send Rae - the Engineer - back to England to supervise the construction of the collapsible 'gunboat'. Only three members of the original Zambesi Expedition were left; the two Livingstone brothers and Doctor Kirk. Kirk like all the others, had only agreed to serve on the expedition for two years, and was therefore also free to go home, but he recorded that he would not think of leaving Livingstone at this time, despite the fact that he could see nothing ahead but fatigue and hardship.

The three men returned to Tete to collect Livingstone's original porters, but found that the majority did not want to return to their native village. They had all taken local 'wives' and they knew that their womenfolk at Linyanti would have given them up for lost and would have been taken by new 'husbands', and they were happy where they were. Thus, when Livingstone set out up-stream, he had only about sixty of the original one hundred and fourteen porters with him, and of these, thirty deserted him and went back to Tete as soon as they reached the Kebrabasa gorge.

Livingstone eventually reached Linyanti in August, where he was greeted with the news that Mr and Mrs Helmore, their son and daughter, and an infant of Mr Price, had all arrived at Linyanti, but had all died within two months of their arrival.

Holloway Helmore had been a missionary in Southern Africa since 1839 and he was to have had two assistants - Price and Mackenzie - but Mackenzie's wife was expecting a baby so he stayed behind in the south for the time being.

Although Livingstone had made no firm promise to guide the missionaries, and

had only told the Society that he would help if he happened to be there at the time, Helmore and Price, together with their respective wives and young children, had set off early for the long overland trek to the Zambesi expecting to meet Livingstone there. They had arrived in February 1860, a particularly bad time of the year for malaria, but of course Livingstone was not there to meet them - he had by then discovered the impassability of the Kebrabasa gorge, and was making plans for his new mission on the Shiré Highlands.

Helmore and Price and their families had not been kindly welcomed by Chief Sekelutu, who seemed to think that Livingstone was the only white man he could trust. They had been robbed of their stores, and clothing, and denied access to the healthy Batoka plateau where Livingstone had planned to build the Mission. All of them had caught malaria, and within two months, Helmore and his wife, and Mrs Price and five out of the seven children, had all died.

Price and the surviving children had eventually given up waiting for Livingstone and had started to trek southwards again. Had they not met with Mackenzie, the third missionary bound for the Zambesi, they too would surely have died in the bush. The dream of establishing a Mission on the Batoka plateau had become a ghastly nightmare.

In his Journal dated 17th August 1860 Livingstone records:

"The missionary party to Linyanti consisted of 22 persons in all - 9 Europeans and 13 coloured people. Of these 5 Europeans died of fever in the course of 3 months, and one went away very sick of fever. Four natives died too, the mortality being of all 9 in 22...."

Livingstone probably realised that, had he not cut a corner on his first east-bound journey, and had he seen the Kebrabasa gorge, he would not have so readily propounded the theory of the Zambesi being 'God's Highway' to the new Mission field, but he soon convinced himself that the disaster was yet another of God's way of directing that the new mission should not be on the Batoka plateau at all, but in the Shiré Highlands, so he turned and went back downstream, reaching Tete at the end of November 1860[1].

Here he found a number of letters awaiting him, including one from the Foreign Secretary, firmly rejecting Livingstone's proposal for 'colonising' the Lake Nyassa region. Another letter told him that a replacement for the *MaRobert* was on its way, and another told him that the first members of the Universities Mission expected to arrive at the mouth of the river in January 1861.

Early in December Livingstone, his brother Charles and Doctor Kirk set out for the Zambesi delta in the *MaRobert,* but as they neared their destination on 21st December 1860, the little launch sank to the bottom of the river. Her crew were given enough warning to enable them to off-load their stores and equipment, but they had to continue their journey on foot, and spent a miserable month in a native hut waiting for the arrival of the missionaries.

On 31st January 1861, *HMS Sidon* was sighted, towing the replacement for the *MaRobert*; a Royal Naval launch, the *HMS Pioneer*. A week later, the Universities Mission arrived, consisting of Bishop Charles Mackenzie and four assistants. The Bishop, although only thirty six years old, was an experienced African missionary, having previously worked amongst the Zulus in Natal.

He and his fellows were somewhat alarmed, and not a little surprised, when they saw the sand bars across the mouth of the river, but Livingstone assured them that it was safe to cross, so having crossed they expected to be taken immediately up-stream to their new Mission field on the Shiré. This was not to be however because Livingstone told the Bishop that they must wait whilst he tried to find an alternative route to the Shiré, explaining that the Portuguese might object to large numbers of Protestant clergy going directly up the Shiré river. The Bishop, who had been assured that the Portuguese would co-operate, objected strongly at the delay, but as usual Livingstone won the day, and left everyone at the mouth of the Zambesi while he took the new launch up the coast to explore the River Rovuma. He knew that this river had already been surveyed by the Royal Navy whose surveyors had found it only to be navigable for about forty five miles when the river was in flood, and only thirty miles when the river was low, but Livingstone was not satisfied with this, and wanted to see for himself, claiming that an alternative route to the Highlands must be found.

He didn't return until April, but confirmed what the Navy had said - the river

---

[1] At this point we must leave the problems presented by the Cabora Bassa rapids as they no longer have any direct relevance to the story. Sufficient to say that in 1974, the massive Cabora Bassa reservoir began to fill, making Africa's largest man-made power producing barrage, and drowning foreverall evidence of Livingstone's disasterous adventure on the Zambesi river.

Rovuma was *not* navigable, so at long last, on 1st May 1861, *HMS Pioneer* steamed up-stream towards the Shiré. It was not a particularly happy or comfortable voyage. The launch kept running aground on mud banks and Livingstone had to off-load some of the stores to lighten ship. With a reduced draught, the Pioneer made better progress and they reached the Murchison cataracts in July.

In mid-July 1861 the whole party set out on foot for Magomero, a village which Livingstone had selected as the best site for the mission headquarters, and the Bishop strode ahead, a gun in one hand and his crozier in the other encouraging idle porters by poking them with it.

They encountered a party of slaves, eighty four men, women and children, roped together in a pitiful 'crocodile', their necks held in forked wooden 'taming' sticks. The slave drivers ran away when they saw the white men coming and, of course, the missionaries released the slaves. Thus, before they had even reached the site of the new mission, the Bishop had obtained eighty four potential 'converts'. Within a few days, fifty seven more slaves had been rescued in a similar fashion. One of these was called 'Chuma'.

CHAPTER TWELVE

I t was not long after their arrival at Magomero, that the Bishop and his team first experienced the inter-tribal warfare which raged in the area, about which they had not been warned. They heard that an attack on a 'friendly' village about ten miles away was imminent, and Livingstone and the Bishop - accompanied by a number of armed porters and some local tribesmen - set out to defend the villagers, by attacking the would-be attackers in their own village. On their way they passed a number of burnt-out villages, and could see others in the distance - still burning - and when they reached their destination, their chosen victims shot poisoned arrows at them, killing one of Livingstone's men. The missionaries returned fire, rushed into the village, and burnt it to the ground!

This foolish action placed the mission in great danger, because surviving tribesmen would certainly seek revenge, so before setting out with Kirk to make a thorough survey of Lake Nyassa to try to prove that the river Rovuma flowed out of it, Livingstone recommended that the Bishop build a defensive stockade around his embryo mission station.

When Livingstone and Kirk returned, having discovered that the Rovuma did not flow out of the lake, he learned that the Bishop, not waiting to be attacked, had twice taken action against the hostile tribesmen, and had temporarily driven them away. Then, quite unexpectedly, a young missionary by the name of Burrup arrived to reinforce the Magomero team, bringing news that *HMS Gorgon* was soon to arrive at the mouth of the Zambesi with his newly married wife, the Bishop's sister and her companion - and, to Livingstone's delight, his own wife, Mary.

David Livingstone decided that he should go down-stream in the *Pioneer* to meet the new arrivals, and suggested that the Bishop should stay at Magomero for the time being to fight off an expected counter-attack from the hostile natives. The Bishop did not agree, and Livingstone wrote in his Journal on 30th October 1861:

"....The bishop does not realise his position, as he intends leaving his most important post at this critical time to bring up his sisters! He seems to lean on them. Most high church people lean on wives or sisters....I hope the bishop will remain at his post; if he doesn't, he is a muff to lean on wife or a sister. I would as soon lean on a policeman...."

Before he and Kirk left on the 15th November 1861, Livingstone arranged for the Bishop and Burrup to come to meet the *Pioneer* on her return journey at a point where the River Ruo joined the Shiré. The plan was then to steam as far up the Ruo as possible, before off-loading the women, who could then trek overland to the mission. This was agreeable to all parties, and Livingstone and Kirk steamed down river. After they left, the Bishop changed his mind and decided to open up a 'path' from the mission at Magomero towards the River Ruo, so that the womenfolk would have an easier journey once they had come ashore. The Bishop allocated the job of 'path clearance' to two of his assistants who, with a number of 'friendly' natives, set about the task with a will, but the working party was attacked, the two white men narrowly escaped with their lives, and the native labourers were either killed, captured or ran away. The Bishop, always ready for a fight, mounted a punitive expedition and burnt down another village. This action delayed the Bishop's and Burrup's departure for the rendezvous, but when at last they got there, they were told by local natives that the *Pioneer* had last been seen steaming downstream, and had certainly not called to off-load any white women.

The two men were puzzled. They had been late arriving at the rendezvous, so perhaps Livingstone and Kirk, finding that they weren't there to take charge of the female party, had for some inexplicable reason decided to go back to the mouth of the Zambesi. (The Bishop was not to know that the *Pioneer* had run into a lot of trouble, had kept grounding on sandbanks and, when seen by the locals, was still on her way to meet the women!)

When, at last, Livingstone reached the delta, he found that the *Gorgon* had been unable to ride at anchor because the weather was too bad and had sailed down the coast to find a safer anchorage. Livingstone and Kirk could only wait for the *Gorgon's* return.

Meanwhile, the Bishop and his companion awaited developments. They dared not return to Magomero because they expected Livingstone and the women to

arrive at any time, so they just had to wait. A local chieftain allocated them a hut on a small, mosquito-ridden island in the middle of the river and there they stayed. Neither man had been well even when they left the mission and as they had paddled down the Ruo towards its junction with the Shiré their canoe had capsized and they had lost all their medicines, including their quinine. Both men soon became seriously ill with malaria and associated diarrhoea, and by the end of January the Bishop's condition worsened, he began to bleed from the mouth, and died on 31st January 1862. Burrup buried him on the island in an unmarked grave and soon the young missionary, now alone and helpless, ran out of food. He had no idea of what could have happened to Livingstone and the womenfolk, and decided to return to Magomero for reinforcements. He got back to the mission on 14th February but died a week later.

On 31st January 1862, of course totally unaware of the tragedy, Livingstone saw *HMS Gorgon* arrive carrying Mr Rae and the dismantled hull, engine, and fittings, of the anti-slaving patrol boat built with six thousand pounds of Livingstone's own money.

The next day the brig *Hetty Ellen* arrived carrying Mrs Livingstone, the Bishop's elderly sister, young Mrs Burrup, two female servants and some additions to the staff of the mission. Since the *Pioneer* was quite unable to carry so many persons, Captain Wilson of the *Gorgon* offered to take the women and their baggage to the proposed meeting place up stream. Kirk was to go with the advance party as guide and Livingstone and Rae were to follow in the *Pioneer* when they had finished off-loading the makings of the patrol boat which Livingstone named the *Lady Nyassa.*

Wilson and his party, finding no one to meet them at the designated spot, pushed on overland to the Mission, where they learned the dreadful news of the death of the Bishop and Mr Burrup.

Even after hearing about these misfortunes, Livingstone did not change his plans, because time allowed by the Foreign Office for the Zambesi expedition was running out. He came to the conclusion that the women should first be got out of the way and that he would then take the *Pioneer* and steam up to Johanna Island - one of the Comoros group which lie between the African coast and the northern tip of Madagascar - where there was a Royal Naval base, and a British Consul who would replenish supplies to take him and his enlarged 'team' into 1864. He had already intended to take his wife with him to Johanna Island, and to leave her there for the time being, before having another look at the river Rovuma which, despite all the evidence to the contrary, he was still determined should provide him with an alternative route to Lake Nyassa.

Instead, he first took the two bereaved women and their servants back to the mouth of the Zambesi, and eventually put them on board *HMS Gorgon* for a passage back to England. He then returned to the junction of the Zambesi and the Shiré, and started work on assembling the *Lady Nyassa*.

On 21st April 1862, Mary Livingstone fell ill. Six days later she died. But even his wife's death didn't make Livingstone change his plans. He buried her under a baobab tree, and continued with his work. By the end of June the hull of the *Lady Nyassa* was assembled and launched, and leaving her behind to be 'fitted out' by a team from the *Gorgon*, Livingstone set off on his extraordinary journey for Johanna Island; some six hundred miles of open sea in *HMS Pioneer*, a small, open, steam-driven launch designed only for work in coastal waters. Nevertheless, he got there, obtained his stores, and made his way back down the coast to the mouth of the Rovuma. Here there was so little water that he couldn't get the *Pioneer* very far, but he continued in two canoes; he and his brother Charles in one and Kirk and Rae in the other. After five days it was obvious that they could go no further, because the river was less than one foot deep, but still Livingstone persisted, and they carried the canoes up-stream, until at the end of September they came to cataracts where even he had to admit defeat.

The exhausted men returned to where they had left the *Pioneer,* and by mid-December 1862, they were re-united with the party from the *Gorgon* working on the hull of the *Lady Nyassa*.

The *Pioneer* with the *Lady Nyassa* in tow finally got under way by mid-January 1863, reaching the Murchison cataracts on April 10th. The next task was to take the *Lady Nyassa* to pieces again, to transport her over the cataracts and to re-assemble her for her duty on the Lake, but before this work could begin, Thornton, the geologist (who, it will be remembered, had been dismissed in 1859, but who had been allowed to return to the team), died. This was the 'last straw' for Charles Livingstone and even for the faithful Doctor Kirk, and they both decided to leave, but then Livingstone himself fell seriously ill, so they stayed with him until he recovered.

Kirk and Charles Livingstone finally left on 19th May 1863, leaving only Doctor Livingstone and Rae as survivors of the original Zambesi Expedition. However, the two men had the assistance of Lieutenant E.D.Young of *HMS Gorgon* who had volunteered to stay behind and help assemble the *Lady Nyassa.*

Young then told the Doctor that before the *Lady Nyassa* could be carried in pieces over the cataracts, a road, thirty miles long, would have to be built. This, he calculated, would take one hundred labourers a full year to achieve. Livingstone was still arguing about this, when it became apparent that food stocks were running low and whilst the three men were debating what to do next, a dis-

patch was received from the Foreign Secretary, re-calling the expedition. Lord Russell said:

"Her Majesty's Government fully appreciates the zeal and perseverance with which you have applied yourself....cannot however conceal from themselves that the results to which they had looked from the expedition....have not been realised....there is little to show that the results actually obtained can be made presently serviceable either for the interests of British Commerce or of humanity in general...."

Her Majesty's Government have accordingly decided that the Expedition....shall within as short a period as may be practicable be withdrawn...."

Livingstone had no option but to accept the re-call, but before he left, decided that he would wait until the waters of the Shiré rose sufficiently to take the two vessels safely downstream. Leaving his companions behind, he then trekked seven hundred miles along the shores of Lake Nyassa before finally embarking on the two little ships and steaming down-stream to the mouth of the now rather discredited 'God's Highway'. They reached open water in February 1864, and both small vessels were taken in tow by a Royal Naval ship and taken up the coast to Mozambique.

Meanwhile, in the disunited and warring States of America, the 'Dixie Greys' had joined up with other Confederate units at Corinth in Mississipi in March 1862 and soon there were forty thousand men under the command of Generals Beauregard and Johnston facing the Federal army of General Grant, who had almost fifty thousand troops at his disposal. The two armies met on April 6th 1862, and forty eight hours later, four thousand men on both sides were dead, and another seventeen thousand wounded. Many of the confederate troops were taken prisoner - including Stanley - and they were transported to a Prisoner of War camp near Chicago. This camp, like many others at the time, was riddled with disease and vermin, and Stanley decided that the only way of escape was to change sides and join the Federal Army, which he did without delay!

In June 1862 he took the oath of allegiance, and became a member of the Illinois Light Artillery, but soon after getting his new blue uniform, Stanley fell ill with dysentery, and was discharged from the Army. By this time he had had enough of America and decided to go back to Wales, so he signed on as a crew member on a merchant ship bound for Liverpool.

CHAPTER THIRTEEN

In India, at about the time when the Zambesi expedition was being recalled, Mary Jane Lugard saw that her brood of children was beginning to wilt in the heat and dust of Madras, and after much thought and prayer, in 1863, she and her husband decided that for the children's sake, she should take them home to England and that the Reverend Frederick would resign and follow them home as soon as possible. So, on 5th March 1863, Mrs Lugard and the children embarked on the *Trafalgar*, a sailing ship which was taking invalided and sick troops home to England.

It was a horrendous voyage! Their cabin was over-run with red ants and the sick troops on board did not take kindly to the noise of crying children and even threatened them violence. Furthermore, as poor Mary Jane recorded sadly, Freddy was inclined to be 'quarrelsome and naughty', but he seems to have enjoyed the voyage rather more than either his mother or his sisters.

The family arrived in England in July, and Mary Jane, who had been out of the country for many years, quite naturally took her family to York to her elderly mother, Mrs Howard, now seventy-seven years old. She was soon to find out that absence had not made her mother's heart grow fonder and she received a very lukewarm welcome. For one thing, Mrs Howard flatly refused to have anything at all to do with Mary Jane's step-daughters, Lucy or Emma, and she only offered her daughter the use of one room in her house. This was unacceptable to Mary Jane because the children would have had to sleep on the floor, so she parted company once more from her difficult old mother, rented a small house in York, engaged a governess and a housemaid to help look after the children, and settled down to wait for her dearly beloved husband to join her.

It was a very different England from the one which she had left in the 1840's, and it took her many months to settle down and become accustomed to the changes around her. All sorts of things had happened whilst she had been in India and, at first absorbed in her missionary work and later with her growing family, she had been only vaguely aware of them. She was soon to realise that urban populations in Britain had grown beyond belief, as more and more common land was 'enclosed', and dispossessed small peasant farmers and their families continued to flock to the growing cities in search of a better life - as had Livingstone's crofter grandfather, so long ago.

Prince Albert

The repeal of the Corn Laws had not helped the countryman, and everything seemed to be against him, as Victorian England enjoyed in its new-found Industrial might. The Crystal Palace, which had housed the Great Exhibition of 1851, seemed to represent a sort of `Temple` to the God of 'Progress', and Mary was amazed to see the ever-growing network of railways, and the new horse-drawn omnibuses in the London streets. But while all these new inventions must have been bewildering to her, a woman of her character must have welcomed the increasing importance of the role of women in society. The Crimean War, which had hardly affected people serving in India, had highlighted the need for nursing care, and she was delighted that the now famous Florence Nightingale had recently opened a school for nurses in London. Mary, like the rest of the nation, had mourned the death of Prince Albert in 1861, and, being separated from her dear husband, had considerable sympathy for the widowed Queen, but the gloom of the death of Albert had to some extent been relieved by the marriage of the Prince of Wales to the beautiful Princess Alexandra of Denmark shortly before the Lugard family arrived 'home' in England.

On his return to Wales, Stanley didn't get a warm welcome either. He found that his mother was by now the highly respected wife of Robert Jones, landlord of the 'Cross Foxes' Inn and, as the mother of two legitimate children, she wanted nothing to do with her eldest son, whose existence she would have much preferred to have forgotten. However, she produced a meal for him, and gave him a bed for the night, but, in her judgement, maternal duty having been done, the next morning she gave him a shilling, and told him to go away and not come back!

Poor Henry went to Manchester to find the relations of his 'father', Henry Hope Stanley, but they didn't want anything to do with him either! They too gave him some clothes and some money, but also told him to go away. Faced by these rebuffs, Stanley decided that America was not such a bad place after all, even though the Civil War still raged. He went back there as soon as he could, and early in 1863 in New York, he signed on as a deck-hand on an American Merchant ship plying between Boston and the Mediterranean.

Henry Stanley

Livingstone handed over *HMS Pioneer* to Lieutenant Young and told him to take the launch to Capetown. He then embarked on the *Lady Nyassa* - which was his own property - and steamed northwards, up the coast to Zanzibar where he tried to sell her. He could find no buyers, and so this extraordinary man, who had little or no sea experience except as a passenger, and hardly knew port from starboard, decided to steam and sail the little forty-four foot launch (which had a draught of only three feet) to Bombay, across more than two thousand miles of open ocean to try to sell her there. He parted company with the faithful Rae (who got himself a job on a sugar plantation on Johanna Island and died within a year), and set off across the Indian Ocean with a crew of three Royal Naval ratings (a stoker, a seaman and a carpenter) seven African natives who had never seen the sea before in their lives, and two native servants, one of whom was 'Chuma' who had been rescued by the Bishop and Livingstone from slave traders in 1861.

Despite his lack of nautical experience, after forty-four days at sea, Livingstone made landfall only one hundred and fifteen miles south of Bombay. He and his crew were desperately short of water and the monsoon was due any day, but nevertheless, Livingstone turned north and steamed into Bombay harbour forty-five days after leaving Zanzibar - and after a voyage of some two thousand five hundred miles.

Nobody of any importance noticed his arrival in India; indeed he said in a letter from Aden in July 1864 to Sir Thomas Maclear, the Astronomer Royal in Cape Town:

"...Our intense insignificance was amusing. A dense haze obscurred all the land....Then for Bombay and soon saw the big forests of masts....Went up, modestly of course, and anchored alongside the outer ones. Nobody saw us, and no wonder....we were but an atom....and it was only on the second day after our arrival that the custom house officer came aboard...."

Undaunted he made his way to Government House, and introduced himself to the Governor, Sir Bartle Frere, who invited him to stay as his guest whilst he negotiated the sale of his boat. Again, he failed to find a buyer - after all, who wanted a collapsible gunboat? - and so he left her in Bombay, embarked on a ship bound for England and was back in London by the end of July, 1864, where he too, received a very luke-warm welcome.

This time, there were no banquets and no celebrations, and the Foreign Secretary gave him a very cold reception indeed. There was no euphoria in the popular press, but much criticism of the Zambesi Expedition, and of Doctor Livingstone himself. Several leading newspapers pointed out that there had been a dreadful waste of public money because no commercial advantage had come from the expedition and several leading churchmen complained about the lack of converts and the total failure of the Universities Mission, blaming it all on Livingstone. Even the Royal Navy complained about misuse of Naval personnel, and stores and the Treasury announced that Livingstone had cost the nation an extra three thousand pounds for having failed to abort the expedition sooner! It was another not very happy homecoming!

Early in August, a poor, dejected David Livingstone went to Scotland to spend some time with his children. He had never even seen the youngest daughter, little Anna Mary, who had been born at Kuruman in 1859 when he was occupied on the Zambesi and he took her a black dolly as a present. Even this went wrong! The little girl didn't like it, and made it plain that she would have preferred a white one. There was worse to come! In June he heard of the death of his eldest son Robert who had gone to America, joined the Federal Army, had been wounded, captured, and had died as a prisoner of war.

Livingstone started to write another book to try to recoup, his fortunes but in September 1864 he interrupted his writing to go to Bath to a meeting of the British Association for the Advancement of Science, at which the main topic of interest was to be a debate between Richard Burton and John Speke about the true source of the River Nile; a problem in which Livingstone as a 'geographer' and explorer, was keenly interested.

The origins of the river Nile had been a matter of speculation and wonder for over two thousand years. Men had long asked themselves how a river, with no known tributaries could continue to overflow its banks in Egypt, when everybody knew that it had come through a great barren desert for hundreds and hundreds of miles? Where, they asked, did all the water come from?

In about 460 BC, the Greek historian Herodotus (484 - 425 BC), had gone upstream as far as the first cataract looking for its source, but had failed to find it. The notorious Roman Emperor Nero had sent two centurions to take charge of

an expedition to find the source, but they had come back empty-handed, saying that the river disappeared into an impenetrable swamp.

Legend had it that a Greek merchant on his way home from a visit to India had landed on the east coast of Africa, had gone inland for twenty five days and had seen great lakes and a range of snow-capped mountains! A Syrian geographer, Marinus of Tyre, had picked up this story and had decided that these mountains and lakes must be the source of the mighty river. In the second century AD, Claudius Ptolemaeus, an Egyptian mathematician, astronomer and geographer (better known perhaps as Ptolemy), using the Syrian's records, produced

Herodotus

a map showing a range of Mountains - the 'Mountains of the Moon' and two lakes from which the river flowed. This map had never been confirmed or seriously challenged until in 1848, when two German Missionaries, Krapft and Rebmann, travelling inland from Mombasa, had reported having seen snow on the mountains of Kilimanjaro and Kenya. Although many armchair geographers claimed that the two men must have had a touch of the sun and were 'seeing things' because - of course - they scoffed - there could be no snow on the Equator, someone had remembered old Ptolomey's 'Mountains of the Moon', and began to wonder if he - and the two Missionaries - had been right after all!

Until 1856, all explorers of the Nile had, quite logically, travelled upstream looking for the source, but in that year Burton and Speke had decided to try to find the source by travelling inland from the east coast of Africa, as had the Greek merchant some two thousand years before.

Speke claimed that he had found the source, Burton denied it, and they had agreed to air their differences in public.

It was to hear this debate that Livingstone went to Bath.

CHAPTER FOURTEEN

Richard Francis Burton (1821-90) and John Hanning Speke (1827-64) had both served in the Indian Army - Burton in a rather unorthodox way, but Burton was a rather unorthodox officer! He liked to disguise himself as a native, dyeing his face and hands, and creeping about in bazaars gathering intelligence. As a result of these activities, he had predicted that the army was on the verge of mutiny, but nobody would heed him.

He was five feet eleven inches tall, robust, weather-beaten and muscular with a huge black moustache. He was bad-tempered and impatient and did not suffer fools gladly, but beneath this frightening exterior, he was a scholar and a remarkable linguist. Since leaving the Indian army, Burton had travelled widely and, in 1853, disguised as a Muslim pilgrim, he had even entered the Holy City of Mecca. He spoke many 'native' tongues including Arabic and towards the end of his life it was claimed that he could speak twenty-two different languages.

Speke, his chosen companion, was a very different character. He too was tall, but as Burton was heavily built, Speke was slender, as Burton was naturally tough, Speke was a fitness fanatic. He ate well but drank no alcohol and never smoked and during one of his visits to Africa, he once walked barefoot to 'toughen himself up'. He too had travelled widely since leaving the army and was a keen big-game hunter. He came from a West Country family which could trace its history back to the Saxons, and unlike Burton, who had a rather raffish reputation, Speke was highly respectable, steady, abstemious and methodical.

The two men had already had an adventure together in Somalia, and Burton,

having decided to look for the source of the Nile, had obtained a grant of one thousand pounds from the Foreign Office and the backing of the Royal Geographical Society. He invited Speke to join him, and the two men had arrived in Zanzibar at the end of 1856, at just about the time when Doctor Livingstone had returned in triumph to Britain after his trans-African trek. They took their time in preparing for a long expedition and didn't leave Zanzibar for the interior until June 1857, shortly after they had heard the news of the Mutiny of native soldiers in India - news which must have tempted Burton to say 'I told you so!'.

Richard Burton

They reached Kazeh (now Tabora in central Tanzania) on 7th November, where they fell in with a number of Arab slave traders with whom Burton immediately became friendly and to whom he talked at length in his fluent Arabic. Speke, who couldn't understand a word of what was going on - became restless and urged Burton to press forwards, but it was not until early December that the two men left Kazeh marching westwards, deeper into the unknown heart of Africa.

Both men fell ill, Speke was almost blind and Burton had an ulcerated jaw, but eventually they reached Ujiji on the eastern bank of Lake Tanganyika on 13th February, 1858. Here they had hoped to find the source of the great river, but observations taken with their barometer showed that the lake was only two thousand five hundred and thirty five feet above sea level, far too low to be the origin of the Nile, so they returned to Kazeh to recuperate, to record their discoveries so far and decide what to do next.

Speke, having recovered his sight, was anxious to search further and have a look at another lake, which the Arabs called 'Nyanza'. They told him, that it lay some three weeks trek away to the north of Kazeh, and after some discussion, it was agreed that Burton would stay behind with his Arab friends and that Speke should go ahead and try to find Lake Nyanza. He reached its shores on 3rd August 1858 and was so impressed by its size and altitude that here at last, he was sure - he later said that he had no doubts at all - here was the source of the Nile! He stayed by the lake for only three days before rushing back in some excitement to Burton at Kazeh.

Burton, altogether a more pragmatic character, had demanded proof that the great lake was the source of the Nile, but Speke had no such proof and it soon became clear that he had simply made an assumption and had no other grounds for his claim.

Speke was very disappointed by Burton's disbelief but they set out for the coast at the end of September 1858 reaching Zanzibar on March 4th 1859. Here they caught up with the news of the outside world and learned that the Indian Mutiny had been put down with much ferocity. As former officers of the Indian Army they were glad to learn that three-quarters of the native Indian soldiers had remained loyal to the Crown, but their mood was still sombre, and there existed a certain antagonism between them.

Burton and Speke then sailed for Aden, where Burton decided to stay for a while. Speke went on to England by himself, then on his arrival in London, Speke went to see Sir Roderick Murchison, the President of the Royal Geographical Society, and told him of his 'discovery' of the source of the Nile. Murchison invited him to return to Africa to confirm his findings and the sum of two thousand five hundred pounds was quickly raised to finance an expedition. Speke arranged that the Royal Geographical Society also would mount a 'back-up' expedition which would travel southwards up the Nile to meet them and bring them fresh supplies after they had confirmed the source of the river. This was a rather haphazard arrangement since, in those days before radio, it was impossible accurately to estimate when, or where, the two expeditions would meet. Nevertheless, this was the arrangement, and the British Vice Consul in Khartoum was given one thousand pounds with which to buy boats and supplies.

Speke engaged a companion - another Indian Army Officer, Captain James Augustus Grant - to go back to Africa with him. Grant was a very cool character. He was a professional soldier who had fought in several campaigns in India and had taken part in the relief of Lucknow, but he was also an accomplished artist and botanist. He was devoted to Speke, whom he regarded as the expedition's leader, and - unlike Burton was the perfect companion.

John Speke

Speke and Grant went back to Africa in 1859, eventually reaching Kazek, and there trekked northwestwards into the native kingdoms of Karagwe, Buganda and Bunyoro on the shores of the huge lake Nyanza - by now called 'Victoria Nyanza' in honour of Queen Victoria. Speke and Grant were astonished at what they found in these remote inland kingdoms. The peoples there had achieved an extraordinary level of 'civilisation' without any contact with the outside world. Their houses were beautifully made, they had a wide variety of musical instruments, and their forms of government were highly sophisticated. Punishments were unbelievably cruel, but the rule of law obtained. Roads had been cut through the bush and in Buganda the young King, Mutesa had established his capital on a hilltop a few miles from the lake shore. The two men stayed in Buganda from February until July 1862, and 'discovered' a waterfall which Speke named after Lord Ripon, one time President of the Royal Geographical Society. They continued to trek northwards, and in December they were met by an advance guard of Egyptian soldiers who accompanied them to their garrison at Faloro where they were royally entertained. The commander of the garrison, Mohammed Wad-el-Mak, was a slaver, and he refused to go northwards towards Gondokoro until he had rounded up all available slaves that were for sale in the area. But at last, in January, 1863, the cavalcade set out, with Speke and Grant heading a disorderly mob of freshly captured (or purchased) slaves, which grew steadily as more and more slaves were added to the haul. In February 1863, this caravan reached Gondokoro where they met several other European explorers who had travelled up-stream from Khartoum to meet them - including Sir Samuel Baker, and his exotic blond-haired wife whom he had purchased from a slave market in Hungary.

Speke had sent a cable to London saying that the question of the source of the Nile had been 'settled', but Burton was furious and set about destroying Speke's claim. Had Speke or Grant circumnavigated the Lake to make sure that no other rivers flowed into it from the real source of the Nile? The answer was 'No'. Had they followed the river all the way down-stream to Gondokoro to make sure that a greater stream had not joined it from the true source of the Nile? Again the answer was 'No'. (Speke and Grant had travelled overland from the lake, and had assumed that the river, when they saw it, *was* the Nile.)

Other members of the Royal Geographical Society joined in the argument and a certain James M'Queen, a geographer of note who had never been to Africa, suggested that Speke had somehow made the Nile flow up-hill! He further accused poor Speke of condoning the slave trade and of all manner of other unpleasant things, generally turning many people against him, with precious little justification.

Livingstone, by now back in England after the Zambesi fiasco, also believed that Burton, was right and agreed that Speke had assumed too much. He thought that the true source of the Nile lay much further to the south.

It was to settle this argument that the British Association for the Advancement of Science had invited Burton and Speke to their meeting in Bath, and the two former companions were to meet face to face on the platform on 16th September 1864 to argue their points of view in public. Doctor Livingstone, despite his unpopularity, was determined to be there.

On the day before the debate, Speke went with his cousin and a gamekeeper to shoot partridges. At about four o'clock Speke's cousin heard a shot and saw Speke fall from the top of a low stone wall. The cousin ran to his assistance and found him with a ghastly wound in his chest. It seemed that he had been climbing over the wall, had carelessly pulled the gun up after him and it had accidentally gone off. He was still conscious when his cousin and the gamekeeper reached him so, leaving the gamekeeper with the injured man, the cousin ran for a doctor. When he got back, Speke was dead.

Despite the inquest finding that death was the result of an accident, many ill-natured people, particularly those who believed that he had *not* found the source of the Nile, preferred to suggest that he had committed suicide rather than face Burton in public debate.

Speke's death meant that the true source of the Nile was still in doubt, and Murchison turned to Doctor Livingstone and asked if he would be prepared to go and settle the question once and for all. Livingstone agreed, and Murchison asked how he would proceed - up the river Rovuma and around the southern end of Lake Tanganyika? Who would go with him? John Kirk? Livingstone asked Kirk, with whom remarkably he still had friendly relations, to accompany him, but Kirk was engaged to be married, and declined. Livingstone decided to go alone.

Astonishingly, despite the failure of the Zambesi Expedition, the Foreign Office was still prepared to back him, if not generously. He was given a grant of five hundred pounds (this was later increased by another one thousand pounds), the Royal Geographical Society donated another five hundred pounds and Livingstone paid the balance from his own funds. He was appointed as 'Consul for Central Africa' (a non-stipendary appointment), and in August 1865 he set off on his last journey, travelling from Folkestone via Paris and Cairo to Bombay. (He wanted to go to Bombay, because the *Lady Nyassa* had still not been sold, and in any case, he wanted to re-employ the Africans whom he had left there.)

Whilst in Bombay, the Governor, with whom he stayed, recommended that he recruit some porters from a Government-run school for freed African slaves at Nasick, one hundred miles or so north east of Bombay. All pupils at this school had been enslaved as children, and had been liberated on the high seas by anti-slaving patrols of the Royal Navy. Because these unfortunates could not be sent 'home' - since they had no home to which to go - the Church Missionary Society had established a school for them, where they could be taught to read and write and be brought up as Christians. 'Nassik' boys despised people who could neither read or write, and they generally regarded themselves as being far too superior to indulge in manual labour. Nevertheless, Livingstone selected eight young men to go with him back to their native Africa. He was also persuaded to take

with him a dozen sepoys, and a havildar to take charge of them. He then sold the launch for two thousand three hundred pounds (it had cost him six thousand pounds!) and sailed for Zanzibar with a team of thirty-five men.

In Zanzibar he recruited ten more porters and purchased a number of water buffalo, six camels and four donkeys. By the time he had obtained a passage for his expedition from Zanzibar to the mainland in mid-March, 1866, most of the water buffalo had died.

CHAPTER FIFTEEN

Dispirited, unloved and unwanted, Henry Stanley spent the rest of 1863 as a deckhand before deserting in Barcelona, where he joined another ship bound for New York. Here he went ashore and got a job as a 'clerk' to a judge who lived in Brooklyn, but this didn't last long, and in mid 1864, when the American Civil War was still raging, Stanley joined the United States Federal Navy as a clerk, signing on for three years.

In the Navy, he became friendly with a lad some years his junior - Lewis H. Noe, with whom he was later to go adventuring - but he soon deserted, and went back to New York, this time looking for a job as a journalist. He had no experience of journalism although he had a natural flair for writing. He didn't find a job, so in mid-August 1865. The dreadful war having ended, Stanley went to San Francisco, still looking for work on the staff of a newspaper. From thence he went to Denver, where he got a job, not as a journalist, but as an apprentice 'printer'!

In Denver, Stanley met a freelance journalist, William Harlow and together the two young men decided to 'go round the world'. To 'test themselves' to see if they were tough enough for such an undertaking they built a raft and floated some six hundred miles down the river Platte from Denver to Omaha, where they boarded a steamboat bound for St. Louis. At St. Louis they caught a train for New York where Stanley collected young Lewis Noe and the three of them obtained a passage on the barque *E.H.Yarrington*, bound for Smyrna (Izmir) in Turkey.

Once ashore, Stanley and Cook bought horses - Lewis Noe had to walk - and the three of them set off in high spirits, intending to cross Asia to China on the first 'leg' of their 'round-the-world' journey. They didn't get far because they were kidnapped by a band of brigands who held them to ransom.

Somehow the whole party was captured by the Turkish authorities, and the three young 'Americans' were released. Leaving Cook behind to serve as witness at the trial of the kidnappers, Stanley and Noe went on to Constantinople where Stanley obtained an interview with the American Minister from whom he obtained a loan of one hundred and fifty pounds secured by a 'promissory note' in the name of his - entirely fictitious - father, who, he said, lived at an equally fictitious address - Number 20, Liberty Street, New York.

Stanley spent some of the one hundred and fifty pounds on an American-style Naval Officer's uniform which was made for him by an obliging Turkish tailor, and then he and Noe sailed for Liverpool, where they obtained lodgings with the relations with whom Stanley had lived before running away to America in 1858. These people must have been very forgiving - or very gullible - since he had left them without even bothering to say 'good-bye', but they seem to have accepted him. He left Noe with them whilst he went back to Wales for the second time to see his mother.

This time he did things in style. Wearing his bogus American Officer's naval uniform, he hired a carriage and a pair of horses from an inn at Mold in Cheshire and drove to Denbeigh where he told his Mother that he was now an 'Ensign' in the American Navy. Elizabeth was duly impressed, and Stanley then drove off to the workhouse at St Asaph where he was received with due respect and where he treated all the children to tea and cakes, before changing back into civilian clothes, and catching a train for London. Here he went to see the representative of the *New York Herald,* and tried, unsuccessfully, to persuade him to give him a job as a reporter.

Frustrated, he went back to Liverpool, collected young Noe and once again returned to America. He found his way to Missouri where, at last he did get a reporter's job on a local paper called *The Democrat* and he was assigned to cover General Winfield Scott Hancock's campaign against the Indians in Kansas and Nebraska. The Editor was pleased with his efforts and Stanley was sent to report on the 'Peace Commission' at Medicine Lodge Creek, Kansas, which followed the campaign. His highly critical reports, in which he expressed pity for the dignified but helpless Indians, attracted the attention of a number of leading American newspapers, including the editor and founder of the *New York Herald,* James Gordon Bennett. Stanley persuaded Bennett to employ him as a reporter and to send him to cover the activities of a British campaign against the Emperor of Ethiopia. Before leaving England, Livingstone had discussed the Nile

question with Sir Roderick Murchison. They had both come to the conclusion that poor Speke had been wrong and that the Nile rose much further south, flowing from the northern end of Lake Tanganyika, via Lake Albert into Victoria Nyanza and that unless Lake Tanganyika was fed by yet another river it, and not Lake Victoria, Nyanza was the true source of the Nile.

Murchison had advised Livingstone to check the connection between Lake Tanganyika and the newly discovered Lake Albert, before searching for a river which might or might not flow into Lake Tanganyika, but Livingstone was so convinced that the link existed, that he didn't bother to make this check.

James Gordon Bennett He and his expedition landed just north of the mouth of the river Rovuma, which, despite all evidence to the contrary, Livingstone was *still* sure flowed from Lake Nyassa (it *still* didn't!), and he and his small army of thirty five men marched inland towards the lake, intending to cross it by canoe and make for a smaller lake which the natives called 'Bangweolo', which Livingstone had convinced himself was the true source of the Nile.

He had intended to pick up some more porters on the mainland, but all the natives in those parts were terrified of being captured by slavers and Livingstone had to abandon a lot of his stores, an action which he was later to regret.

He was soon to realise that the recruitment of the Indian sepoys had been a big mistake, for they wouldn't keep up with the rest of the caravan, they stole from people in the villages through which the caravan passed, and - worse still - they ill-treated the pack-animals. The camels proved to be an even bigger liability than the sepoys! They were slow and were incapable of penetrating thick bush unless a path was cut for them, a time-consuming and troublesome task. Soon Livingstone found that he could not buy food. Not only had there been a severe drought, but he had entered an area much troubled by slave raiders from hostile tribes. Everywhere he saw distressing evidence of the beastly trade, including slaves too ill to march, tied together and left to die.

In July, an Arab slaver, hearing that Livingstone was short of food, diverted his caravan, and went to find and help him. This was not the first and certainly not the last time, that Arab slavers came to the rescue of European explorers in Africa despite knowing that these 'mad' white men were strongly opposed to the slave trade. It is even more surprising that Livingstone, with his strongly held views about the slave trade, accepted the help offered, and frequently actually travelled in the company of slavers.

Shortly after this encounter, the Indian sepoys killed and ate a buffalo calf from amongst Livingstone's pack animals claiming that it had been killed by a 'tiger' - they told the Doctor that they had seen its stripes! There are, of course, no tigers in Africa and Livingstone knew that they were lying so he dismissed them all and sent them back to the coast - all except the havildar who begged to be allowed to stay. With the dismissal of the Indians, Livingstone's party was reduced to twenty-three, but they moved on and early in August, reached the shores of Lake Nyassa. His reputation had gone before him. Natives in the region still remembered his activities in 1861 when he had freed many of their slaves and they didn't trust him. They refused to hire him a dhow in which to cross the lake because they guessed that he would burn it when he reached the far shore. Undeterred, he trekked around the south side of the lake, but many of his porters deserted him. With only eleven men left, he continued his trek but was frequently ill and had to rest.

Musa, the headman of the deserting porters, reaching Zanzibar, told the Sultan that Livingstone had been murdered and that his faithful porters had returned - in sorrow - with the news. This information soon reached London where flags were flown at half mast, and obituary notices appeared in the papers, but the notices were seen by Lieutenant Young of the Royal Navy (who, had worked with Livingstone on the *'Lady Nyassa'* and had taken the 'Pioneer' to Capetown). Young clearly remembered Musa as a congenital liar and volunteered to go to Lake Nyassa to get to the bottom of the matter. Remarkably, with the backing of the Royal Navy, a small sailing boat was built for him and taken to the lake where he picked up Livingstone's trail. Although he did not make contact with the explorer, he found out enough to prove that Musa's story had been false, and then a letter written by Livingstone long after his reported death, reached Zanzibar, telling the true story of the porters' desertion, Musa was arrested by the Sultan and imprisoned in irons for eight months. In January 1867, a porter carrying Livingstone's chronometers slipped and fell and in so doing damaged them so badly that the Doctor could no longer use them for accurate calculations of longitude. (Subsequently it was found that for the following eighteen months, all his positions were some twenty miles west of the position calculated.)

Two weeks later, the porter carrying Livingstone's medicine chest deserted and took the chest with him leaving the Doctor without any medical supplies at all, but he wandered on, northwards, searching for the river which he was certain flowed northward from Lake Bangweolo into lake Tanganyika. By this time he was in much pain and suspected that he had rheumatic fever, but had no means of treating himself for this disease.

Early in February 1867 Livingstone encountered an Arab slave caravan heading

for the coast and he asked the Arabs to take a packet of letters to Zanzibar for him, one of which requested the British Consul there to send more supplies to Ujiji on the shore of Lake Tanganyika saying that he hoped to be there in a couple of month's time. He reached the lake much about on schedule on April Fools' day 1867 but he was told that 'war' had broken out between local tribes and some Arab slavers so he had no option but to try to make a detour to avoid getting mixed up in the fighting. He didn't get far and fell ill with malaria, during which illness he was faithfully attended by two of his 'boys', 'Susi' and 'Chuma', (Chuma, it will be remembered, was the youngster whom he had rescued from slavers in 1861).

Having more or less recovered from the fever, he made for the nearest Arab encampment to try to find out how serious the 'war' was and reached it towards the end of May. He stayed with the Arabs until mid-September when he set out again, this time in company with a half-cast Arab trader called Hamid bin Mohammed, better known as 'Tippu Tip', and together they reached the shores of Lake Moero on 8th November 1867.

CHAPTER SIXTEEN

Theodore II, Emperor of Ethiopia[1], was the son of a relatively unimportant chieftain, but he had claimed that he was of 'royal' blood and he spent much of his early life fighting and killing anybody who opposed him.

By 1855 he had defeated most of the other ruling chieftains and had declared himself Emperor. As we have already seen, Britain's shortest route to India depended on the security of Egypt which, in turn, depended on the security of the River Nile.

The 'Blue' Nile rose in the mountains of Ethiopia, and since British ships enter-

---

[1]*Many writers tend to use the names 'Abyssinia' and 'Ethiopia' as being interchangeable. Some show the country either as 'Abyssinia (Ethiopia)' or as 'Ethiopia (Abyssinia)'. This is confusing and except in quotations directly referring to 'Abyssinia' - see Queen Victoria's letter to the Emperor Theodore. The name Ethiopia is used throughout this book. Nevertheless the origins of the two names is not without interest. The romanised pronunciation of the ancient Arabic name for the area which contains modern Ethiopia was HABASHAT. This name is said to have been 'latinised' in the seventeenth century to ABYSSINIA, probably via the process of believing that the name 'ABYSSIN' was the nearest 'western' equivalent of the Arabic 'HABASHAT', <u>plus</u> the addition of the suffix 'IA' so frequently used for names of countries - (see for example, RHODES-IA and NIGER-IA).*

The OED records that the name ETHIOPIA comes from the Greek AITHIOPS, (probably for ATHEIN, to burn + OPS, face), hence a sunburnt or 'black' man. This was 'latinised' to AETHIO-PIA, and was originally used to describe swarthy peoples in other parts of the world. (In 1861 it was said that there were three principal races of man, Caucasian, Mongolian and Ethiopian.).

For reasons which are far from clear, in general the British called the country 'Abyssinia' (and continued so to call it up to and including the 'Abyssinian War' in 1935), but the native people called it, and still call it 'Ethiopia'.

ing the Red Sea from the Indian Ocean had to sail close inshore along the Ethiopian coast, events in that wild country were of considerable interest to Britain, and it paid her to establish good relations with the Emperor, no matter what his background.

Mr W.G. Plowden, an Englishman who, had chosen to live in Ethiopia, was friendly with Theodore and was appointed British Consul to Ethiopia, and given instructions to enter into a treaty of friendship with the Emperor. Britain's official recognition of Theodore gave him and his country a respectability not hitherto enjoyed and, as a result, a number of Christian missionaries from various European countries went to Ethiopia to try to introduce their particular 'brand' of Christianity, seemingly ignoring the fact that Ethiopia had been a mainly Christian country since the fourth century A.D.

In 1860, Plowden was killed by rebel tribesmen and the Emperor mounted a savage punitive expedition, killing some two thousand warriors in the process. Britain had sent Captain Charles Duncan Cameron as a replacement Consul, and he arrived there in 1862 bringing with him a gift from Queen Victoria - a pair of pistols inscribed:

"Presented to Theodore, Emperor of Abyssinia, by Victoria, Queen of Great Britain and Ireland, for his kindness to her servant Plowden, 1861"

Theodore was delighted! He was so pleased that he wrote an extraordinary letter to the Queen, which started:

"In the name of the Father, of the Son, and of the Holy Ghost, one God in Trinity, chosen by God, King of Kings, Theodore of Ethiopia, to her Majesty Victoria, Queen of England.."

and ended:

"I wish to have an answer to this letter by Consul Cameron, and that he may conduct my Embassy to England. See how Islam oppresses the Christian"

The letter eventually reached the Foreign Office in London by hand of Cameron, but it was set aside - or overlooked - and nobody sent even an acknowledgement. To make matters worse, the Foreign Office directed Cameron not to return directly to Ethiopia, but to go via the Sudan to see what action was being taken to suppress the slave trade, there and to look into the possibility of growing cotton on the banks of the Nile to replace American cotton which had doubled in price as a result of the Civil War.

Theodore was angry! Not only had the Queen failed to acknowledge his letter

but she had deliberately sent her servant Cameron back to Ethiopia via an Islamic country which Theodore regarded as being an enemy. He immediately imprisoned all Europeans and when, at last, Cameron returned, he was thrown into prison in chains, and tortured. Then, when a Mr Kerans, a young Irishman, arrived in Ethiopia from Britain as a consular assistant he too was imprisoned, although he knew nothing of the cause of the Emperor's fury.

Thedore II News of these events eventually reached Colonel Merewether, the British Political Agent in Aden, who advised the Foreign Office to reply to the Emperor's letter. A reply was drafted for the Queen's signature, expressing continued friendship but requesting the immediate release of all European captives and of 'her servant' Cameron.

This letter was taken to Ethiopia by a member of Merewether's staff, Hormuzd Rassam, an Iraqi who had adopted British nationality, and Rassam, accompanied by Doctor Henry Blanc and Lieutenant Prideaux, went to Massawa in Egypt, regarded then as the 'gateway' to Ethiopia, and sought permission to enter the Emperor's kingdom. This was not forthcoming until August 1865, and even then Rassam went first to Cairo to purchase gifts for the Emperor, whom he finally met in January 1866. Theodore accepted the gifts and then threw Rassam into prison!

Theodore released one of the German missionaries and, whilst still holding his wife and children hostage, sent him with letters to Queen Victoria asking her to send skilled artisans to his country to help him 'modernise' it. The German reached England in July 1866, but the Government was very much preoccupied with the question of electoral reform; Earl Russel's Whig Government having just been brought down by the issue. Lord Derby's minority Tory Government was having difficulty with its own supporters, as well as with the general public, and there were riots in Hyde Park where the Police had to be reinforced by a unit of the Life Guards. All this, plus a cholera epidemic, tended to give a low priority to the problems of a handful of Europeans being held by an African potentate in a country of which the majority of people in the country had never heard. However, somebody must have taken notice; some skilled artisans were recruited, and a polite letter was drafted *The Emperor's Seal*

Lt General Sir Robert Napier

for the Queen's signature. Gifts for the Emperor were purchased, and the poor German Missionary, who must have been deeply worried about the fate of his wife and children, was instructed to go with the artisans - and carry the Queen's letter and her gifts to Ethiopia - but to make sure that Theodore released all prisoners before the gifts were handed over or the artisans set to work.

The letter was signed by the Queen in October and the missionary was just about to set off on his thankless task when the news of Rassam's imprisonment reached England. A fresh letter was therefore drafted - this time in stronger terms - and given to the hapless missionary to deliver. He arrived back at the Emperor's court in December 1866, but Theodore still wouldn't release the prisoners - indeed he made their lives even more miserable.

The British Government was unable to do anything constructive and simply hoped that the Ethiopian problem would fade away, but of course, it didn't and by July 1867, when the British public became aware of problems and demanded that something be done.

A further letter was sent to Theodore telling him to release the prisoners immediately, but it remained unanswered and the Government decided to argue no more but to declare war on this incredible upstart!

General Napier had told the astonished Government that he would require twelve thousand fighting men, almost twice as many supporting staff, some twenty thousand mules, and a fleet of two hundred and eighty ships, to carry the expedition to Africa.

By mid-October 1867 an advance guard was sent to construct a port at Zul, a small town on the Red Sea, and slowly the invasion force was assembled. It finally consisted of four thousand white officers, nine thousand native troops - mostly Indians - nineteen thousand supporting staff of one sort or another plus sixteen thousand mules, four thousand seven hundred camels, two thousand five hundred horses and forty-four Indian elephants to carry the guns, together with twenty thousand sheep and bullocks to feed the troops.

Mr. Rassam. Mr. Stern.   Mr. and Mrs. Rosenthal   Pietro.   Capt. Cameron.
    Lieut. Prideaux.   and child.   Dr. Blanc.

Hostage Crisis 1866
A contemporary engraving of the hostages themselves

This was the campaign that Henry Stanley was sent to cover on behalf of the *New York Herald*. The editor, Gordon Bennett, had told him that he would be paid only by results and that he must write exclusively for the Herald.

Stanley accepted the terms, and sailed once again for Liverpool. Travelling via London, Paris and Marseilles, he reached Suez at the end of January 1868, where he hired a servant, bought a horse and applied for a passage to Zula. Before he left Suez he came to an understanding with someone in the local telegraph office, and bribed him to give priority to all his dispatches. He then went and caught up with Napier's army, but he was not well received, and was regarded by many of the officers as a 'howling cad'. This made no difference to Stanley, who was not interested in other peoples' opinion, and was only concerned with reporting on the campaign in great detail. After a battle in which some seven hundred Abyssinians were killed and twelve hundred wounded - with only twenty of Napier's troops wounded and none killed, the mad Theodore shot himself with one of the pistols sent to him as a present by Queen Victoria. The European prisoners were released, and Stanley, having obtained some souvenirs, including a bloodstained strip of the Emperor's shirt, made for the coast as fast as he could. He obtained a passage on the ship which was carrying a Colonel Millward, who had the official Army dispatches, but the ship was delayed at Suez, and put in quarantine because of a cholera epidemic. Nevertheless, somehow Stanley managed to smuggle his reports ashore to his friend in the telegraph office, and his version of events reached London and New York, before there was any official word in London about the campaign. This made him unpopular with the British establishment - and with the Army - but this didn't worry Henry Stanley. He had achieved his first 'scoop', and had established his reputation as a journalist of some note.

The new editor of the Herald, James Gordon Bennett Jr., was very pleased indeed, and he gave Stanley a permanent post on the newspaper. For the rest of 1868 and for the first part of 1869, Stanley stayed in Europe, reporting from London, Paris, and Madrid, but, having become a bona fide journalist, he decided that his name did not sound sufficiently important, so he 'invented' a middle name, and became 'Henry Moreton Stanley' - the name which he retained for the rest of his quite remarkable life. He also acquired an American passport, and had business cards printed, saying simply:

H.M.Stanley; New York Herald

Meanwhile, Livingstone, almost certainly unaware of events in Ethiopia, had reached the shores of Lake Moero, having heard that a river, which the locals called 'Luapula', flowed into the lake from Lake Bangweolo, far to the south, and that a larger river flowed out of the lake to the North. The natives called this river the 'Lualaba', but Livingstone, convinced that this must be the 'Nile', decided to track it northwards to see if it did flow into Lake Tanganyika, and from thence to Lake Albert. He could not risk making this long journey until he had picked up fresh supplies and medicines from Ujiji, but nevertheless he set out on a brief trek in company with an Arab slaver to check on the in-flow of the river Luapula. By the time he got to the relevant area, however, the rains had started, and prevented further exploration. In March 1868 he decided instead to move north again towards Lake Tanganyika, and by this time he had convinced himself that Lake Bangweolo was the source of the Nile. He even drafted a dispatch to the British Foreign Secretary announcing that he could 'safely assert' that he had found the true source of the mighty river, and that everyone else - including Burton, Speke and Grant - had been looking too far to the north! He reached the shores of Lake Bangweolo by mid July and tried to hire a canoe in which to explore it, but he had run out of 'trade goods', and had nothing with which to pay for the hire. Then he heard that an Arab slaver called Bogharib was planning to visit an area to the northwest of Lake Tanganyika, through which, Livingstone decided, the River Lualaba or infant Nile must flow, so he decided temporarily to abandon his stores at Ujiji, and go with Bogharib. However, more fighting broke out between Arabs and local natives, and as a result their trek was

British troops at the Kafir-Bur Gate,
Magdala, during the Abyssinian Campaign

aborted, so Livingstone, still in the company of Bogharib, made for Ujiji after all.

By January 1869, now nearing his fifty sixth birthday, the Doctor was still making for Ujiji, but he had pneumonia and was often delirious. He would probably have died had it not been for Bogharib, who nursed him and directed that he be carried in a litter. They reached the shores of Lake Tanganyika in mid- February 1869, but it was another month before Livingstone reached Ujiji, by which time he was blistered by the sun, coughing blood, and squeezing live maggots out of his arms and legs! When at last they reached Ujiji, Livingstone discovered that the stores, which had been sent from the coast, had been pillaged, and there was no food, no medicine and perhaps worse still, no letters from the outside world. All that was left, apart from a few trade goods - beads and cloth - was a little sugar, tea and coffee. He was told that the Arabs had helped themselves to his stores because they had assumed that he was long since dead, and wouldn't be wanting them. They had been seen as a gift from Allah, not to be wasted!

Livingstone had two options - either to trek back to the coast to collect replacement stores, or to try to get another message to Zanzibar, where his old companion Doctor Kirk was by now Consul. Still determined to track down the elusive

Nile, he decided against going back to the coast, but instead wrote no less than forty four letters, and instructed some Arab traders to take them to Zanzibar. Despite the kindness shown to him by individual Arabs, many still distrusted him and suspected that he was spying on their activities. They thought that his letters might contain adverse reports to the Sultan, so although they politely took them for delivery, they destroyed most of them, and only one letter addressed to Doctor Kirk actually got to its destination.

By the end of July he was fit enough to trek again to try to find the Lualaba and was determined to prove, once and for all, that it was the infant Nile. He planned to return to Ujiji within six months to collect stores which he hoped that Kirk would send him, but this was not to be, and his health broke down again. He was frequently ill with malaria, he had ulcers on his feet, and was often in great pain. He had lost most of his teeth, and had extracted several stumps by twisting twine around them and striking the twine with a stick to jerk them out of his swollen gums. His progress was not only hampered by illness, but by local 'wars' between Arabs and hostile natives and for the rest of 1869 and for the greater part of 1870 he was confined to his hut, reading his Bible from cover-to-cover four times. During one of these enforced periods of idleness, he heard that one of his porters who had deserted - a lad called James whom he had recruited from Nasick in India - had been captured by natives and eaten. Livingstone was revolted, and he came to the reluctant conclusion that there was nothing to choose between the slave traders and the cannibals whom they captured. If anything, he thought, the slave traders were more 'civilised'! He was still hut-bound early in 1871 when ten porters arrived, having been sent by Doctor Kirk from Zanzibar, bringing fresh supplies of quinine, and some cloth and beads with which he could trade. By mid-February 1871, Livingstone and a party of thirteen men, the ten porters sent by Kirk, plus Susi, Chuma, and another 'Nassick' lad called 'Gardner', reached a town called Nyange, where they saw the Lualaba for the first time. Here the river was at least two miles wide, and it flowed slowly northward - it must be the Nile!

Livingstone tried to hire some canoes so that he could follow the river north. But the Arabs, suspecting that he was either a spy for the Sultan or a rival trader trying to get a share of their lucrative ivory and slave trade, were not helpful. He offered them a lot of money plus all the supplies which - he hoped - awaited him at Ujiji, but whilst the Arabs were considering this offer, there was a fracas in the town, during which Arabs opened fire on villagers coming by river to market. Many people were shot or drowned, and yet another local 'war' had broken out. Livingstone, weak and frequently too ill to trek, was often under attack from hostile natives who thought that he was an Arab slaver, but he reached Ujiji towards the end of October 1871 in a dreadfully weak condition. He found that a caravan from Zanzibar had arrived, but, again assuming that he must be dead, the Arabs had plundered the stores and, yet again there was nothing left!

CHAPTER SEVENTEEN

Although the early reports of Livingstone's death had proved to be false, they had nevertheless aroused world interest in his activities and both European and American newspapers had begun to speculate on his whereabouts. Some said that he was in Zanzibar, others that he was about to cross Africa again, this time at the Equator, but nobody really knew where he was and he had not been seen by any white person for over three years.

Gordon Bennett sent for Stanley and told him to go and find Livingstone and get another 'scoop' for the Herald. Stanley was not pleased, because the Suez Canal was just about to be opened and he wanted to be there when it was. Livingstone would have to wait! The French had built the canal, and Ferdinand de Lesseps' `Compagnie Universelle du Canal Maritime de Suez` had obtained a lease of ninety nine years to date from its opening, after which time, it would become Egyptian property. The canal was to be opened in November, 1869 and although this meant that under the terms of the lease it would not become Egyptian until 1968 - that was far too far ahead for Ismail, the Khedive of Egypt, a spendthrift, and he was determined to have his share of the glory while he could.

The Khedive set about making sure that the opening was a success and amongst other extravagances, he had an Opera House built in Cairo and commissioned an Italian, Giuseppi Verdi, to write an opera to be performed in it. Verdi accepted the commission but, in the event, he didn't complete the work on time, and *Aida* was not performed until 1871! Ismail ordered that the pyramids were to be illuminated with magnesium flares, and in Port Said, three magnificent pavilions were built, one for the more important guests, another for Christian visitors, and a third for Muslim dignitaries. Half way along the canal, a new town was built and called 'Ismailia'. Vast quantities of fireworks were purchased and brought to Port Said, but they were set off by accident with an enormous bang which almost destroyed the town!

Nevertheless, at last all was ready, and on November 17th, the canal was blessed by Muslim, Greek Orthodox, Roman Catholic, and Coptic Christian clerics. To the sound of gunfire, and the music of no less than twenty bands, the Empress Eugénie of France in the Imperial yacht *Aigle,* led the flotilla into the canal, followed by the Khedive in his yacht, and the Emperor of Austria in his. No British 'Royals' were present because the Prince and Princess of Wales had made an official visit some months before, had been present at the opening of the sluice gates into the 'Bitter Lakes', and, having seen this stage of the exercise, didn't want to come back for what they felt, was bound to be a rather vulgar celebration.

The French, Egyptian and Austrian Royal Yachts were escorted by British, Austrian and Russian warships which went to make up a fleet of over seventy vessels. These ships, and another fleet coming from Suez met at sunset at Ismailia and there the guests all went ashore for a banquet. Africa was declared to have ceased to be an 'island', and the Khedive enthusiastically declared that Egypt was now part of Europe!

Henry Moreton Stanley covered all these activities with his accustomed style, and, after the canal had been duly opened, off he went up the Nile as far as the first cataract and wrote a guide book for American tourists. He didn't give Livingstone a second thought. From Egypt he went to Constantinople where, only

The grand opening of the Suez Canal

three eventful years, before he had cheated the American Minister out of one hundred and fifty pounds. Astonishingly he went to see the Minister, who was still in office, apologised for the fraud, and, remarkably, made friends with him. So friendly did they become that when Stanley left for the Persian Gulf, the Minister gave him a present of a repeating rifle, and a set of letters of introduction to authorities whom Stanley would meet on his way to India - his declared destination.

Stanley then trekked overland to the Gulf and slept amongst the ruins of Persepolis, an ancient Persian city, once capital of Darius I (522-486 BC), to the north-east of the city of Shiraz in Iran, and he carved an inscription on one of the remaining pillars. It says - 'Stanley, *New York Herald*, 1870.' From Persia he went on to Karachi, and from thence to Bombay, which he reached in August 1870. Here he learned that Livingstone was still 'missing', and he decided that perhaps he ought now to obey orders and go and find him.

Even then he didn't hurry, but waited for two months for a boat to Mauritius whence he sailed to the Seychelles and finally got to Zanzibar in January 1871. He was to find that nobody in Zanzibar had ever heard of Henry Moreton Stanley or of the financial backing that was to be given to him by the *New York Herald*. He was finally 'rescued' by the American Consul, who assured the Zanzibari business community that any man representing the great *New York Herald* was 'credit-worthy'. He then made careful enquiries and found that still nobody had heard anything of Livingstone's whereabouts, so he set about organising an expedition to go and find him, as directed by his editor.

Stanley and his two companions, a servant whom he had hired on his travels and the Mate from the ship which had brought him to Zanzibar, and whom he had persuaded to join him in his adventure, assembled six tons of baggage and recruited a large number of porters to carry it, and within a very few weeks, Stanley's 'Find Livingstone' expedition numbered almost two hundred souls. By the end of January 1871, this small army crossed to the mainland from Zanzibar, and set out on its journey, with one man in front carrying the American flag - the 'Stars and Stripes' - and with other men firing their muskets into the air as a farewell salute.

Stanley reached Tabora by the end of June but was held up there until September by one of the many 'wars' between Arab slavers and local tribesmen. During this period of enforced idleness he fell ill with malaria but by the end of September the 'war' was over and he was fit to continue his trek. Early in November he heard that natives had seen a very old, and sick white man at Ujiji, and Stanley knew that he had succeeded in his mission. On 10th November 1871 he marched into Ujiji with American and Zanzibari flags flying, and muskets firing, and Stanley met Livingstone at last.

Stanley: The Rising star of the
New York Herald

One might think that the two men had little in common - the one, a deeply religious man, dedicated to serving others, the other an accomplished liar and cheat, a self-made man who cared only for himself and for his reputation as a journalist. Nevertheless, both were incredibly brave and physically tough and both had come from humble beginnings.

It may have been these facts that made them take to each other, or maybe it was because Livingstone gave Stanley a kindly almost fatherly welcome, one will never know, but Stanley, who secretly yearned for love and adulation, soon became very attached to the elderly Scottish Missionary doctor turned explorer, and they sat and talked and talked for hours on end, as only lonely men can talk. Stanley brought Livingstone up to date with news of the outside world. He told him of his adventures in Ethiopia, of the defeat of France by Prussia after the brief Franco-Prussian War and he told of the opening of the Suez Canal. In return, Livingstone told the young journalist of his adventures, and his quest to find the source of the Nile.

There can be little doubt that, from this initial empathy, a true and deep relationship developed - at least on Stanley's part. He later was to say of Livingstone that "I loved him like a son", and from a man who did not know his natural father, and who had run away from the man who had 'adopted' him, this rings true. Stanley's affectionate feeling towards Livingstone was to last for the rest of his life.

Shortly after Stanley's arrival with masses of badly needed stores and medicines, the two men set out together in a canoe to explore Lake Tanganyika, and to see if a river flowed from it into Lake Albert. (None did, and yet another theory about the Nile was exploded). Livingstone might at last have realised that, had he followed Murchison's advice and checked this first, he might have saved himself a lot of time and trouble, but having discovered that the theory was wrong, he was more determined than ever to go back to the Lualaba and prove that here, at last, was the true Nile - even if it didn't connect with Lake Tanganyika!

Stanley tried to persuade the doctor to return to the coast with him, but Livingstone said that he had to finish his task and solve the mystery of the Nile, once and for all. Together they trekked back to Tabora, and parted on March 14th 1872 with Stanley promising to send Livingstone more supplies when he reached the coast. After a forced march, averaging some fourteen miles a day, Stanley reached the coast early in May, where he met an expedition under the command of Lieutenant L.S.Dawson of the Royal Navy which included amongst its members William Oswell ('Zouga') Livingstone, the explorer's second son. This expedition had been sent by the Royal Geographical Society to try to locate Livingstone and bring him relief, but when Stanley told the astonished members that the explorer was alive and that his stores had already been replenished, Dawson decided to abort the expedition and to return to England.

Stanley, together with some of the members of the RGS expedition, chartered a steamer to take them to the Seychelles, but before he left Zanzibar, Stanley gave his dispatches to the Captain of an American ship, bound for New York via the Cape, and when at last he arrived at Aden, on his way back to England, he received a telegram from Gordon Bennett:

"You are now as famous as Livingstone, having discovered the discoverer. Accept my thanks and the whole world's"

"Dr Livingstone I presume"

Stanley's 'scoop' made the headlines in the *New York Herald* before the Royal Geographical Society (whose own expedition had not yet reported), even knew that Livingstone had been located. This caused great offence, and some disgruntled members of the Society, (who still remembered Stanley's outrageous behaviour over the Emperor Theodore affair), claimed that Stanley couldn't have 'found' Livingstone, because Livingstone had never been 'lost'. Others claimed that Stanley had made it all up, that he had not found Livingstone at all, and that the whole thing was another vulgar American journalistic stunt.

Stanley reached Marseilles towards the end of July 1872, and went on to Paris where he was treated as a hero, and feted by leading Americans living in that city, but by the time he reached London he discovered that British newspapers were doing their best to play down his achievement, some suggesting even that his claims were fraudulent. This upset him badly.

During his short and adventurous life Stanley had been a fraud - several times - but this time, when he actually *had* achieved something, it was hard not to be believed, and the unfair criticism undoubtedly influenced his later actions.

It was not all bad news. Queen Victoria sent him a present of a snuff box and summoned him to Dunrobin Castle for a personal interview. This made Stanley feel just a little better, but he returned to America as soon as he could and was greeted by the Mayor of New York, and great crowds who cheered him as a hero. But again, his home-coming was marred! Gordon Bennett was not there and was reported to have said that Stanley might have 'found' Livingstone, but he, Gordon Bennett had 'found' Stanley! Without Bennett, nobody would even have heard of Stanley!

This, like the British newspaper comment, was not fair - Stanley had more or less thrust himself upon the *New York Herald* and had gone to extraordinary lengths to make the connection, but perhaps Bennett Jr. was more than a little jealous and wanted to keep Stanley 'in his place'. No contact was made between the two men until April 1873 when Bennett, who was in Paris at the time, sent for Stanley. After what was said to have been a disagreeable interview, Bennett raised his salary from four hundred pounds a year to one thousand pounds and sent him to Spain to cover the second 'Carlist' war [1].

An illustration from one of Stanley's accounts of his African

---

[1] *Carlists were people who believed that the brother of Ferdinand VII, Don Carlos and not his daughter Isabella, should have succeeded him in 1833. They had fought but been defeated from 1833 to 1839 but a second attempt had been started in 1872 and was still in progress.*

CHAPTER EIGHTEEN

Everyone in the small Lugard household in York appears to have been reasonably happy except poor Mary. She badly missed her husband and found the task of coping with life difficult in cold wet England after years in India. She also found it difficult to cope with her children - particularly with young Freddy - but early in 1864, she received the glad news that Frederick Greuber was on his way home, and she rushed off to Switzerland to meet him.

At last Mary too was happy and together they returned to England where Frederick obtained a temporary Curacy and she became pregnant. In June, 1865 - three months after giving birth to her second son, Edward, and when Freddy was only seven years old - Mary Lugard, rebellious daughter, missionary worker, devoted step-mother, faithful wife, and loving mother, died at the early age of forty seven.

The Reverend Frederick Lugard was broken-hearted at the loss of his third wife, and he soon became almost a recluse.

He was given a rectorship, but no rectory, and for some time, he and his motherless children, including the young baby Edward, lived in lodgings.

Unable to afford to give Freddy a good education, he sent him to a Dame School in Worcester for a year, and then the sensitive and motherless boy whose father no longer gave him any affection, was put into a preparatory boarding school near Manchester where he was bullied by his fellows and frequently thrashed by the masters.

In 1871 he left the 'prep' school and went to school at Rossall in Lancashire, where his treatment was not much improved, but here we must leave him for a while, and return to Livingstone, who was *still* looking for the source of the Nile.

After Stanley's departure, Livingstone had waited for five months, until August 1872, when supplies promised by Stanley, arrived from the coast. He then decided to trek south to find the 'Ancient fountains of the Nile'. All did not go well however. Livingstone was far from well, suffering from malaria and associated ailments, which included much anal bleeding. By January 1873, he was losing a lot of blood, and he and his party, which still included the faithful Susi and Chuma and a lad called Jacob Wainwright, (another 'Nassick' boy), rarely covered more than a mile a day, as they waded waist deep through swamps of mud and standing water. Livingstone frequently had to be carried because he was too weak to walk or ride, but despite these terrible sufferings, he was still determined to prove that the River Lualaba was the Nile. Again he drafted a dispatch to the Foreign Secretary saying - in anticipation of course - that he had reached the 'gushing springs' of Herodotus. (He left the latitude and longitudes blank, to be filled in when he got there!).

By April 1873 he was too weak even to ride a donkey, and Susi and Chuma made him a litter in which they carried him to a village where he asked if the Chief knew of any great gushing fountains in the area. The Chief didn't of course, and on 30th April came to see Livingstone, but the Doctor was in such great pain that he asked him to go away and come back on the morrow. He then went to sleep and did not call for Susi until late evening, when he asked for some boiling water and dosed himself with calomel. It was just before dawn on 1st May 1873 that his servants found him dead, kneeling by his improvised bed, as if in prayer.

At first the servants were afraid to tell the Chief for fear that the death might be regarded as an evil omen, but eventually they told the truth and the Chief joined them in mourning. Then a truly remarkable thing happened. Instead of immediately burying the corpse, the servants decided to 'embalm' it. They opened up the body and removed the intestines and heart, which they buried in a tin box whilst the 'Nassick' boy, Wainwright, who could read and write, read the funeral service from Livingstone's Prayerbook. They then exchanged a quantity of beads for some salt, which they daily rubbed into the cadaver to 'cure' it, first having built a protective fence around the scene of their grisly operations. They daily exposed the corpse to the sun to dry it thoroughly and then they wrapped it in an animal skin and placed the whole thing into a roll of bark, stripped from a nearby tree. Finally they wrapped the result of their labours in sailcloth and painted it with tar which had been intended for painting the hull of Livingstone's canoes. Then they set out for the coast, carrying the corpse with them.

In August, by means of the extraordinary way in which news travelled - and still travels - in the African bush, they heard of an expedition led by a white man, which was searching for Livingstone. This was in fact, the second expedition sent by the Royal Geographical Society - the first having been intercepted by Stanley and aborted in May 1872, but because many members still distrusted Stanley, a second expedition, this time under the command of Lieutenant Verney Lovett Cameron of the Royal Navy, had left England on 30th November 1872. Cameron's party included a former Naval messmate, Doctor Dillon, a Lieutenant Cecil Murphy of the Royal Regiment of Artillery and Robert Moffat - grandson of the famous missionary, and Livingstone's nephew.

Perhaps Livingstone's porters had heard of the first expedition and thought that it had returned. Perhaps they merely assumed that Zouga would be with the second expedition, still anxious to find his father - who knows - but whatever the reason, Jacob Wainwright wrote a letter to Zouga, and sent it by hand of Chuma. A facsimile of the actual letter is reproduced in Cameron's own book *Across Africa* and it is therefore possible to quote it verbatim;

"Ukhonongo October 1873

Sir,
We have heard in the month of August that you have started from Zanzibar for Unyenyembe, and again and again letely (sic) we have heared(sic)your arrival. Your father died by disease beyond the country of Bisa, but we have carried the corpse with us, 10 of our soldier(sic) are lost and some have died. Our hunger presses us to ask you some clothes to buy provision for our soldiers and we should have an answer that when we shall enter there shall be firing of guns or not, and if you permit us to fire guns then send us some powder. We have wrote (sic) these few words in the place of Sultan or King Mbowra.

The writer Jacob Wainwright,
Dr. Livingstone Exped."

This remarkable letter written by a relatively uneducated 'Mission Boy' reached Cameron on 20th October, 1873 when, as he records in his book, he was lying on his bed *".......enfeebled from repeated attacks of fever..."* his mind, he says *".....dazed and confused with whirling thoughts and fancies of home and those dear ones far away...."* Although the letter was addressed to Oswell Livingstone, Cameron opened and read it. It took him some time to grasp the import of the contents, but having done so, he sent a messenger to the coast bearing news of Livingstone's death.

The caravan bearing Livingstone's body arrived a few days later, and it was

David Livingstone's funeral in Westminster Abbey

greeted with as much ceremony as was possible in the circumstances. Susi, who had taken command of the caravan, had brought with him a couple of the Doctor's boxes together with his guns and navigational instruments, and he told Cameron that he had left another box containing books and papers behind at Ujiji.

Cameron, Dillon and Murphy (Moffat had, by this time, died), then debated what to do next. Murphy claimed that the whole purpose of the expedition had now ceased to exist and said that they should return to the coast, but Cameron and Dillon felt that they should continue to Ujiji at least, to collect the remaining box and papers. Having taken this decision, Dr. Dillon became too ill to travel and Murphy, despite his views on the validity of the expedition, volunteered to stay with Cameron. Cameron declined to accept his offer, and opted to go to Ujiji alone so Dillon and Murphy joined the caravan bearing Livingstone's body, and headed for the coast. Shortly afterwards in a delirium caused by malarial fever, poor Dillon went berserk and shot himself.

Cameron eventually recovered Livingstone's papers in February 1874, and then decided, before returning to the coast, to have a look at the River Lualaba, which the old Doctor was sure was the Nile.

The story of Cameron's adventures are well documented elsewhere and have no real place in this story. However, in brief, he did not return to the east coast but pressed on alone, making treaties as he went, and in November 1875, reached Benguela in Angola, becoming the first white man to cross Africa from east to west at this latitude.

He returned to England in April 1876 and wrote a two volume book about his adventures, and that is all we need to say about the gallant Lieutenant Cameron - except to say that he would seem to deserve a larger place in African history than he at present occupies.

In September 1873 an advance force, under the command of Sir Garnet Wolseley (W.S Gilbert's *"...very model of a modern Major-General..."*), was sent to the Gold Coast where British anti-slaving forts and trading stations were under threat from the Ashanti tribes. The Ashanti, who resented what they saw as Britain's absurd attitude towards slavery and who dominated the hinterland, had cut off legitimate trade to the coast. Britain had tried to solve these problems by the apparently simple means of getting rid of the Gold Coast protectorate by giving it self-government, but the Fanti peoples on the coast would have none of it! They wanted British protection, and *didn't* want independence. Several localised wars had been fought between the Fanti and the Ashanti, but Britain had avoided trying to pacify the hinterland until 1873, when the Ashanti had invaded Fanti territory and threatened to overthrow British trading posts. This was too much, and at last, the Government decided that it must act against Kofi Karikari, the Ashanti King, who Wolseley was instructed to 'punish' but not to bring about a complete break-up of his power.

Sir Garnet Wolseley

In November 1873, Gordon Bennett sent Stanley to cover the campaign for the *New York Herald*, but the journalist's reputation had gone before him, and Sir Garnet, no doubt remembering what Stanley had done after the Ethiopian campaign, made sure that neither Stanley - nor any other 'damned journalist' - got any news at all, until official dispatches had been sent on their way to London.

In early 1874 Kofi Karikari was defeated and he signed a treaty with Britain which brought the war to an end. To ensure that there was no further attack by the Ashanti, in July 1874 the Gold Coast Colony was formed, and lasted until it was granted independence in 1957 - when it re-named itself 'Ghana'.

With the end of the Ashanti war, Stanley and a few other journalists were offered a passage on a British warship to the Cape Verde Islands where, to his great sorrow, Stanley heard of Livingstone's death. He made his own way back to London and arrived in time for the funeral in Westminster Abbey.

After the funeral, Stanley decided that it was to be his mission to go back to Africa, to carry on where Livingstone had left off, and to settle, once and for all, the question of the source of the Nile, after which he would then chart the great central African lakes, and try to find the headwaters of the River Congo and follow it to its mouth. He was determined to show members of the Royal Geographical Society, who doubted his word about his earlier African journey, that he was the equal of any other explorer!

Whilst in London, he met and fell in love with Alice Pike, the daughter of an American businessman who was on a visit to England. Alice went back to the States in June 1874, and Stanley went to see the Editor of the London *Daily Telegraph* to seek financial backing for his proposed expedition. (He was, of course, still on the pay-roll of the *New York Herald*, but such considerations were of little importance to Stanley who knew that Gordon Bennett would not give him backing unless pressure was to be brought to bear!) *The Telegraph* promised to give him six thousand pounds, but only if *the Herald* would match the sum. Stanley, nothing loth, sent a cable to Bennett asking if he would get his backing and he received a cabled reply, containing one word: 'YES'.

Stanley began to plan his journey, but he found time to cross the Atlantic to New York where he and Alice entered into a pact of marriage, each promising to be faithful to the other, and to marry on his safe return from Africa.

He returned to England and recruited assistants, two brothers, Frank and Edward Pocock, and a young clerk called Frederick Baker. The four men sailed for Africa and arrived in Zanzibar on 21st September, 1874.

CHAPTER NINETEEN

On November 17th, 1874, Stanley, his three white companions and a caravan of over three hundred Africans, set out from Bagamoyo on the east African coast, heading for Lake Victoria Nyanza, the largest of the central African lakes which had first been 'discovered' by Speke in 1858. Stanley intended to map this lake, and before heading southward, similarly to map Lake Tanganyika.

It was a dreadful journey, during which Edward Pocock died of typhus, but by the end of February 1875 Stanley and his companions reached their first objective. A few days later, leaving Frank Pocock and Frederick Baker behind at a 'base' camp, he set out in a collapsible boat, northwards up the eastern coast, intending to circumnavigate and map the lake. He was attacked from time to time by hostile natives who came out from the shore in their canoes to intercept the invaders. He repulsed them with his rifle, and eventually reached the northern end of the lake, where, on 1st April 1875 he entered the kingdom of the Kabaka Mutesa, King of Buganda. Stanley was quite overwhelmed by the welcome he received. He was given a hut and presented with food and drink for his men and was invited to meet the Kabaka later that day.

Frederick Baker

The Kingdom of Buganda

The Kingdom of Buganda, and its two neighbouring territories of Karagwe and Bunyoro had been isolated from the outside world until the 1840's when an Arab slave trader from Zanzibar had arrived, but it was not until 1861, when Speke and Grant reached there on their quest for the Nile, that Bugandans had first been seen by white men. This isolation made the level of sophistication in the three Kingdoms, of which Speke had spoken at great length, all the more re- markable, and gave the lie to people in Europe who still firmly believed that be- fore white men brought 'civilisation' to Africa, there was nothing there but bar- barism and savagery. Somehow, without any outside influence, the three King- doms had developed a social and administrative structure far more advanced than white explorers had found anywhere south of the Sahara, except perhaps in 'Hausaland' which lay far away to the west.

Houses in the three kingdoms were beautifully built of woven canes and reeds, with the peaks of their roofs often as much as fifty feet high. The people wove baskets which were so fine that they were watertight, and they made a soft and durable 'cloth' from the bark of trees. They washed their hands before eating and their food was varied and good, quite unlike much African food which was dull and unimaginative.

Buganda, low lying, lush and tropical, lay on the northern shore of the great lake, and was the central and most highly developed of the three kingdoms. Its Kabaka was advised by a 'cabinet' amongst whose members was a principal minister, a treasurer, an army commander, and an 'admiral' in command of the war fleet of canoes. Despite this almost 'western' form of government, there were astonishing gaps in the peoples' knowledge, for they had no means of writing, of counting, or of measuring the passage of time. Their law enforcement was unbelievably cruel and primitive, and for the smallest 'crimes' or even 'errors' of etiquette, people were tortured and executed on the spot.

The Kingdom of Karagwe lay to the south of Buganda, much of it more than five thousand feet above sea level. Its King, Rumanika, was hospitable to strangers and kept a strange harem of wives who were so fat that they could not walk. Bunyoro, the third kingdom lay to the north of Buganda and much of it was harsh open scrub land. Its King was an unpleasant young man called Kabarega.

Mutesa, dressed in a black robe girded with a golden belt, received Stanley with courtesy, and accepted the gifts which had been brought him. The two men sat and, through an interpreter, discussed a wide variety of subjects ranging from the events of the outside 'western' world to religion.

The Kabaka was clearly very interested in firearms, and Stanley was able to demonstrate his own marksmanship by shooting dead a small crocodile at a range of one hundred yards. His shooting practice in Arkansas was beginning to pay off!

It was as a self-appointed 'successor' to Doctor Livingstone, that Henry Moreton Stanley, began to preach the Gospel! He tried to persuade Mutesa that the religion of the Christians was far superior to that of the Moslems - apart from any other consideration, it did not involve the painful requirement of circumcision; an important factor to men who owned and kept a large harem.

Whilst Stanley was engaged in his role as evangelist, another white man, Colonel Ernest Linant de Bellefonds, appeared at the court of the Kabaka. Linant was an emissary from General Gordon, who was at that time, employed by the Khedive of Egypt. Whilst nearly everybody must know that General Gordon was killed at Khartoum, perhaps not quite so many know how he got to be there in

the first place. It is a strange and involved tale which indirectly affects the course of this story.

Again, as we have seen, although Egypt was still a part of the Ottoman Empire, it had been more or less independent since 1840, when Turkey's rulers had recognised Mohammed Ali as the 'hereditary ruler' of Egypt. In 1867, his descendent, Ismail Pasha who had succeeded as 'viceroy' in 1863, had been given the title 'Khedive' by the Turks (the word being derived from the Persian *Kediv* meaning 'Prince'). Ismail was a happy man. Egypt was prospering because the American Civil War had boosted cotton prices, and the country's annual income had rapidly risen from around five million, to twenty five million pounds per year. The Khedive who had always been a spendthrift, transferred all his personal debts to the State, and continued to spend money lavishly. He was not only rich, but ambitious and wanted to extend the territory over which he ruled, believing that the whole of the 'upper Nile' to the south of the Sudan should become part of his realm.

General Gordon

During the celebrations which followed the opening of the sluices on the Suez canal in the presence of the Prince and Princess of Wales, Ismail approached Sir Samuel Baker, an explorer (one of the people who had travelled up the Nile to meet Speke and Grant in 1863 and who had accompanied the Royal tour as an interpreter), and asked him if he would take command of a military expedition which was to annex the upper Nile to Egypt.

Baker was a remarkable man in his own right, but whilst he is of considerable importance in the history of pre-colonial Africa, his role in this particular story does not warrant more than a thumbnail account of his adventures in the service of the Khedive. He was told that if he accepted the invitation, he would be made a 'Pasha' (a Turkish 'Lord') and a Major-General in the Egyptian army, with a salary of forty thousand pounds for a four year contract. Baker accepted, and set about his task with a will, assembling his forces at Khartoum, which, although being the 'capital' of the 'Sudan', was a small town on the Nile of which, in those days, nobody outside Egypt had ever heard. In February 1870 he sailed south, up-stream, with something over one thousand armed men, into the area in which he had travelled in 1863 when he met Speke and Grant. In those days there had been clear channels open for navigation, but he found that, after seven years, these channels had been choked with impenetrable weed.

Baker and his men fought the weed as the level of the river dropped, but by

April he was forced to give up and retreat, and to wait until December 1870, before trying again. Then with fifty nine vessels of various kinds and sixteen hundred men, he hacked his way southward, but it was not until early March that, after herculean efforts, they gained open water near Gondokoro. On 26th May Baker held a parade of some twelve hundred of his men, hoisted the Ottoman flag, and formally annexed the surrounding country to Egypt. He called it 'Equatoria'. In January 1872 he trekked further south arriving in the kingdom of Bunyoro by mid-March. Here he built himself a 'Government House', and on 14th May 1872, publicly annexed Bunyoro to the Khedive. King Kabarega of Bunyoro didn't approve of this, and resisted forcibly and Baker had to retreat. After further fighting, he decided to leave a garrison of Egyptian soldiers on the frontier with Bunyoro and withdraw. He reached Cairo in August 1873, resigned his Egyptian commission, and by the end of the year he was back in England.

After Baker's resignation, Ismail looked around for a suitable replacement, and chose a forty one year old Colonel of the British Royal Engineers, Charles George Gordon, who had fought with distinction in the Crimea and in China, where he had defended British trading interests in helping defeat the Taiping Rebellion in 1864, and where he had earned the nickname of 'China' Gordon.

He was offered, and accepted, the post of 'Governor of Equatoria', and on January 28th 1874, the very day that news of Livingstone's death reached England, Gordon left to take up his post. He reached Cairo ten days later, and met the Khedive to discuss what was required of him. He was instructed to build a chain of forts along the River Nile from Gondokoro to Buganda, and to annexe Buganda to Egypt, abolishing slave trading in the areas he crossed. Gordon's army consisted of Turkish, Sudanese, and Egyptian soldiers, and his staff included Americans, Frenchmen and Italians as well as Englishmen. He was directed to work under the Egyptian Governor of the Sudan (which had been conquered by Mohammed Ali in 1821), who had his headquarters in Khartoum.

When Gordon reached Gondokoro he found that the garrison left behind by Baker had gone to pieces. There was no discipline, many of the officers were actively engaged in slave trading and, in general, chaos reigned. He sailed back down the Nile to Khartoum where he demanded that 'Equatoria' be separated from the rest of the Sudan, and that he be appointed as Governor General. The Governor of the Sudan wouldn't agree, so Gordon went on to Cairo where he persuaded the Khedive to meet his demands. He was Governor General of Equatoria until 1879 when he resigned and returned to England.

Ernest Linant de Bellefond was a Protestant Frenchman on Governor General Gordon's staff, and he seemed to have approved of Stanley's attempts to introduce the Kabaka to Livingstone's brand of Christianity. When Linant was about to leave to return to Equatoria, Stanley gave him letters addressed to the editors

of the London *Daily Telegraph,* and to the *New York Herald*, claiming that if Christian missionaries were not sent to Buganda, the whole area would fall to Islam. Linant duly dispatched these two letters at Khartoum, and when they were published they proved to be a 'watershed' in the history of Africa.

Soon after Linant's departure, Stanley took his leave of Mutesa, and returned to his base camp, where he discovered that Barker had died, and that the sole British survivor of the original team was Frank Pocock. Together they sailed down the western side of the lake to the Island of Bumbiri where natives attacked his boat, and destroyed his oars. Stanley repelled them with his elephant gun, sank two 'enemy' canoes, and killed five men. He then improvised paddles and got himself out of danger, but vowed to return and take revenge for the attack. He sent an ultimatum to the Chief responsible for the area saying that if compensation were not paid, he, Stanley, would attack. His demands were not met so he sailed within fifty yards of the 'enemy' and opened fire. Losses were never confirmed, but Stanley proudly claimed in his dispatches to London and New York that thirty three natives had been killed and over one hundred wounded. These revelations were received with indignation and outrage by the *'Aborigines Protection Society'*, and amongst all those who were beginning to think in terms of what today we would call 'human rights' for all men, even for the so called 'savages' in Africa.

After this encounter, Stanley had intended to leave Buganda and go on to survey and map Lake Albert, but Mutesa declared war on tribes at the northern end of Lake Victoria, and Stanley volunteered to go and help him! During September 1875, Stanley spent his time in fighting the Mutesa's enemies using modern firepower against spears and arrows, and in what little spare time he had, he started to translate the Gospel for Mutesa.

Between them, Mutesa and Stanley won the little 'war', and on November 26th Stanley's expedition at last got under way. By early 1876 he was passing through wild and inhospitable country, was frequently under attack from hostile natives, and didn't reach the shores of Lake Tanganyika until the end of May. He went to Ujiji to see if there was any mail for him - there wasn't - so he sailed around the lake until the end of July, no doubt remembering his voyage in these waters with his hero, Doctor Livingstone. In mid-September he set out to find the river Lualaba, and reached the banks of the mile-wide river by mid-October. Here he met with Tippu-Tip, one of the half-caste Arab slavers with whom Livingstone had made contact, and he entered into an arrangement whereby he would pay the slaver five thousand dollars to be allowed to trek in his company for sixty days. Tippu-Tip agreed and added his caravan of two hundred armed men to Stanley's small army of one hundred and fifty.

Together they trekked down the river bank, often very slowly, because the

War Canoe

slaver, whilst starting to move at dawn, usually camped for the day by mid-morning. This pattern continued until one of Tippu-Tip's favourite concubines died of smallpox whereupon the slaver abandoned his contract, leaving Stanley to his own devices.

On 28th December 1876 Stanley's boat - which he had called the *Lady Alice* after Alice Pike - together with twenty two canoes loaded with trade goods and equipment, set off down stream, with one hundred and forty three men, women and children.

Soon after New Year's Day, 1877, Stanley was told that rapids and cataracts lay ahead.

At each of these, his boat and all the canoes had to be unloaded, roadways had to be cut through the forest along which the vessels and their loads had to be carried until relatively smooth water was reached. The craft were then put back into the river and re-loaded.

They then continued down-stream until the next rapids were encountered, when the whole process had to be repeated. It was a back-breaking, painfully slow progress, but by the end of January they were well downstream of the cataracts and waterfalls - Stanley later named them the 'Stanley Falls'. From this point the river flowed westwards, and it became obvious that the Lualaba, Livingstone's 'Nile', was not the Nile after all, but almost certainly the headwaters of the River Congo, and when eventually Stanley crossed the Equator and the river turned

Stanley Falls

The Stanley Falls Station

southwest, he was sure of it.

His expedition followed the course of the great river, for much of the time fighting hostile natives who feared the invasion of their territory by so large a force, but by early March Stanley reached the village of Bolobo, some one thousand miles downstream of 'Stanley Falls'. There the river ran into a circular lake which was so large that it was difficult to see the far side - Stanley called this 'Stanley Pool'. Downstream of the pool, there were more cataracts, and it took him five months to by-pass them. In one of these rapids, Frank Pocock was drowned and several canoes and their contents were lost, but Stanley had no option but to continue. On July 31st 1877, Stanley decided to abandon the river and to march overland towards the coast, and because his supplies were running low, he sent a runner ahead with a letter addressed to 'Any Gentleman who speaks English', in which he asked for food and supplies to be sent to meet him.

On 7th August, 1877, just as he was making camp for the night, a caravan arrived from the west coast, carrying food. His letter had reached civilisation and the journey was nearing its end. Refreshed and encouraged, he marched on, first to the town of Boma on the north side of the mouth of the Congo, and then to the coast.

In late September, Stanley and his party were given a passage around the Cape of Good Hope to Zanzibar, arriving on November 26th, 1877 when Stanley collected his mail. It included a letter telling him that Alice Pike had jilted him and had married someone else in January 1876!

CHAPTER TWENTY

A s a boy, Freddy Lugard had wanted to be a clergyman like his father, but after a while at his Public School, he was persuaded to try to enter the Indian Civil Service instead and he was put into the school's 'Army' class which coached lads both for entry to Sandhurst, and the Indian Civil Service.

In 1877, at the age of nineteen, Freddy went to London to take the Civil Service entrance examination, and stayed with his uncle, General the Right Honourable Sir Edward Lugard, PC, GCB, who had fought with distinction in the Sikh wars and during the Indian Mutiny.

From 1861 until 1871, Sir Edward had been Permanent Under Secretary of State for War and had been President of a Commission which had given rise in 1871 to the 'Army Regulation Act' which abolished the practice of wealthy but inexperienced and sometimes unsuitable young men purchasing Commissions in the Army.

At about this time there was mounting tension in the Balkans where Christian peasants in Bosnia and Herzegovina had rebelled against their Muslim Ottoman overlords. There was also public outrage in Britain in 1876, when news was received of atrocities perpetrated by Turks against Bulgarian Christians.

Russia had intervened to help the Bulgars, and, despite British diplomatic efforts to avert conflict, had then declared war on Turkey. When war broke out, Britain remained neutral but she was on her guard because there were signs that sooner or later she would have to become involved and although the British public didn't approve of Muslim troops killing Christian civilians, it couldn't approve of Russia becoming too powerful either. A popular music hall song of the day, by G.W. Hunt which introduced the word 'Jingoism' into the English language, summarised the situation:

> *"We don't want to fight, but by Jingo, if we do;*
> *We've got the ships, we've got the men, we've got the money too!*
> *We've fought the Bear before, and while we're Britons true,*
> *the Russians shall not have Constantinople!"*

No doubt the gallant Sir Edward told his nephew of the glory that might come his way, were he to join the Army instead of becoming a mere Civil Servant and Freddy, much impressed, decided more or less on the spot, that he would not try to enter the Indian Civil Service after all, but would become an Army Officer like his uncle.

One of about one thousand candidates, he duly sat the Sandhurst examination, and when the results were published, he looked in vain for his name at the lower end of the list and spent two miserable days wondering what to do next until a friend drew his attention to the fact that he was looking at the wrong end of the list. He had passed - sixth from the top!

In February 1878, when Lugard was twenty years old and about to go to the Royal Military Academy at Sandhurst, Turkey was still at war with Russia, but the war ended in March, when Turkey was forced by Russia to sign a Treaty at San Stefano, which freed most of the Balkans from Turkish influence, and made Bulgaria a client State of Russia.

The San Stefano Treaty upset many European Powers; Austria for example, coveted Bosnia and Germany also wanted to curb Russian expansion. Furthermore, despite the fact that Britain and France were rivals, both were more afraid of Russia than they were of each other, Britain feared that a powerful Russia might force her way through Turkey and Persia and invade India, and France feared a Russian advance on the Mediterranean where her own influence was growing.

The 'shield' against Russian advances, both to India and to the Mediterranean, was the rapidly crumbling Ottoman Empire, and although the majority of Turks embraced Islam and most Russians were Christians, Britain, and France, set aside moral and religious considerations, and were determined to uphold the Turks against the Russians, come what may.

In January, ships of the Royal Navy had been sent to anchor off Constantinople to protect it from Russia and only eight weeks after entering Sandhurst, all Cadets were commissioned and ordered to join their Regiments. Second Lieutenant F.J.D. Lugard was posted to the 1st Battalion of the 9th Regiment, the 'East Norfolks' in Ireland where, even in those days, British troops had to be stationed to protect the populace from a further Fenian uprising[1].

More or less at the same time as Lugard joined his regiment, the major European Powers met in Berlin to discuss the possible consequences of the San Stefano Treaty. The outcome of the Berlin Congress enabled the British Prime Minister, the Earl of Beaconsfield, (formerly Benjamin Disraeli), to declare that we had won 'peace with honour'. Russia was required to return to Turkey most of the territory ceded under the Treaty of San Stefano and Austria was given a Protectorate over Bosnia. Nobody knew it at the time of course, but the seeds of the Bosnian Civil War of the early 1990's had been sown!

As another result of the Congress, Britain was given the right to occupy and administer the Turkish island of Cyprus although it remained under Ottoman sovereignty. This provided Britain with a useful 'springboard' from which troops could be sent quickly to Turkey - or to Egypt should this become necessary[2]. War was averted, but by then, Lugard was established in his regiment, and was not required to go back to Sandhurst. His Army career had begun.

Despite the abolition of the practice of purchasing Army Commissions, the majority of Army Officers still came from wealthy upper class families and had private incomes with which to supplement their Army pay, to enable them to keep their own stables, to hunt, and generally to enjoy all the pleasures of the mid-Victorian leisured classes. Lugard had no such private income, and was soon to discover that he could not possibly live on his pay as a subaltern, so he applied for, and obtained, a transfer to the 2nd Batallion of his Regiment, which was stationed at Peshawar on the North West Frontier of India, ready to defend India against any possible Russian incursion.

Having returned to the land of his birth, he soon became involved in what is now known as the 'Second Afghan War', and he marched with General Sir Charles Gough's Brigade, through the Khyber Pass to secure the frontier against an expected Russian attack, but whilst in Afghan country he caught what was then called 'Peshawar Fever' (probably typhus), and was made to report 'sick'.

---

[1]The Fenians, forerunners of the IRA, were members of the Irish Republican Brotherhood founded in America in 1858 who had taken an oath to

"..renounce all allegiance to the Queen of England, and to take arms and fight at a moment's warning to make Ireland an Independent Democratic Republic".

[2]Cyprus was later annexed to Britain when Turkey entered the World War on Germany's side, and eventually became a British Colony in 1925.

He was carried back to Peshawar and sent to hospital where, two weeks later, he heard that General Gough's Brigade had gone to the rescue of General Roberts' Column which had been surrounded by the Afghans.

Lugard tried to get out of bed and go to join his brigade, but the Doctors prevented him, and told him that unless he continued to receive treatment, he would surely die.

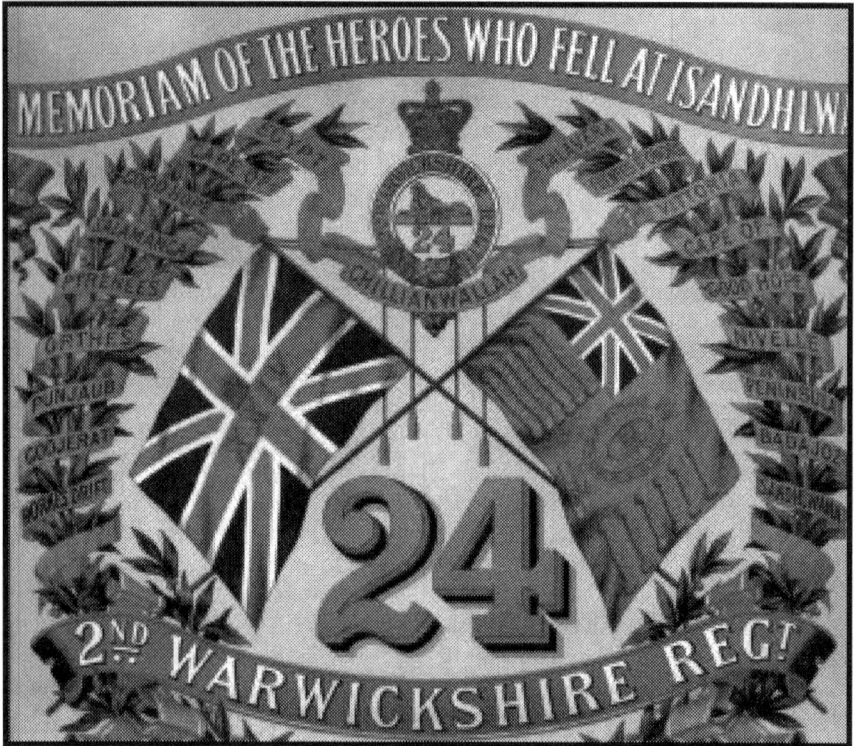

By the time he was fit for duty, the fighting was over, but nevertheless he went to Kabul in Afghanistan, and spent the winter with his regiment. He was promoted to Lieutenant in January 1880, but then a medical Board invalided him back to England where he spent a year before returning to India.

This was not a happy time for the British Army. In January 1879 Zulu impis had overwhelmed the British troops at Isandhlwana in Natal, and whilst in England Lugard heard of the appalling business at Majuba Hill in Southern Africa where a force of fifteen hundred trained British troops suffered a crushing defeat at the hands of a bunch of sharpshooting Afrikaner farmers soon to be known to the world at "Boers". More than three hundred British troops were killed, including Sir George Colley who led them - he was shot through the middle of his fore-head.

The Army, which was trained for battle of a more conventional nature, not for fighting naked savages or angry Dutch farmers, was outraged and ashamed by these reverses and demanded that it should immediately be allowed to wipe out this latest affront by a massive counter attack. The British Government did not agree and, to make matters worse in the eyes of all soldiers, in August, 1881, signed the Pretoria Convention which gave the Transvaal its independence.

Lieutenant Lugard returned to India at the end of this morale crushing year for the Army where, instead of being allowed to go and teach the Boers a lesson, as all British Army Officers yearned to, he spent three years of 'peacetime' soldier-ing. He was still very short of money, and, despite his move to India, found it hard to live on his Army pay. He did everything he could to increase his income and studied both Hindustani and Urdu, hoping to pass language examinations, and get a little more pay as an interpreter. He passed both exams, but the army abolished the 'post' of interpreter and he was no better off - except that he now spoke two native languages!

He simply had to do *something* to improve his finances, so he applied for a course in 'Army Transport' where the officer in charge was a Captain Willcocks, with whom he struck up an immediate friendship which was to last a life-time. He finished the course and passed the examination and actually acted as a Transport Officer for a while. Willcocks recommended him for a permanent ap-pointment and in the meantime - although Lugard worked very hard - he also played hard, attending race meetings, riding in gymkhanas and playing polo, living a life, which, he said, would not have met with approval from either his father or his mother.

CHAPTER TWENTY ONE

The little country of Belgium, having been ruled in turn by a number of European countries, including Austria, Spain, and France, and having been joined to the Netherlands during the Napoleonic wars, became independent in 1830, when the National Congress elected Prince Leopold of Saxe-Coburg to be King Leopold I of Belgium.

Leopold had been married to Charlotte, daughter of King George IV of Great Britain and might well have become Britain's Prince Consort, had poor Charlotte not died giving birth to a still-born child in 1817. Having thus lost any opportunity to influence the British throne, Leopold married again, this time to Louise, daughter of Louis-Philippe of France. She presented him with a son who succeeded to the throne of Belgium in 1865 as King Leopold II.

As a youth, many years before he succeeded to his father's throne, young Leopold had developed a taste for foreign travel, and had visited Egypt, India and China. He had long since decided that if the small and newly independent Belgian nation was to achieve recognition on the world stage, she would simply *have* to have an overseas colony.

When he came to the throne, Leopold II was determined to acquire some overseas territory - although his advisers were against the idea - and he first approached Spain to ask if that Government would lease the Phillipines to Belgium. The answer was 'NO', so he then asked the Portuguese Government if it would lease Angola or Mozambique - or Timor, or anywhere else - but again the answer was 'NO'! He then tried to get Britain to lease him a foothold in New Guinea, but Britain wouldn't agree either, but despite these rebuffs he continued his search, until one day he read of Lieutenant Cameron's journey through Central Africa, and of his adventures in the Congo Basin.

In 1876, the year in which Queen Victoria had become 'Empress of India', Leopold II had invited a number of famous explorers - including Cameron - to Brussels for what he chose to call a 'Geographical Conference' on Central Africa. This conference opened on 12th September and three days later delegates had agreed to the formation of an International African Association, to be governed by an international commission. This agreement gave Leopold II considerable importance and international popularity. Here, it was said, was a King who was actually prepared to spend his own personal fortune in a 'crusade' against the dreadful internal slave trade of Africa, but what the world didn't realise, was that his real motive was to get himself - and Belgium - what he himself called 'A slice of the African Cake'!

King Leopold II

Leopold decided that there was only one man who was ruthless and brave enough to go and *cut the cake* for him - none other than the now famous Henry Moreton Stanley, and in January 1878, two representatives of King Leopold approached Stanley to find out if he was willing to discuss the Congo with their King. Not surprisingly, Stanley jumped at the opportunity and by December was committed to going back to the Congo for five years to administer the '*Comité d'etudes du Haut-Congo*' as the International Association had come to be called. He was sworn to secrecy, and told that all communications with the King were to be strictly confidential.

In February 1879, Stanley, travelling under the assumed name of 'Monsieur Henri', left Brussels for Suez where he was to join a chartered steamship, the *Albion*. This ship reached Zanzibar in April 1879 and by the time Stanley sailed north again in her, she was carrying sixty hand - picked Zanzibari porters. Before leaving Zanzibar, Stanley chartered another vessel to carry two thousand packing cases, containing some eighty tons of stores and sent this to the mouth of the Congo. However, when the *Albion* reached Aden, Stanley received a telegram saying that the *Comité d'Etudes du Haut-Congo* had gone bankrupt and he was instructed to return to Brussels immediately. King or no King, he refused and replied that he must be met at Gibraltar by one of Leopold's representatives with whom he would discuss the situation. The King agreed. Stanley was met by Colonel Strauch, who told him that Leopold had personally come to the financial rescue of the Committee, and that the expedition could go ahead as planned. Stanley went ahead reaching the mouth of the Congo on August 14th 1879, with instructions *not* to attempt to create a Belgian 'colony', but to establish a powerful independent African state.

His difficulties and adventures there have no direct bearing on this particular story. Sufficient to say that his principal difficulty came from constant interference from Brussels. Stanley finally appealed directly to the King who told his representatives to give him a freer hand. It was a frustrating time however and Stanley became depressed and ill, but despite his failing health, by 1882 he had built a road past the cataracts, had established three trading stations on the river and had launched two vessels, one of them a steamer - on 'Stanley Pool'. Believing that he had done all that was asked of him, he returned to Brussels at the end of September 1882, but it was soon pointed out that his contract was for five years and that he had to go back to Africa and administer the project.

Stanley claimed that he was too ill to return and went to see the King himself who sympathised but told him that he was not merely interested in buying and selling ivory, and other local produce or raising revenue by the collection of taxes from the natives, but that he was alarmed by possible French rivalry in the area. France, he told Stanley, had sent one of her naval officers to make treaties in the Congo area, and Leopold didn't like it. (The French naval officer was in fact an impoverished Italian aristocrat, Count Giuseppe Savorgnan de Brazza, who was serving with the French Navy.) King Leopold told Stanley that de Brazza had already entered into treaties with tribes on the northern shores of 'Stanley Pool' and had claimed the territory for France. Stanley seemed to collect the blame for this intrusion, and the Belgian Ambassador to London even suggested that Stanley had failed in his duty to the King and should have hunted down de Brazza and shot him!

Stanley was justifiably annoyed at this criticism, but was persuaded by the King in person to return to the Congo to consolidate what he had already achieved, and to combat any further expansion by France. Stanley got back to the Congo in December 1882 to find that, in his absence, all the stations which he had established had been allowed to fall into disrepair. It took him many months to restore order but then he set about treaty-making on behalf of the King. He was tired and ill and he tried to get a 'deputy', suggesting to Leopold that he should try to recruit General 'China' Gordon who had recently finished his stint with the Khedive of Egypt. Leopold agreed. Gordon accepted the appointment and after discussions with King Leopold was ready in February 1884 to sail for the Congo to team up with Stanley. He never reached the Congo however, because the British Government asked him to return to the Sudan where a revolt which threatened the security of Egypt, had assumed serious proportions. Gordon returned to Khartoum, never to return, and Stanley didn't get his deputy. Stanley finally left the Congo in 1884, having established trading stations as far as one thousand miles up stream at 'Stanley Falls'. He had negotiated more than four hundred treaties with local chieftains, had launched a flotilla of steamers on

'Stanley Pool' and had recruited one hundred and twenty Europeans and six hundred Africans into the King's personal service. He returned to London, remaining in Leopold's service but living in a flat off Piccadilly where he wrote books on his exploits and from whence he went on numerous lecture tours. In the summer of 1886 he was invited to visit America where he was introduced as *'An American Citizen, caressed and complimented by half the crowned heads of Europe'.*

CHAPTER TWENTY TWO

Since Lugard will play an increasingly important role in this story, it is necessary to understand what had been happening at the scene of his next appearance - Egypt and the Sudan.

Britain and France both regarded Egypt as being of considerable strategic importance, and what psychologists would probably call a 'love-hate' relationship had developed between the British and French Governments as they behaved like a pair of nervous hounds, circling one another, furiously wagging their tails in token friendship but ready at all times for a fight.

After the Crimean War, the Sultan of Turkey had borrowed heavily from both Britain and France - rather more from France than from Britain - and, in 1876, unable to repay these loans, the Sultan had been declared bankrupt. This had had a serious effect on the spendthrift Khedive Ismail of Egypt who, with the help of Baker and later that of Gordon, was expanding into the upper Nile with his greedy eyes on Buganda.

When all European banks had shut their doors to Turkey, Britain and France had become very concerned, not only over the weakness of the Ottoman Empire, but of the effect that this would have on her dependency, Egypt. Neither country could afford to see Egypt collapse and British and French financial controllers (sometimes called the 'Debt Commissioners') had been appointed, and sent to Egypt to try and sort out the financial muddle. Their duties were once likened to those of puppeteers, who had to pull the strings without ever appearing on the stage, but the Commissioners inevitably became involved in Egypt's internal affairs, to the displeasure of the growing number of Egyptian Nationalists, who wanted 'Egypt for the Egyptians'.

In 1878, France had demanded a complete revision of Egypt's fiscal system, and Britain had reluctantly gone along with this proposal. In return for a new loan, the two nations had made the Khedive give up his autocratic powers, and his hitherto private revenues and estates, and hand them over to a Ministry run jointly by a French and a British 'Minister'.

In February 1879 there had been a mutiny in the Egyptian Army led by a dedicated nationalist, Colonel Arabi Pasha. The Khedive Ismail, seeing this as a means of regaining power from the British and French, had supported Arabi, and had expelled both the Financial Ministers. Britain and France had been outraged and had persuaded the Sultan of Turkey to dismiss Ismail and appoint his eldest son Tewfik as Khedive in his place. Tewfik had reinstated both Ministers and Anglo/French financial control had been reimposed but despite this, the French wanted to mount an expedition to take over the country and so prevent further troubles of the kind. Britain had mistrusted any direct interference by France, but didn't want to become involved herself, and had tried to persuade Turkey to take the necessary action because, it was argued, Egypt was still a Turkish responsibility.

Arabi Pasha

France would not agree. She feared that Colonel Arabi's revolution could herald an Islamic uprising which might affect the rest of Mediterranean North Africa in which the French had a growing colonial interest, and had demanded action to stop the nationalist movement completely. She invited Britain to join in the issue of a declaration which upheld the new Khedive and Anglo/French financial control. Britain's Prime Minister, Gladstone, whilst doubting whether this would have much effect on Arabi or the Egyptian Nationalist movement, had agreed, and a joint declaration was presented to Egypt on 8th January 1882. Colonel Arabi and his fellow nationalists who had more or less treated this as a declaration of war, overthrew Twefik on 5th February and an extreme Nationalist Government came to power with Arabi as its Minister for War. France was determined to put down the Egyptian Nationalist movement, but Britain still wanted to act with caution, and again called upon Turkey to act. France did not agree with this approach and the already fragile Anglo/French alliance had been placed under great strain.

Then, in February 1882, French policy changed. France repudiated the use of force, and did not even want the Sultan of Turkey to invade Egypt, saying however, that even if a landing should become necessary, it should be by Turkish Troops under Anglo/French control! Britain on the other hand had proposed that a Turkish Commissioner should be appointed to arbitrate between the Nationalists and the Khedive, and that a 'Naval Demonstration' by the two European powers should be staged to reinforce Turkish authority. France would not at first agree with this, but after intense diplomatic activity, it was decided that an Anglo/Franch Naval force should be sent to Egypt to show the Nationalists that Britain and France meant business.

By 15th May, a joint fleet of British and French warships was on its way to Alexandria and this had given the Khedive Tewfik sufficient courage to try to dismiss his Nationalist Government. He did not succeed however, and popular opinion brought Arabi and his supporters back within days. The arrival of the Anglo/French fleet had done nothing to overawe the Nationalists and indeed on 11th/12th June, fifty Europeans had been massacred and the British Consul assaulted. London was still urging Paris to agree to Turkish military intervention, when Admiral Sir Beauchamp Seymour, who was in charge of the British part of the fleet at Alexandria, had reported that the nationalists were installing gun batteries which were a threat to his fleet. He had requested permission to issue an ultimatum saying that he would fire on these batteries if their construction did not immediately stop. France would not agree, and had withdrawn her part of the joint fleet, leaving the Royal Navy in sole command.

Only half of Gladstone's (Liberal) Cabinet had been in favour of allowing Seymour to do as he proposed, but ministers were already at loggerheads with one another over the vexed question of Home Rule for Ireland, and Gladstone was on the point of resignation, when someone had pointed out that events in Egypt endangered the Suez Canal. It is curious, but this does not seem to have occurred to anyone earlier! Seymour had therefore been authorised to send his ultimatum, and the Cabinet had instructed the War Department to prepare troops for an invasion of Egypt. As a result, an expeditionary force of some twenty thousand men under the command of Sir Garnet Wolseley, had been placed on 'stand-by'.

Seymour's ultimatum had been issued, and ignored, so on 11th July, the Royal Navy had bombarded the gun emplacements. This had merely served to fan the nationalist blaze, and Arabi responded by declaring a 'Jihad' or Holy War against the infidel British. Meanwhile, the Khedive Tewfik had fled from Cairo to Alexandria to place himself under the protection of the Royal Navy.

Arabi had said that, in defence of Egypt, he would, if necessary, destroy the Suez Canal, and Britain asked France and Italy to join in immediate action to

put down the Nationalists and protect the waterway. France agreed to help protect the canal, but would not become involved in Egypt's internal affairs, and Italy refused to help at all! Then France had changed her mind, and even refused to help finance an expedition to protect the canal, so since eighty two percent of all trade passing through the canal was British, Britain had decided to 'go it alone', and Wolseley's expedition which landed on 16th August 1882, had broken the Egyptian Nationalist Army at the Battle of Tel el Kebir on the 13th September, and had taken Arabi prisoner. Khedive Tewfik had then returned to Cairo, but Britain was in effect now in control of Egypt.

Britain had no desire at all for any long-term occupation of the country, and had even produced a timetable for the withdrawal of her troops. Indeed the main body of troops had *been* withdrawn leaving only a small garrison to protect Tewfik and to train the Egyptian army and police. France continued to be difficult and would not agree to anything that Britain proposed, and finally Britain had decided to take matters into her own hands, and had expelled France from the dual control of Egyptian affairs. The fragile entente had finally been broken.

Meanwhile, in the Sudan, the shadowy figure of Mohammed Ahmed Ibn el Sayyid Abdullah was emerging. He declared himself to be the 'Mahdi' (Arabic: 'He who is guided aright' - the leader expected by Moslems one day to appear - some thinking that he will be a reincarnation of the Prophet Mohammed, some claiming that he will be a reincarnation of Jesus - for whom the Muslims have a great respect - but only as a 'prophet'.)

The Mahdi had declared that the Sudan should be cleansed of all corrupt Egyptians, and that its people should return to a strict observance of the 'true faith' . Nowadays no doubt, he would be called an 'Islamic Fundamentalist' - and whilst Britain's invasion of Egypt was taking place, the 'Mahdi' had laid siege to the town of El Obeid which fell to him in January 1883. His triumphant followers had massacred the Egyptian garrison and many of the townspeople and had captured a huge quantity of arms and ammunition and money. Britain feared that the Mahdi's uprising threatened the headwaters of the Nile, for it was *still* thought in 1883 that any power holding that area could somehow cut off the river, bring Egypt to its knees and threaten the route to India.

The Mahdi

In order to strengthen the Khedivate, Sir Evelyn Baring was appointed as British Consul General in Cairo and became 'Viceroy' in all but name, but Britain was still anxious to extricate herself from Egyptian affairs and many Liberal Ministers recommended a rapid withdrawal. Queen Victoria did not agree - neither did Baring who thought that Britain should be prepared for a long stay. He could not have known how long!

Tewfik had then decided to re-capture Kordofan (an area to the south and west of Khartoum) from the Mahdists, and ten thousand men of the Egyptian Army, under the command of another British Army Officer in Egyptian employ, Colonel William Hicks, had been sent to achieve this. Hicks, who was known to the Egyptians as 'Hicks Pasha', and his force had marched out of Omdurman on September 8th 1883, but was annihilated on 5th November.

This defeat had sent shock-waves throughout both Egypt and Britain. Once again, the route to India was in danger. The Mahdi simply had to be prevented from entering Egypt or from taking any of the Sudanese ports on the Red Sea, particularly the port of Suakin. There were also still loyal Egyptian and Sudanese garrisons in the Sudan and these could not be allowed to suffer the same fate as that of El Obeid. Someone had to organise their withdrawal but who? That was the question!

Then, in an interview with the Editor of the *Pall Mall Gazette*, General Gordon, who was preparing to leave for the Congo as Stanley's deputy, expressed the view that there should be no question of withdrawal of these troops. After all, he said, who was this 'Mahdi' fellow anyway? Surely just another troublesome Arab who could be dealt with by the Egyptian Army - if properly led! The *Pall Mall Gazette* had published Gordon's views, and this had an immediate effect on public opinion. Why not send good old 'China' Gordon himself to the Sudan? He'd soon sort out the Mahdi and his rabble! After all he had already once led the Egyptian army and must know what he was talking about! The Government had gone along with public sentiments, and had approached Gordon, who agreed to go and help organise the evacuation of loyal Egyptian and Sudanese troops, if King Leopold would agree to defer his appointment as Stanley's deputy. The King agreed, and Gordon had left for Egypt early in 1884, where the Khedive appointed him 'Governor General' of the Sudan.

Gordon, away from London - and Cairo - had reverted to his original opinion and decided that it would not be right to evacuate loyal troops, or to leave the Sudan without a proper government, because if the troops were evacuated, the Mahdi would certainly enter Khartoum, and from there he would constitute a real threat to Egypt. Gordon decided that if this threat was to be avoided, there was only one answer. The Mahdi must be *'smashed up'* - his very words - and he had asked for another one hundred thousand pounds and two hundred Indian troops to assist him. However, before any action could be taken on his request, tribes to the north of Khartoum had joined forces with the Mahdi. Suakin was besieged, Khartoum was cut off, and the telegraph went dead.

At first, nobody was particularly concerned. Gordon had some thirty four thousand people in Khartoum, of whom eight thousand were soldiers armed with rifles and some field guns. He had plenty of ammunition and enough food for at least six months, but in March, Baring and Wolseley warned the British Government that Gordon was in grave danger, and had pressed for an expedition to go and rescue him but it was not until August that an expedition had been authorised. In September Wolseley had raised a force of ten thousand men and in October had set out for Khartoum to relieve Gordon.

The Assassination of General Gordon

Meanwhile, reinforcements were sent to relieve Suakin. This force consisting of thirteen thousand men drawn from Britain, Australia, and India, was under the command of General Graham. The young Lieutenant Frederick Lugard was appointed as 'Transport Officer' to the Indian contingent. After a number of reverses Wolseley's troops had reached Khartoum on 28th January 1885, but it was too late. The town had fallen and Gordon had been killed on the 26th! Wolseley sought permission to mount a counter attack, using General Graham's force to attack the Mahdi's forces to the east of the Nile, but this was refused and he was ordered to retreat back across the border into Egypt leaving the Sudan to the mercy of the victorious Mahdi (who was not to live long to enjoy his triumph over the infidels because he died in June 1885). The Mahdi was succeeded by the Khalifa Abdullah, a ruthless cruel and despotic man who bathed in the reflected glory of the now dead Mahdi. He marked the start of his own career as leader by building the Mahdi a magnificent tomb at Omdurman, across the river from Khartoum.

The Indian contingent with which Lieutenant Lugard served, had reached Suakin in March 1885 and had taken part in some action against the Mahdists in which some fifteen hundred 'dervishes' were killed. Fifteen British officers, and three hundred other ranks were also killed or injured before being withdrawn. In this action, Lugard 'won his spurs' as a Transport officer. Meanwhile, in April 1885, the news reached Britain that the Russians had captured Penjdeh in Af-

Frederick Lugard

ghanistan. As a result, Russia and Britain were once more on the brink of war. Gladstone, the Prime Minister, asked the House of Commons for eleven million pounds to buy war supplies, and the Indian contingent from Suakin was rapidly sent back to India to defend the North West Frontier.

CHAPTER TWENTY THREE

Soon after his return from the Sudan, by now a highly regarded Transport Officer, Lugard had been posted to take charge of Army Transport at Lucknow where there was a large British community. Here in 1886 he met a sexy divorcee, not only beautiful but vivacious, dashing and amusing, and Lieutenant Frederick Dealtry Lugard fell in love. Who she was, we do not know, except that she was known to her friends as 'Clytie'.

In his twenty seven years, Lugard had never had much time for the fair sex, but 'Clytie' changed his life - in more ways than one! In October 1886 he was parted from her and posted as Transport Officer to a field force in Burma where Britain was busy securing territory against possible infiltration by the French who, having been driven out of the Indian sub-continent by the British at the end of the eighteenth century, had long been interested in securing alternative trading bases in the Far East.

After losing the Franco-Prussian War, in an attempt to regain some of her national pride, France was busy establishing herself as a colonial power on the eastern side of the land which lies between India and China - an area influenced by both Indian and Chinese cultures and which Europeans called `'Indo-China'. In 1863, France had annexed Cambodia, in 1867 she had occupied Cochinchina (now part of Vietnam) and in 1884 also had occupied both Tonkin and Annam (now both part of Vietnam) and was showing interest in land further to the west, particularly territory in Burma (now Myanmar) which bordered British India.

In 1852, the Governor-General of India had annexed much of Burma into the British Empire, and in 1885, when Burma's King Thibaw had confiscated a British trading company working in Burma and offered it to the French, Britain protested and sent him an ultimatum. When he refused to negotiate, Britain had invaded, deposed King Thibaw and annexed the whole of Upper Burma to the Indian Empire. It was in support of the aftermath of this campaign that Lugard was sent to Burma.

Towards the middle of 1887, Lugard received a telegram telling him that his 'Clytie', whilst trying to drive a coach and four through the gateway of the officers' mess in Lucknow, had overturned it and badly injured herself. He immediately applied for leave to go and see her, but his application was rejected, so he decided to resign his commission and leave the army. His Commanding Officer referred the resignation to General Lord Roberts who directed that Lugard be given immediate leave on 'urgent private affairs'. He left Burma as soon as he could but by the time he reached Lucknow, he discovered that 'Clytie' had recovered sufficiently to go back to England. Lugard hurried after her, but when he reached London, he found that she had completely recovered, and was bestowing her charms on someone else. She wanted nothing more to do with a penniless young Army Lieutenant.

Lugard was shocked, broken hearted and almost suicidal, but as suicide was not a gentlemanly or honourable way to solve his problems, he joined the newly formed London Fire Brigade and sought death by volunteering to attend all the more dangerous fires. Fate wouldn't oblige him however, and he lived on. In December he was recalled by the Army and instructed to join the 1st Battalion of his Regiment at Aldershot, where he discovered that he had been made a member of the Distinguished Service Order (DSO) for his services in Burma. This honour did nothing for his broken heart. Indeed his return to army life only served to remind him of happier days in Lucknow. He was so deeply depressed that he fell ill, and was eventually given indefinite sick-leave, and was free to find one way of forgetting his sorrows.

Lugard had been a fifteen year old schoolboy when Livingstone had died, but he, like everyone else in the country had been thrilled and inspired by the Doctor's exploits, and knew - of course - of his hatred of the internal African slave trade. He also knew that despite Livingstone's efforts, slavery still flourished within Africa and that Doctor Kirk - now Sir John Kirk - who had been with Livingstone on the Zambesi Expedition, was British Consul in Zanzibar, and was a dedicated anti-slaver. Lugard, still trying to find an honourable way out of his misery, decided to offer his services to Sir John in his battle against the evil trade.

A British Consulate had first been established in Zanzibar as long ago as 1841, because despite Britain's efforts, slave trading continued to flourish on the island and in the Sultan's territories on the mainland. In 1845, Britain had begun to apply pressure on the Sultan and by 1847 had managed to stop the trade with

slaves that were sold outside the Sultan's own territory. Internal slave trading continued however, and in the early 1850's Zanzibari Arab slave traders had reached Buganda.

The Omani Sultan of Zanzibar, Seyyid Said, had ruled that, on his death, one of his sons, Majid - should rule Zanzibar, whilst another son, Thuwaini should rule Oman, But when Seyyid died in 1856, Thuwaini decided that he would much rather rule Zanzibar than Oman and prepared to take the island by force. His bid was frustrated by the appearance of ships of the Royal Navy, and after that Majid had ruled Zanzibar more or less under British protection. His younger brother, Bargash, had then tried to overthrow him, but with British assistance, Majid had captured his brother who was sent to exile in India. When Majid died in 1870, Bargash came home and became Sultan, and was supported by the British.

Doctor Kirk had eventually been made British Consul at Zanzibar, and had become a firm friend of Bargash. However, when the British Government had drawn up an anti-slave treaty which was delivered to the Sultan by Bartle Frere - still at that time, the Governor of Bombay and, as such, responsible for all activity in the Indian Ocean - Bargash had rejected the treaty and, as a result, the Royal Navy had blockaded all 'slave' ports along the east African coast. Frere had then threatened that if the treaty, wasn't signed, the Navy would blockade Zanzibar itself. Bargash gave in and promised to abolish slavery throughout his territory.

In 1878 in Glasgow in Scotland, the 'African Lakes Company' had been founded by businessmen who wished to fulfil Livingstone's dreams for Lake Nyassa and 'to advance the Kingdom of God by honest trade'. In the same year, William Mackinnon, another Scottish businessman, leased territory from the Sultan of Zanzibar and created the 'British East Africa Company'.

The first Christian missionaries had gone to Buganda within seven months of the publication of Stanley's letters to the *New York Herald,* and the London *Daily Telegraph* and not only Protestant, but also Roman Catholic missioners, flocked to Africa to 'save' Buganda from Islam.

Amongst the first Church of England clergy to be sent in answer to Stanley's plea was the Reverend James Hannington, the incumbent of a quiet parish near Brighton. He set out for Africa on the understanding that he would become the first Bishop of Buganda. He didn't get far. He and four other young, recently ordained clergymen joined a caravan managed by Charles Stokes, an Irish Protestant, who had gone to Africa as a lay missionary. The five clergymen were totally confused by Africa, they knew nothing of the problems which faced them, and could not even supervise their cooks because in Victorian times, young gentlemen - and certainly young men of the cloth - knew nothing of domestic matters. As a result their food was often uneatable, and they complained pathetically to Stokes, at the same time criticising the 'un-Christian' way in which he treated his native staff. Stokes resented their criticism and made little effort to help them and is even recorded as having threatened to put one of them in chains if they dared interfere again with the management of the caravan!

Rev James Hannington

Before they had gone far, they received advice from a missionary already in Buganda that it was unsafe to proceed further because the Kabaka was ill and dying and there was likely to be trouble with his successor, so, disappointed but not sorry to part company with Stokes, they joined an Arab slave caravan and returned to Zanzibar, and Hannington went back to England.

In 1884 Mutesa, the Kabaka of Buganda (with whom Stanley had made contact in 1875, and who had leaned towards Christianity), died. He was succeeded by Mwanga, over whose succession there was some dissent. On his succession, some of his elders prophesied that his kingdom would be overthrown by 'whitemen'.

In 1885 the British Church Missionary Society appointed Hannington 'Bishop of Buganda', and sent him back to Africa, but he and his staff were all murdered before they reached their destination. It was generally believed that the killings were carried out on the orders of the new Kabaka.

In Buganda matters went from bad to worse. The Kabaka's court had traditionally included a number of sons of provincial chieftains who were trained for high office when they grew up. European commentators, unable to find a better way to describe these children have called them 'Pages'.

Both Protestant and Catholic Missionaries had seen these young men as being fertile soil into which to sow the seeds of Christian religion in the hopes that, through his 'Pages', they could convert the Kabaka, or at least ensure that future generations of local Chiefs were Christians. Some Bugandan elders, who were deeply suspicious of the activities of the missionaries, decided to put an end to this intrigue and on 3rd June 1886, thirteen 'Protestant' and thirteen 'Roman Catholic' Pages were publicly burnt alive as a warning to others not to embrace this 'new' religion. This dreadful act temporarily united the Protestant and Catholic missionaries and the Muslims, and the monotheists began to prepare for war. They purchased arms and ammunition from Stokes, who having been sacked by the Missionary Society had become a trader and arms dealer, buying up arms from the African Lakes Company and selling them at a huge profit to anyone with sufficient money - or ivory - to pay for them.[1]

---

[1]After Stokes' wife, an English Mission Nurse had died in childbirth, he had married an African girl and been dismissed from the Church Missionary Society as a result. He ultimately extended his 'gun-running' activities to the Congo where he was captured by a small Belgian force, unlawfully tried and condemned to death, by a one-man 'Military Court'. He was hanged on 15th January 1895. When, at last, news of his death reached England it caused quite a stir. Britain protested to the Belgians, who recalled the Military commander responsible for the illegal 'court' who was formally charged with murder, but was acquitted.

CHAPTER TWENTY FOUR

L ugard was still wondering if he should offer to help Sir John Kirk in his battle against the evil slave trade, when he heard that the Italians were about to invade Ethiopia from their impoverished coastal territory of Eritrea. On impulse, he packed his bags, took all his money with him - a total of only forty eight sovereigns - and set out to try to join the Italian force. The British Embassy in Rome told him that this was out of the question, and that if he went to Ethiopia, he might easily be captured and shot as a spy. Dejected, he reverted to his original plan of offering his services to Sir John Kirk, and went to Naples intending to catch a ship to Suez and from thence to Zanzibar, but he discovered that the First Class fare from Naples to Suez was thirty pounds, which clearly, he couldn't afford. However, he found that he could travel as a deck passenger for only three pounds and ten shillings (three pounds and fifty pence), and he chose a course, normally unthinkable for a Victorian English officer and gentleman - he booked the deck passage sleeping among a scruffy crowd of Italian and Arab labourers, negotiating with the ship's cook for two meals a day at the cost of two shillings (ten pence). These meals were nothing more or less than greasy left-overs but they kept him alive - although, at this stage, he still didn't much care whether he lived or died.

By the end of February 1888 he had reached Massawa on the Red Sea, where, despite the warning received from the Embassy in Rome, he went ashore and tried to catch up with the invading Italian force, determined to become involved in the fighting if he could. Travelling some of the way by train and the rest of it on foot, he eventually reached the Italian lines where he met the war correspondent of the *London Times* and the *Italian General* in command of the expeditionary force. Both men were very kind to Lugard, but again warned him to stay away from the front. At last he decided that he was beaten, and he retraced his steps, returned to the coast and took a ship to Aden where he went ashore and stayed in a local bug-ridden 'hotel' waiting for a ship bound for Zanzibar. He tried to get another 'deck' passage, but the `British India Steam Navigation Company` would not allow Europeans to travel as deck passengers - in those days, such things were just not done east of Suez - so he was forced to buy a second class ticket which cost him thirteen pounds and ten shillings (thirteen pounds and fifty pence) from his rapidly dwindling finances.

Another passenger on the ship - travelling first class of course - was Colonel Euan-Smith, Sir John Kirk's successor as Consul to Zanzibar, and although the gulf between first and second Class passengers was enormous, Lugard finally managed to meet the Colonel who promised to put his name forward as a suitable candidate for employment with the newly formed `Imperial British East Africa Company` - originally the 'British East Africa Company'. This was all very well, but Lugard was nearly penniless and he simply had to find some means of making money on which to live - or die. Then he heard that the 'African Lakes Company' was looking for elephant hunters who would go and collect ivory for them, so he sailed on from Zanzibar to Mozambique where he met HenryO'Neill, the British Consul, a one-time naval officer who had served on anti-slaving patrols. O'Neill had just returned to base from a visit to Lake Nyassa where he had assisted the British traders to defend their newly built trading post against hostile Arab slavers who resented and feared European interference.

O'Neill explained to Lugard that the object of the African Lakes Company, originally called the 'Livingstonia Central Africa Company', was to try to fulfil one of David Livingstone's dreams of establishing legitimate trade and Christian Missions on the Shiré river, and on the shores of Lake Nyassa. All profits from the Company, after payment of a dividend of five percent to shareholders, were to be re-invested in missionary work. The Company had built a 'road' - called the 'Stevenson Road' - from Karonga on the northwest corner of Lake Nyassa to join up with an isolated mission station on the southern edge of Lake Tanganyika and had established a trading post at Karonga. This had not pleased the Arabs, who were led by a half-caste called Mlozi, who had decided that Karonga was an ideal slave trading base and wanted no interference from European do-gooders. The Company had built three fortified villages near the trading post, and on either side of the 'Stevenson Road' in which they gave sanctuary to potential, or escaping slaves. Mlozi had decided to rid himself of these tiresome Europeans, and had spread the word that all natives in the area had been called by the traders to a meeting at Karonga. When people began to congregate, Mlozi had rounded them up and slaughtered them all.

O'Neill and a hunter employed by the Company, had arrived at Karonga early in November 1887 the previous year, to try to help the traders beat off attacks by the slavers, and had been joined by the two brothers Moir who were Company Managers. Between them they had even attempted a counter-attack on Mlozi

Lake Nyassa and Lake Bangweolo

and his men, but this had failed. One of the Moir brothers had been badly wounded, and O'Neill had had to return to Mozambique leaving the matter unresolved.

This news excited Lugard. Here was a situation in which he could lose himself and his miseries by facing an honourable death and he volunteered to go and organise the European traders in their fight against the evil slavers. It is doubtful whether he knew or cared about the attitude of the British Government towards the activities of the Company, which was operating in what was widely regarded as a Portuguese sphere of influence. The Government was, as usual, happy to see traders and missionaries opening up 'heathen lands afar', so long as they didn't involve the Mother Country, but this was not all! Britain was holding long and involved diplomatic negotiations about various claims to African territories which related to the balance of power in Europe. The situation was complicated because not only were the Shiré and the Zambesi rivers in Portugal's sphere of influence, to make matters worse, many Portuguese companies were financed by British capital, so any conflict with Portugal could cause problems. What was more, Germany was also showing an interest in the north-west end of Lake Nyassa, and Britain did not want to jeopardise German support either in the Mediterranean and on the river Nile.

It was all very involved, but one could not expect an idealistic young Army Officer to bother too much about European balances of power. He, like most idealists, had 'tunnel vision'. He hated slavery. He blamed everybody for not doing more to stop it, and was prepared to put his life in danger to show that if 'officials' wouldn't act, he, Lugard, would!

He left Mozambique at the end of March 1888, bearing a letter of recommendation from O'Neill to the Lakes Company, and travelling by canoe or on foot, he reached a Mission in a village which had been re-named 'Blantyre' in honour of Livingstone. He was astonished by what he saw. The Mission house and the Church, which looked like a miniature English Cathedral, was built of brick, the whole station, church and all, having been designed by the Missioner, the Reverend David Clement Scott who, with his charming wife, made Lugard very welcome. They invited him to a very 'English' afternoon tea, presided over by Mrs Scott, complete with silver tea service, which somehow seemed incongruous in the circumstances.

Lugard met both Moir brothers and gave them his letter of introduction from O'Neill, upon reading which they immediately employed him, imploring him, as a professional soldier, to take command of a campaign against the slavers. Lugard was very happy to accept this commission, but he said that he really ought to have 'official' blessing on his endeavours. Mr Hawes, the British Consul, normally in Blantyre, was on leave in England but his 'stand-in' was John Buchannan, who was 'British Consul for the Lakes'.

Buchannan told Lugard that he had recently received very clear instructions from the Foreign Office in London that in no circumstances should Britain become officially involved in action against Arab slavers, because Lake Nyassa was not a British Protectorate nor even within a British 'sphere of influence'. Despite this, Lugard was still ready to take arms against the Arabs and argued that Hawes, on leave in London, could not possibly know of the local crisis and said that if London knew that British lives were at risk, he was sure that permission would be given. In the end, poor Buchannan said that if the white community would call on him for assistance, he would 'tone down' his official opposition, and since the white community consisted almost entirely of the traders who were under threat, this presented no difficulty.

In the end, Buchannan wrote to Lugard and said that whilst H.M. Government could not be held responsible for any action taken against the slavers, he, Buchannan approved of what was proposed. Armed with this 'authority' Lugard and some employees of the Trading Company went, up-stream in the Mission boat the *Ilalla* - reaching 'Livingstonia' a Free Church Mission on the edge of the lake. Here they took in tow a small metal-hulled boat belonging to the missionaries, and both boats being loaded with white and native volunteers, they steamed up the lake towards Karonga, stopping off to attack and burn an Arab camp on the way. On arrival at Karonga, Lugard set about improving the station's defences and then went on a reconnaissance of Arab positions. He was seen by the Arabs, and there was an exchange of fire.

A few days later, another trader arrived with one hundred and ninety armed natives, and three nubile female slaves whom he had liberated from their captors *en route* to Karonga. These girls were causing some problems, and tended to take the minds of Lugard's 'troops' off more important matters, so he arranged to return them to the tribe from which they had been captured, and work on the defences resumed.

He had other problems with his 'troops'. He had been used to dealing with properly disciplined soldiers, but these men, both black and white, knew nothing of military discipline, argued when given orders, and squabbled amongst themselves.

It was a very ragged army.

CHAPTER TWENTY FIVE

Having assembled his 'army', Lugard tried to instil some order into the chaos, and he issued all his men with a strip of brightly coloured cloth to be worn on the head, or as an armband, as a kind of 'uniform', and a means of identifying friend from foe. In preparation for the battle which was to follow, he selected what he called a 'hospital' tree to which all injured or wounded men should be brought for collection after the fight.

Early on the 19th June 1888, he and his 'troops' crept towards the Arab stockades, and Lugard personally led a charge intending to blow up the stockade wall, but the man with the explosives failed to charge with him and he was forced instead to try to get his men to storm the walls. The attack was a dismal failure, and he was almost immediately shot and wounded. He tried to reach the 'hospital' tree but failed and lay bleeding on the ground until he was found by his personal servant who carried him back to Karonga some fourteen hours later.

Once back in relative safety, Lugard inspected his wounds. He had been so close to the Arab who had shot him that his right arm was blackened with powder burns, and two lumps of the wadding (that had been put in the barrel of the ancient weapon to hold the musket ball in place) had been imbedded in his flesh. The musket ball had passed through his arm, narrowly missing an artery, and had entered his chest, where it had been deflected by a rib before exiting above his right breast.

Lugard took stock of the situation; five of his native troops had been killed, and nine more badly wounded. Of the twenty five white men who had taken part in the assault on the stockades, two were seriously wounded, and even the doctor was delirious. Lugard's own wounds had to be dressed by someone whose only 'medical' experience came from having once attended a First Aid class. Soon other members of his 'army' fell ill and - one by one - Lugard's force broke up. One of the Moir brothers and a white trader from Natal offered to go to Cape Colony to try to obtain a cannon with which to storm the slaver's stockades, but when the mission launch arrived, almost everyone else just wanted to 'go home'.

Lugard waited until the launch returned on 5th July when he decided that he was serving no useful purpose in staying at Karonga, so he retreated to Blantyre to recuperate, and to draw up plans for suppressing slave trading on Lake Nyassa. Whilst at Blantyre he received a letter from the Imperial East African Company offering him employment and an opportunity to lead an expedition into the interior of the territory leased from the Sultan of Zanzibar. Lugard was very tempted to accept the offer, but he felt that his work on Lake Nyassa had not been completed, and that he simply had to stay where he was.

Towards the end of October, he returned to Karonga and spent much time travelling around the area, making plans, and conducting a number of minor sorties against Arab strongholds. On Christmas Eve, 1888 when he was camped on a small island in the lake to the south of Karonga, an Arab dhow appeared after dark and started to off-load arms and ammunition for the slavers. Lugard and some twenty five local tribesmen attacked it and drove it off, full of holes and carrying a number of dead and wounded Arabs. Early in January 1889, the mission launch arrived carrying a small cannon which the Moir brothers had obtained from Cape Colony. Lugard was delighted, assembled it, and opened fire on the stockades. But unfortunately the gun fired such high velocity shells that they passed right through the wooden walls of the stockade, and out the other side, to explode harmlessly in the bush beyond. He made a second attempt to destroy the Arab stronghold but again failed, and was wondering what to do next when he heard that the Lakes Company had failed to get any support from the British government, and was likely to go bankrupt. This news forced him to decide that there was little point in his remaining on Lake Nyassa, so he packed his bag and prepared to leave. Just before he left, the remnants of his 'army' clubbed together and presented him with a ceremonial sword, which remained one of his most prized possessions for the rest of his adventurous life.

He was paddled downstream in a canoe to Quilimane, and on to Zanzibar where he met Consul Hawes, who was on his way back from leave. Lugard tried hard to persuade the Consul to agree to accept responsibility for continuing action against the Arab slavers, but he was told that the British Government was adamant and would neither send military assistance nor extend a Protectorate over the Lake. The British Prime Minister himself had made it clear that the office of Consul represented a compromise between the wishes of the missionaries to obtain protection, and the determination of the Government not to be involved in

expensive operations. The Prime Minister had further declared that the Consul's only 'weapon' was 'bluster'. In short, the missionaries and the traders were on their own. Hawes was angered to learn from Lugard about his 'war' against the Arabs and claimed that the fraças had been caused by the traders themselves who had provoked their Arab neighbours. He told Lugard that if he wanted to argue, he had better go back to England and discuss the situation with the directors of the Lakes Company. This unwelcome advice was almost immediately followed by a telegram from the said directors, telling him to return to England immediately.

On his arrival in London he discovered that O'Neill in Zanzibar, and Hawes in Blantyre, had both sent telegrams to the Foreign Office reporting on his private 'war', and that even the Prime Minister knew all about it. All concerned had agreed that H.M. Government could accept no responsibility whatsoever for Lugard's actions, and here the matter would have rested had Lugard not decided to appeal.

He made speeches on the subject to the Royal Geographical Society and the British Association, and discussed the problem of Nyassa with Sir John Kirk, now back in London. He wrote and published a number of articles in which he described the scenery and the peoples of Lake Nyassa and their struggle against the Arab slavers, and was causing considerable embarrassment to the Government by generally making a nuisance of himself when a formidable potential ally, Cecil John Rhodes, appeared on the scene from South Africa, where much had happened since Livingstone landed there in 1840.

After the Battle of Blood River, the Boers had driven Dingane from Zululand and had declared Mpande to be the new King of the Zulus, but Britain had refused to recognise the new Republic which they had created (the Free Province of New Holland in S.E. Africa), and in May 1843 the Governor of Cape Colony had announced that Queen Victoria intended to adopt Natal as one of her Colonies, and a High Commissioner was sent to Durban to put this into effect.

This High Commissioner went to see Mpande to try to establish good relations between the Zulu Nation and the new British Administration, and Mpande had been persuaded to stay north of the Tugela river and to the east of its tributary, the river Buffalo. In February 1845, Britain had changed her mind and Natal did not become a separate Colony after all, but was regarded merely as a province of Cape Colony. Three years later, Britain had annexed the land between the Orange and Vaal rivers, leaving only scattered settlements of Boers on the far side of the river Vaal - known to the Boers as the 'Transvaal'.

Between 1848 and 1851, large numbers of British immigrants were encouraged to go to Natal as a deliberate policy of `watering down` the Boer population and

making the territory more British, but in 1852, Britain had recognised the Boer Republic of the Transvaal and in 1857 had withdrawn from beyond the Orange river. The 'Orange Free State' had thus been formed and then Natal province had, at last, been made independent of Cape Colony.

Cteshwayo

In 1872, Mpande had died and Theophilus Shepstone, the British Secretary for Native Affairs agreed, in the name of Queen Victoria, to have Cteshwayo (sometimes spelled Cetewayo, but the spelling given here is truer to the correct sound) crowned King of the Zulus, but before the Coronation, which took place on 1st September 1873, Shepstone required the assembled company to promise to mend their ways, not to shed blood indiscriminately, not to condemn criminals without trial, and to accept the replacement of the death penalty by the confiscation of property. All the Zulu Chiefs - except Cteshwayo - agreed, but even before Shepstone had left Zululand, Cteshwayo had a man put to death for stealing!

There had followed many arguments and confrontations between Zulus and Boers which threatened the fragile peace of the region, and, after having been assured that the majority of Boers would be glad to have British protection, Britain annexed the Transvaal.

The new Governor of Cape Colony, none other than Sir Bartle Frere, (who had been the Governor of Bombay when Livingstone arrived there in 1864), then wanted to annexe Zululand but a Boundary Commission recommended that most of the lands surrendered to the Boers by the Zulus after the battle of Blood River, should be regarded as being part of Zululand.

Bartle Frere feared - with justification - that if the Boers got to hear of this, there would be trouble, for these very lands had been 'won' from the Zulus after the 'covenant' made with Almighty God by the Boers on the very eve of the battle. Notwithstanding his fears, the British Government confirmed the findings of the Commission and in December 1878, Frere instructed Shepstone to call all Zulu chiefs together and tell them of the decision. Determined to have the last word, Frere insisted that Shepstone issue an ultimatum demanding that the Zulu army be disbanded and that every Zulu male be allowed to marry when he reached the age of puberty instead of having first to join the army and to 'wash his spear' in blood before being allowed to take a wife. The ultimatum - which was clearly unacceptable to the Zulus - expired and on 11th January 1879, British troops had crossed the Tugela River. The 'Zulu War' had begun. After several humiliating British defeats, The Zulus were eventually overpowered, the Royal Kraal surrounded, Cetshwayo taken prisoner, and sent to England to make his peace with the great white Queen.

Despite having been rescued from the Zulus by the British, the ungrateful Boers in the Transvaal expelled those Burghers who had supported annexation by Britain, and had tried to re-claim their independence. A virtually unknown Boer by name of Kruger had raised an armed rebellion and in 1881 a small British force had been annihilated by the Boers at the Battle of Majuba Hill - the second dreadful shock for all the British Army.

In that same year, Cecil John Rhodes, who had gone to Natal in 1870 to work on his brother's farm, and from thence had gone to Kimberly to the diamond mines, had entered the Parliament of Cape Colony, and in 1885 was involved in placing a British Protectorate over Bechuanaland.

CHAPTER TWENTY SIX

Whilst he was in England, Frederick Lugard must at least have *heard* of the Emin Pasha Relief Expedition, but it is doubtful whether he knew any more about Emin than most other people at the time. He certainly could have had no idea that Emin's affairs would be of the slightest personal interest to him, and he was so deeply involved in his efforts to do something for the Lake Trading Company, that he took no notice at all of the excitement caused in some quarters by this curious little man.

'Emin Pasha' came into the world as Eduard Karl Oskar Schnitzer, when he was born into an Austrian Jewish family in Oppeln in Silesia on 28th March 1840. He had studied medicine in the Universities of Breslau, Königsberg, and Berlin, but although he qualified as a Doctor in 1864, he failed to apply in time for permission to sit an examination which would have allowed him to practise medicine in Germany, and instead he had wandered across Europe to Turkey where, - remarkably for a Jew - he embraced Islam and adopted the name 'Hairoullah Effendi'. He was employed as a District and Port Medical Officer by the Turkish authorities, and later moved on to Khartoum, where he adopted the new name of 'Mohammed el Emin' (Emin means 'the faithful one'), and managed to obtain employment as a Medical Officer with General Gordon.

In July 1878, for the want of any other candidate, Gordon made Emin Governor of that part of the southern Sudan which Baker had named 'Equatoria', and he was given the Turkish title of 'Pasha', which was reserved for military oofficers of high rank and for governors of provinces.

Emin Pasha governed the vast area of Equatoria, with the assistance of two battalions of Sudanese troops under the command of Egyptian officers. He married an Ethiopian woman and had a daughter by her, amassed a huge personal fortune in ivory and when not involved in gubernatorial duties, happily spent his time collecting and classifying plants and animals, for he was a dedicated naturalist. The British Museum (Natural History) in London *still* lists several species of plants and animals attributed to him.

The Mahdi's revolution, and Egypt's withdrawal from the Sudan had isolated him and his Province from the outside world, and although he had at first had some thoughts of surrendering, he was protected from the Mahdi's forces by the swamps of the Sudd, and as he still had two steamboats under his control, he decided to retreat further south, up the Nile to Wadelai, downstream from Lake Albert. Here he established his headquarters.

Nobody in the outside world knew what had happened to him or his garrisons until 1886, when a Russian explorer reported that he had seen Emin alive, and well at Wadelai with four thousand 'loyal Egyptians'. As a result of this meeting, Emin was able to establish contact with a Scottish missionary in Buganda, to whom he sent letters from time to time. It seemed that Emin urgently required ammunition and stores, but he was told that since the Egyptian government could no longer assist him from within Egypt, he was to retreat with his garrison to the east African coast, where he would be safe from the Mahdi.

By now, his 'garrison' of Egyptian and Sudanese troops plus their wives, children, 'hangers-on' and slaves, numbered over ten thousand, and the prospect of getting this number of souls safely across a thousand miles of unfriendly territory to the coast was daunting and indeed, quite impossible, unless someone sent porters and pack animals to help him.

His wife had died, but he still had his daughter Farida to keep him company, and he was quite content to stay where he was and get on with his collection of plants and animals - until he broke his spectacles which, because he was very shortsighted, made his natural history research difficult. He became very frustrated, his letters reflected this, and he began complaining about the world's indifference to his plight, and he appealed for assistance.

When the acting British Consul in Zanzibar received news of Emin Pasha, he had cabled to the Foreign Office suggesting that an expedition should be mounted to re-supply Emin, but the British Government was not impressed. Who was this Emin Pasha? they asked. If it was true that he was a German, then why not let the Germans rescue him? Sir John Kirk, at home in London for consultations with the Foreign Office, was appalled at the suggestion, for once again the situation in Africa was being affected by considerations of the balance of power in Europe. Britain could not hope to get Egypt's finances in order with-

Collapsable boat (From Stanley's `In Darkest Africa`)

out support from Germany, and Bismarck had taken advantage of this knowledge by challenging Britain's trading position in southern Africa. Germany wanted her share of the cake, and began to back her traders against those of Britain.

As long ago as 1883, Bismarck had asked Britain whether she was prepared to protect a German settlement at Angra Pequina (now Luderitz) in south west Africa, but Britain, receiving objections from the Government of Cape Colony, stalled and didn't give a satisfactory reply. In early 1884 the Germans had created their own Protectorate over Angra Pequina, and in July 1884 had declared Protectorates over Togoland, and the Cameroons in West Africa. After much negotiation, an Anglo-German Agreement was reached in October 1886, whereby the German African Company gained control of Dar-es-Salaam and Pangani on the East Coast, and the Sultan of Zanzibar's territory was arbitrarily divided between the two spheres of influence; Britain having the northern area and Germany the south. Kirk feared, with some justification, that if Britain were to be foolish enough to encourage a German expedition to 'rescue' Emin Pasha, Equatoria might easily become a German Protectorate also, not only giving Germany control of the headwaters of the Nile, but leaving Buganda ripe for the picking also.

Mackinnon, the businessman whose East African Company was interested in trade with Buganda, joined forces with Kirk to try to persuade the Foreign office

"The expedition sailed from Zanzibar for the mouth of the Congo on 25th February 1887". (Page 179)

to act but, having failed, between them they formed the 'Emin Pasha Relief Committee'. Mackinnon decided that the only man capable of taking charge of an expedition to rescue Emin was Henry Moreton Stanley, who was already working for King Leopold of the Belgians. Nevertheless Mackinnon contacted Stanley - who expressed interest in the project - and went to see his royal employer. King Leopold was not in the least worried over the fate of Emin Pasha as an individual, but he was interested in Equatoria and wondered if he could some- how tag it on to 'his' Congo territory and thereby gain access to the Nile. Whilst pro- testing loudly that it would be very incon- venient for him to release Stanley he said that - out of the kindness of his heart - he would do so provided that the relief expedi- tion approached Equatoria via the Congo, making use of his 'flotilla' of steam boats.

After a private meeting between King Leo- pold and William Mackinnon, this was all agreed and Stanley set about recruiting his team, which consisted mainly of a number of British Army officers, who, in those days seemed to be able to get extended leave without difficulty to enable them to serve

Tippu Tip

on all kinds of expeditions. He also assembled a huge arsenal of weapons which included five hundred Remington rifles, a Maxim machinegun, one hundred and fifty thousand rounds of ammunition, and two tons of gunpowder. His other stores included tents, the makings of a boat which could be put together from a number of portable sections, quantities of food and medicines, and forty large hampers of delicacies from Fortnum and Mason! Stanley clearly believed in the adage known to all those of us who have served in Africa, that 'any fool can be uncomfortable in the bush!'

Stanley's first stop was Egypt where he recruited sixty two Sudanese soldiers and obtained instructions for Emin Pasha from the Khedive. He then sailed to Aden, where he was joined by most of his team before going on to Zanzibar. In Zanzibar, Stanley discussed business with Tippu Tip; the half-caste slaver with whom first Livingstone and later Stanley had travelled. Tippu Tip, who seems to have recovered from the loss of his concubine, agreed to cooperate with Stanley, and the expedition sailed from Zanzibar in Februuary 1887. On behalf of King Leopold, Stanley offered Tippu Tip the Governorship of the area of the Congo above 'Stanley Falls' in exchange for supplying porters to carry relief stores to Emin Pasha. They were then to return bearing Emin's huge stock of ivory, which Tippu Tip would then arrange to sell to everybody's advantage.

The expedition sailed from Zanzibar for the mouth of the Congo on 25th Febru- ary 1887, and consisted of nine white men, six hundred and twenty three Zanzi- bari porters, Tippu Tip and ninety seven of his Arab followers, sixty two Suda- nese soldiers supplied by the Khedive, twelve Somali soldiers, two interpreters, and Stanley's own personal servant - a total of eight hundred and six men.

This small army reached the mouth of the Congo on 18th March 1887, where Stanley discovered that Leopold's 'flotilla' now consisted of only one serviceable boat, (remarkably it was called the *Stanley*), but that all the rest had been allowed to fall into decay. Stanley was furious and appealed for help from the resident British missionaries who reluctantly handed over a steamer called *Peace*. The American missionaries on the Congo wanted nothing at all to do with Stanley because they feared him and despised his record of brutality with the native population, but a Belgian officer requisitioned one of their craft, which was called the *Henry Reed* and handed it over to Stanley anyway. After many delays, the expedition eventually steamed up stream on 1st May 1887, with the *Stanley*, the *Henry Reed* and the *Peace* towing improvised barges, made out of the hulls of several of Leopold's otherwise unserviceable steamers.

Because of the shortage of river transport, Stanley decided to leave a rearguard behind and to go ahead with a reduced party to find Emin. Having done so, the rearguard could catch up, bringing the bulk of the stores. In June 1887 Stanley marched eastward, with a man in front proudly carrying a flag, not that of Britain or America or Belgium, nor yet that of the Sultan of Zanzibar, but the flag of the 'New York Yacht Club' (Said to be a compliment by Stanley to his erstwhile editor, Gordon Bennet!)

Having left the majority of the expedition behind at 'basecamp' Stanley's advance party finally broke through the rain forest early in December 1887, and marched on towards the southwest corner of Lake Albert, where, on April 18th 1888, Stanley received a letter from Emin offering to come to *his* assistance! Stanley sent one of his staff ahead to find Emin and bring him back to the 'relief column'.

When Stanley was finally 'rescued' by the man he had come to rescue, he was astonished! Emin and his staff were dressed in neat white uniforms, they had two river steamers, the *Khedive* and the *Nyanza,* both in good condition with brasswork sparkling. The 'relief expedition' was cared for and given better food than its members had eaten for months, and Emin even arranged for his tailor to make them new clothes, and his cobblers to repair their footwear.

It was all a bit of an anti-climax. To Stanley's surprise, Emin didn't seem to want to evacuate his headquarters! He was delighted to have made contact with the outside world but it soon became obvious that he did not really want to leave his 'people', or to go to the coast with his 'rescuer'.

Stanley spent some time trying to get Emin to agree either to joining Equatoria to the Congo Free State, or at least to hand it over to the growing British sphere of influence in east Africa, but Emin could not make up his mind, and did not now seem to want to make any move. In May, 1888, Stanley decided to go back

and bring up his rearguard with the remainder of the relief stores, but he left Mounteney Jephson, a young man who had trained to be a Merchant Service officer, to go with Emin on one of his steamers, to start to evacuate his northern-most 'stations'. When Emin and Jephson arrived at the first three of these stations, they were received with courtesy and honour, but in August they were placed under house arrest by mutinous troops who didn't want to leave Equatoria and go back to Egypt - a country which many of them had never even seen.

Meanwhile Stanley, having fought his way back through the rainforest, finally reached his base camp to find that the officer in charge had been murdered, three others had retired (one was at that time, dying somewhere down-river), and that only one European had survived. A hundred native porters and troops had also died and forty five of the remainder were on the point of death. Nevertheless Stanley led the survivors back towards Lake Albert, and arrived there early in January 1889 to find a letter dated 7th November 1888 from Jephson explaining that he and Emin had been taken prisoner by the mutineers, and had only been released because of the arrival of some Mahdist forces.

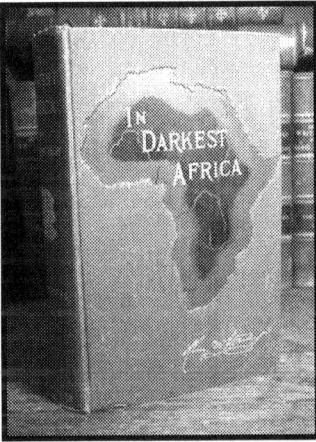

Stanley wrote a furiously worded letter to Jephson ordering him to rejoin the expedition, and saying that Emin must make up his mind about whether or not to withdraw to the coast. Jephson, having received the letter, returned to Stanley's camp on 7th February, followed, a week later by Emin and his daughter but only eight soldiers. Emin begged for more time, and Stanley relented and gave him until April to get ready.

Stanley then fell ill with gastritis, but by early May, Emin was ready to move, having persuaded only one hundred and ninety Egyptian soldiers to come with him - the bulk of his 'army' having refused to leave Equatoria. Added to this were three hundred and eighty women and children, and Stanley's own force, which had by now been reduced to three hundred and fifty men, making a total of nine hundred and twenty souls. Porters had to be obtained to carry loads and equipment for this large group, and when it finally moved towards the coast, it numbered almost two thousand.

It took until December 1889 for the huge caravan to reach Bagamoyo on the coast where, as a result of the Anglo-German Agreement, the Germans had established themselves in a neat looking 'town'. The German Commissioner for East Africa rode out to meet Stanley and Emin, and accompanied them into the town where a salute was fired by guns at the fort, and from German warships at

anchor off the coast.

Stanley and Emin were fêted, and Emin, having perhaps had too much to drink, wandered off and fell to the ground from a first floor balcony, cracking his skull in the process. Stanley, who, by this time, was somewhat tired of Emin, and his problems, waited for a couple of days to see if he would survive and then took his remaining men and crossed over to Zanzibar. Soon afterwards, he left for Cairo and never heard from Emin again.

In Cairo, Stanley wrote another book - *In Darkest Africa* - and eventually returned to London, more or less bringing to an end his part in this story. It was however, by no means the end of this remarkable man's career. When he arrived back in England he was praised by

Emin Pasha

everyone for his exploits. Queen Victoria offered him a Knighthood, which he had to refuse because he was at last, *really* an American citizen, having taken out formal American citizenship in 1885 to protect copyright on some of his books!

In 1890 he married, and in May 1892 took the Oath of Allegiance, and became (once more) a British subject. To please his ambitious wife he stood for Parliament as a Liberal candidate, but was defeated. He stood again in 1895 and was elected, but did not much enjoy his time in the House of Commons - it was far too dull for him to be an ordinary 'back-bencher'.

At the end of 1899 he was knighted, and shortly afterwards, the workhouse boy from Denbeigh, *now* the much respected Sir Henry Moreton Stanley, took his wife and retired to a house near Pirbright in Surrey. In 1904 he fell ill with pleurisy and was taken to London in an ambulance where, on the morning of May 10th, he died. His name as soldier, sailor, journalist and adventurer has lived on and his deeds continue to change the face of Africa and to affect the lives of millions.

Emin survived his fall and took service with the Germans with the rank of Reichskommissar and, with a strongly armed force, set out on April 26th 1890, for Buganda and Equatoria, to claim both territories for Germany. But an Anglo-German treaty on East Africa was signed on 1st July, and made his journey to Buganda fruitless (although the news of this didn't catch up with him for five months). He then camped for a while at Bukoba on the eastern shore of Lake

Victoria, and then set out for Equatoria, skirting around Buganda on the way.

In July 1891, he found the remainder of his 'Army' consisting of those troops who had mutinied and refused to go with him and Stanley to the coast in 1889. A Major, Selim Bey, was in command and had maintained a high standard of discipline and good order. All rifles were clean, and well oiled, and the soldiers had remained loyal to the Khedive of Egypt. Emin explained that he was now in German employ, and invited the troops to join him in the service of the Kaiser, but the troops declined saying that they would never serve a Christian king.

After much debate however, three officers and twenty six other ranks agreed to go with Emin and off they went, heading westward, intending to claim the 'hinterland' of the Cameroons for Germany[1].

The journey ended in disaster. Most of his soldiers and many of their families and camp followers died of smallpox and Emin himself was murdered by Arab traders in November 1892, when he wandered into what they considered to be 'their' territory. Most of the world has forgotten this strange little man, his only epitaph being the inclusion of 'Emin' in the scientific names of certain mammalian species listed in the British Museum (Natural History) in South Kensington.

---

[1] In the winter of 1884 Bismark invited the representatives of fourteen nations to attend a conference in Berlin to try to settle differences of opinion over tropical Africa. As a result of this conference, all participating nations, acquiring possessions or protectorates on the coast of Africa agreed to tell the other signatories of their acquisitions. In addition, the concept of the 'Hinterland' was introduced and the word passed into the English language, (being defined in the OED as 'the district behind that lying along the coast'). It was agreed that the Hinterland could only be claimed if the local chief had signed a treaty agreeing to hand over sovereignty to, or to seek protection from the European Power, and if the hinterland was physically occupied by representatives of the European Power. The Conference did not define how far inland the hinterland could be deemed to stretch but the concept was important and will be referred to later in this story.

CHAPTER TWENTY SEVEN

R hodes, always known as 'C.J. Rhodes' or as 'Mr Rhodes' - it is claimed that nobody ever dared to use his Christian names - had been born in England and had gone to Natal for health reasons. He was a strange man, a patriot and an Imperialist whose ambition was to bring the whole world under British rule. He even wanted to bring the United States of America back into the British Empire, and dreamed of world domination by the 'Anglo-Saxon race'. His ambition was to build a railway from Cairo to the Cape of Good Hope, and to paint - as he put it - the whole map of Africa 'red' (the colour used in those days by cartographers for all British, or British dependent territories).

When Lugard arrived back in London from his east African adventures, Rhodes was there also, trying to get a Royal Charter for his 'British South Africa Company'.

Rhodes was an intolerant and impatient man who didn't wait for things to happen - he *made* them happen, and whilst Lugard was trying to raise official support for the Nyassa region, Rhodes decided that the British Government must be forced to secure it for Britain. The area which people were beginning to call 'Nyassaland' was on the route of Rhodes' dream railway from Cairo to the Cape, and he immediately offered to buy the 'African Lakes Company' and amalgamate it with his British South Africa Company. The Directors of the Lake Company told Lugard that they were

Cecil Rhodes stands astride the whole of Africa

only prepared to sell to Rhodes if he got his Royal Charter, but anyway, Lugard went to see Rhodes and put his plans before him. Rhodes asked if Lugard would be prepared to put these plans into operation, and Lugard said 'yes'.

Exactly what went wrong is not clear, but when Lugard went back to see Rhodes to discuss the next step, he discovered that the great man had sailed for South Africa without attempting to make any further contact with him. Lugard was furious, not only with Rhodes, but with the directors of the Lake Company, whom, he considered, had ruined everything by their procrastination, and he published an angry article which ended with a Latin 'tag' which meant:

'All that work and nothing to show for it!'

This naturally displeased the directors of the Lake Company, and Lugard was dismissed.[1].

Lugard had another string to his bow. He was still on extended leave from the Indian Army, and he accepted employment offered to him by the 'Imperial British East Africa Company', and sailed for on 5th November 1889, this time as a first class passenger.

Frederick Lugard arrived to take up his duties with the Imperial British East Africa Company in Mombasa on December 6th 1889, only two days after Stanley and Emin had arrived at Bagamoyo some two hundred miles to the south. There is no reason to believe that he knew anything of Emin's 'rescue', or that even if he did, that it would have been more of passing interest to him.

It did not take him long to get started and - without waiting for Christmas to be over - on December 20th he set out towards an isolated Trading Post at Machakos, some three hundred and fifty miles inland with instructions to build a series of stockaded 'forts' along the way.

His first expedition on behalf of the Company was not without incident. He built the first fort without any particular difficulty, and continued to trek towards Machakos, but then he fell into an animal trap dug by local tribesmen and only narrowly escaped death when he was attacked by a crocodile whilst bathing in a river. Before long he crossed into the country of the dreaded Masai and entered into a blood brotherhood with a number of chiefs - a process which involved mingling the blood from an incision in his arm with that of his 'brother' who had made a similar incision before putting some of the mixed blood on a piece of meat and eating it! A ceremony which would not find much favour in these days of AIDS.

---

[1] Nyassaland was finally made a British Protectorate in 1891, thus going some way towards achieving Livingstone's post-Zambesi' dream, and meeting Lugard's ambition for the area.

At the end of March 1890 he started out on his return journey, reaching one of his 'forts' on the 19th April to find a number of letters waiting for him. One of these brought him up-to-date on events in Buganda, an area in which, his employers, the IBEA Company, had an interest.

He learned that, after the burning of the Christian 'pages' in 1886, the combined monotheistic forces, Christian and Moslem, had attacked the Palace of the Kabaka, had overthrown the pagan courtiers, and had captured the Kabaka Mwanga. Then, somehow, the Kabaka had escaped and had sought refuge in a mission station run by the 'White Fathers' who, remarkably enough seemed to have given him shelter.

H.H. Danieri Basamula-Ekkeri Mwanga II Mukasa, Kabaka of Buganda; 1884-1888 & 1889-1897

This upset the alliance between Christians and Moslems, and the Moslems, who were far better armed than either the Protestant or Catholic Missionaries or their supporters, had soon evicted all Christians from the Palace, and had put a 'pretender' on the throne. Thus, despite Stanley's efforts to bring Christianity to Buganda, for the time being at least, the country was under Moslem rule!

The Catholic missionaries who still held (or protected) the deposed Kabaka Mwanga, had once again joined forces with the Protestant Missionaries and had stormed the Palace with a combined force of around two thousand warriors. The attack had been spoiled by sectarian squabbles between the Catholics and the Protestants. The Moslems had been able to repel the attack and had driven the combined Christian force back to the lake. Here, once again, the Christians had temporarily settled their differences, and mounted a counter-attack, slaughtering all the Moslems that they could find reinstating Mwanga as the rightful Kabaka. Having done so, however, the two Christian factions had fallen out, yet again, and the Protestant missionaries had appealed to the IBEA Company for protection.

By this time, there were four quite separate 'groups' active in Buganda. The first group consisted of the indigenous pagan people, of whom the Kabaka was King. They had held sway in Buganda since time immemorial - until the Moslems from the coast, Egypt, and the Sudan, had begun to take an interest in the area, and until Speke, and later Stanley, arrived from the 'West'. They known as the

'Futabangi', or the 'Wa-Bangi', because they smoked hashish or bhang.

The second group consisted of the Moslems, the 'Wa-Islami', who wanted to claim Buganda for Islam and the third and fourth groups were affiliated to the Catholic and Protestant missionaries who had rushed to Buganda as a result of Henry Stanley's appeal in 1875. Because the majority of the Catholic missionaries were French, their supporters were known as the 'Wa-Fransi'. The Protestants, on the other hand were mostly British and were known as the 'Wa Ingereza' the 'English' - the leading ones were in fact Scots, but the Baganda could not be expected to know the difference![1]

Because the influence of the Catholics was strong, and because the French were in general anti-British, the IBEA Company feared that they might well welcome German intervention, that Buganda would fall into German hands and that the IBEA would lose all its influence there. For this reason, the Company wanted to get a representative into Buganda as soon as possible, and to secure a treaty with Mwanga before the Germans did.

Lugard read all this with the greatest interest as he plodded slowly back towards Mombasa. He assumed that he would be given the job of sorting out the Company's problems in Buganda so he pressed on as hard as he could, towards the coast, but he was in poor physical shape. His Nyassa wounds were festering again and his feet were giving trouble, he walked bare-foot for several days to try to relieve the pain. He was finally carried into Mombasa in a hammock, but when he got there he discovered that he was not to negotiate a treaty with the Kabaka after all, but that Major General Sir Francis de Winton, a much older man and recently the Commissioner in Swaziland, was to be given the job. Lugard - whose army leave had been extended for the purpose - was simply to open up a route to Buganda for de Winton.

Lugard was very upset and tried to resign. Although he was younger and less experienced than de Winton, he felt that he should have been chosen, and that de Winton was an 'intruder'. There was then an exchange of letters between the two men, and in the end, Lugard was persuaded to stay in east Africa and do as he was told! He was instructed to find the shortest possible route from Mombasa to Lake Victoria and - at all costs - to get to Buganda before the Germans, so off he went, first to Zanzibar to recruit experienced porters.

He was about to start his journey to Buganda, when news reached Mombasa, that a treaty had been signed on 1st July 1890 between Britain and Germany, in which the Germans renounced all interest in Buganda, and in Zanzibar Island, and gave up their small protectorates to the north of Mombasa, in exchange for the small British island of Heligoland, which lies off the west coast of Den-

mark[1].

Under the same treaty, the Germans gained access to the Zambesi river from their south west African protectorate via a corridor of land about four hundred and fifty kilometers long[2], and it was further agreed that the German sphere of influence in east Africa should be south of a line running from the coast, north-westward, through the middle of Lake Victoria to a point where it cut latitude one degree south of the equator[3]. The British sphere of influence was to be north of this line.

To some extent, the Anglo/German treaty took the urgency out of the situation, but nevertheless the Company was anxious that a treaty be signed with the Kabaka of Buganda before politicians could change their minds. Lugard was instructed to go ahead, to establish two 'stations' between Machakos and Lake Victoria, and then await de Winton's arrival. He reached Machakos towards the end of September 1890, and marched on to the edge of Kikuyu country, where he built a stockaded fort at Dagoretti (which was near the present site of Nairobi in Kenya). There he waited, and on October 18th he received the news that de Winton was not, after all, coming to Buganda. Lugard was ordered to proceed instead and get a treaty signed by the Kabaka as soon as possible. He was delighted. This, after all, was what he had wanted in the first place, and he left Dagoretti on 1st November with three hundred men, of whom two hundred seemed incapable of even using a rifle, let alone the battered Maxim machine gun which Lugard had been given during his visit to Zanzibar. (This was the very same machine gun which Stanley's men had hauled across Africa from the mouth of the Congo when 'rescuing' Emin Pasha!).

Lugard and his 'army' reached the borders of Buganda on 13th December, 1890, where he received letters of welcome from the Kabaka and from both Protestant and Catholic missionaries in the area. He marched on towards Mengo, the hill

---

[1] Heligoland had been ceded to Britain in 1814 but the German Kaiser, who had just dismissed Bismark and appointed Count von Caprivi as the new German Chancellor, had appointed himself Admiral of the German fleet, and he badly wanted this island as a naval base. It is said that Queen Victoria did not approve of the transfer since it handed over some of her 'loyal subjects' to another, possibly less scrupulous power. Nevertheless the exchange was seen to be advantageous to Britain, and it was once described by someone as being "a trouser button (Heligoland) for a whole suit of clothes" (Buganda etc.)

[2] Known as the 'Caprivi strip', being named after General Georg von Caprivi, the new chancellor.

[3] Originally this line from the coast passed to the south of Mount Kilimanjaro, but Queen Victoria was concerned that this would 'rob' her grandson, Kaiser William, of a mountain and the line was re-drawn so that Mount Kilimanjaro came within the German sphere of influence. This extraordinary gesture is still reflected in the present day boundary between Kenya and Tanzania. The German sphere of influence included the present day countries of Rwanda and Burundi, scenes of Civil War and unrest in the 1990's, but Germany did little or nothing with these tribal territories which were handed over to Belgium after the Great War of 1914 - 18, at the same time as Tanganyika was handed over to British adminsitration.

on which the Kabaka's palace was built, and like Speke and Stanley before him, Lugard was impressed by the high degree of 'civilisation' which he found in Buganda. The roads were well kept, passers-by were well dressed and respectful, and he was met by an envoy from the Kabaka who came, accompanied by the Royal Band, which contained not only drums and flutes, but various stringed instruments as well. At each halt along the way, Lugard was entertained by dancers, and there was a generally festive atmosphere.

The Kabaka had suggested that Lugard should make camp outside his capital on Mengo, but Lugard ignored this and selected another hill called the 'Hill of the Antelope' (Kampala), where he established his headquarters on 18th December 1890, and went to meet the Kabaka on the following day.

On Christmas day he met some of the Europeans who were already in Buganda. These were Ernest Gedge, a junior representative of the IBEA, who had been sent to Buganda a year earlier, and two resident Church of England Clergymen. The French missions were represented by Father Brard and there was also a German representative, a medical Doctor, Lieutenant Stuhlmann, who declared that he was in Buganda as a guest of the Kabaka. .He was in fact Reichskommissar Emin's second-in-command, and was probably really there to 'pick up the pieces' for Germany should the British bid for a treaty fail!

But it didn't fail, and on Boxing Day, 1890, the Kabaka put his mark to a treaty with the IBEA which granted the Company suzerainity over Buganda for a period of two years. Under this treaty, slave trading was forbidden, arms trading was to be controlled by the IBEA, foreign traders and missionaries were to be free to settle and freedom of trade was to be protected. The Kabaka was to form a standing army which was to be trained by Company Officers, and the Company's Resident representative had to be consulted by the Kabaka on all 'grave and serious affairs and matters connected with the state'.

Having achieved his treaty, Lugard set about consolidating his headquarters, and in his first report to the Directors of the IBEA he asked for a British 'Resident' and four or five capable Assistants or Clerks together with five hundred trained troops under the command of a British Officer. His report ended on a negative note. He said that in his opinion, the value of trade with Buganda and the surrounding territories had been overestimated. There was nothing to export except ivory and the distance from the coast meant that no trade goods could be brought in - or out, except on the heads of human porters.

CHAPTER TWENTY EIGHT

As Lugard settled down in his camp at Kampala, he realised that he might as well be in the middle of a hornet's nest. Despite the treaty - or perhaps because of it - nobody loved him *or* the IBEA which he represented. Worse still, the four 'groups' of peoples within Buganda were at constant loggerheads with one another. The French 'White Fathers' who were supported by their Wa-Fransi followers, resented Lugard, not only because he was British, but because he was also a protestant, and they feared that he would take sides against them. Although the British (protestant) missionaries had appealed to the IBEA for assistance, they saw Lugard and the Company as a threat to their brand of Christianity and they feared that he would be too open handed towards their Catholic rivals. The Wa-Islami disliked Lugard because he was a Christian, and because they felt that Buganda should have close ties with the Sultan of Zanzibar or the Khedive of Egypt and not with Britain, and the Wa-bangi, the pagans, hated everyone, because, they argued, it was their country anyway and they wanted neither Christians, nor Muslims, neither Egyptians, nor Zanzibaris, nor French, nor English, to tell them how to run it! It was not a happy situation with which to deal and Lugard must often have wondered if Henry Stanley's appeal for Christian missionaries for Buganda had been such a good idea after all!

He received some reinforcements from the coast, not the five hundred 'trained troops' for which he had asked but a contingent of seventy five Sudanese and one hundred Swahili troops, under the command of Captain W.H. Williams of the British Royal Regiment of Artillery, together with a second Maxim gun, and stores carried by untrained porters. This itself caused some embarrassment since, in Army terms, Williams was senior to Lugard, but he and his troops had been sent to support Lugard as a Company official, and the fact that he was an Army Officer on extended leave was - in Lugard's opinion - irrelevant. Williams accepted the argument, and turned out to be a splendid second-in-command and was a great source of strength to Frederick Lugard.

In February 1891, Lugard was told by the Kabaka that war between the Wa-Fransi and the Wa-Ingereza was imminent, and the Wa-Fransi were seen to be taking up positions on Mengo, the Kabaka's Palace hill. Lugard marched up with his Sudanese troops, and threatened to open fire with one of his Maxims on anyone who started trouble. This temporarily dampened everybody's enthusiasm, but the next day the Wa-Fransi were on the warpath again, this time waving a huge French tricolor, and again Lugard was forced to threaten them with his Maxim guns.

By the end of March, a second batch of reinforcements arrived, and although the majority of the men were unarmed, they brought with them valuable trade goods and presents for the Kabaka from the IBEA. These, at least temporarily, won the Kabaka over to Lugard's side since he began to believe that the British were not intending to oust him from power, but to support and uphold him. Then an opportunity arose whereby Lugard could perhaps win favour with both the Wa-Fransi and the Wa-Ingereza, and strengthen his position with the Kabaka. The Muslims, after having been defeated by the combined Christian forces, had retreated to neighbouring Bunyoro, and had now started to raid Bugandan territory from their stronghold. Lugard promised the Kabaka to mount a punitive expedition against these troublesome people, and, leaving Captain Williams in charge at Kampala, he marched against the Muslims, leading the Kabaka's 'army' into battle. As it marched, further tribesmen swelled its numbers, and by the time it reached the Muslim encampment, it numbered about twenty five thousand men, mostly undisciplined Bugandans who swarmed across a river and put the Muslims to flight. Lugard's troops only fired a few shots to help them on their way, but there was little that he could do to take control of the situation.

Khedive Abbas Helmy II

The son of Khedive Tewfik, he was born in 1874. He ruled from January 8, 1892 till September 19, 1914. Due to his reform policy and tendency to fight the British occupation, they dethroned him in December 1914 and declared Egypt a British protectorate.

It is not clear how Lugard got to hear of the existence of the remnants of Emin's 'army'. Perhaps Lieutenant Stuhlmann, the German Doctor, has told him, we shall never know, but Lugard decided to go to Equatoria to try to persuade these Egyptian and Sudanese troops to join him. After all he argued, they were real soldiers and the thought of adding trained men to his forces was irresistible. Therefore having routed the Muslims, he did not return to Kampala but marched on towards Equatoria.

He marched westward entering into further blood-brotherhoods with a chief and making 'friends' with the native population as he went. In July he came across a party of Swahili men marching under the German flag, who claimed that they were on their way to find Reichskommisar Emin. Lugard arrested the men and sent a letter to Emin protesting at their intrusion into what he claimed was a British sphere of influence. He then built a small 'fort' on a ridge of the Ruwenzori Mountains, named it 'Fort George' before setting off again in search of Emin's troops. Early in August he encountered a large force of hostile natives, but he put them to flight with a burst of machinegun fire and continued northwards building another fort en route, which he named 'Fort Edward'. From there he sent a runner back to Williams at Kampala with letters and detailed reports. He left a small garrison behind at his new 'fort', and continued his search for Emin's lost troops but he didn't find them - they found him!

On September 6th 1891, three officers and a number of other ranks walked into Lugard's camp on the shores of Lake Albert. A few days later they were joined by their Commanding Officer, Major Selim Bey, who told Lugard that although a few of his troops had joined Emin, the remainder had remained loyal to their master, the Khedive of Egypt.

They had maintained themselves in good disciplined order since Emin left them, and Selim had instituted his own system of promotions which had kept the troops happy but had produced rather more 'Chiefs' than 'Indians'. When Lugard was invited to inspect the garrison he found that it contained two Majors, three Captains, five Lieutenants, three Sergeants Major, five Sergeants, seven Corporals, fourteen Private Soldiers, - and one bugler.

Many of the men had been wounded at one time or another and their standard issue uniforms had long since worn out, but they had manufactured uniforms out of 'bark' cloth, and Lugard was impressed by their loyalty and discipline. He explained to Selim that Britain and Egypt were allies, that Egypt had abandoned the Sudan and that they were therefore free to go with him back to Kampala. At first Selim would not budge unless he received written orders from the Khedive, and Lugard had some difficulty in explaining the impossibility of getting such a written instruction from Cairo. Reluctantly therefore, Selim agreed to a 'temporary attachment' to Lugard's force on the understanding that all orders to his troops should be made through him and by nobody else. Lugard had no option but to agree, but he then discovered that although there were only forty soldiers, each had a harem of women, that each woman had a bevy of children, mothers, fathers, grandmothers and all had household slaves. Furthermore, he discovered that grown-up families of soldiers had also taken wives and they too had children, mothers, fathers, grandmothers, and household slaves and that all these people - including the household slaves - required porters to carry their effects to the coast. Finally he discovered that the garrison had attracted a number of hangers-on, and that they too had to be catered for. By the time they had all been counted, there were over nine thousand souls!

This extraordinary caravan eventually set out for Kampala, but soon afterwards, smallpox broke out, and poor Lugard found himself responsible for numbers of squalling infants whose parents had died by the wayside. He must have felt like the Pied Piper of Hamelin! He stopped and built another 'fort', managed to persuade some of the civilians to remain there until they were collected, and then pressed on towards Fort Edward.

He was within reach of Kampala on Christmas Day 1891, when a runner brought him a message from Captain Williams back at base, saying that the IBEA was in serious financial trouble, and that he was to retire from Buganda and return to the coast. Lugard simply couldn't believe it, but he marched on reaching Kampala on the 31st December 1891 when Williams showed him the letter. It was dated 10th August 1891, and it was accompanied by a personal letter to him saying that Buganda was costing the IBEA forty thousand pounds a year to maintain and that there was little sign of any return on this investment. On Lugard's own evidence, no return would ever be received, until or unless a

railway was built from Mombasa to Buganda. The Company had hoped that the British Government would guarantee the cost of such a railway but the anti-Imperialist wing of the Liberal party was opposed to the idea, and the best that the Government would promise was a 'survey' to see if the building of a railway was feasible. Meanwhile, Buganda would have to be abandoned and that was that!

Lugard and Williams sat up well into the night discussing the situation. There was a huge gulf between the Company's financial interests and their own attempts to bring peace to the troubled region. This sort of conflict of interests was frequently to happen in Africa for whilst commercial, economic, and political considerations loomed large in the minds of directors in Board rooms in Manchester and in Government Offices in Whitehall, to the men on the ground, the priority was, usually genuinely, the welfare of the people whom they were trying to govern or help. Lugard and Williams both knew that if they obeyed orders and withdrew from Bugands there would be certain civil war between the Protestant and Catholic factions, and, after much discussion, Williams told Lugard that he would donate his entire personal fortune of four thousand pounds to enable Lugard to stay in Kampala and 'hold the fort' whilst he, Williams, went to London to explain the situation and beg for more time. Lugard accepted Williams' extraordinarily generous gesture, and started to write an explanatory report to the Company, explaining the situation.

CHAPTER TWENTY NINE

L ugard was still writing his report when he was interrupted by visits from representatives of both Protestant and Catholic missionaries, each of whom complained that Captain Williams had shown unacceptable bias towards the other faction during Lugard's absence. He was still trying to sort out these clearly unjustified complaints, when a runner from the coast arrived with a telegram cancelling the August directive, saying that private subscriptions had been received and that the Company could continue to operate in Buganda until December 1892, when it would *have* to withdraw.

Lugard and Williams were jubilant and were just beginning to relax a little and to make plans for the next twelve months, when a follower of the catholic Wa-Fransi faction murdered a protestant Wa-Ingereza.

Realising that this murder could lead to riots or even to outright war, Lugard went to see the Kabaka to demand that the murderer be executed, but the Kabaka kept Lugard waiting in the blazing sun and then refused to see him. Lugard stormed back to Kampala, leaving one of his Sudanese officers behind at the palace to discuss the matter with the Kabaka - if and when he was ready to talk.

Eventually the Kabaka sent a message to Lugard saying that the murderer had acted within Bugandan law, since the man he had killed was a thief. Lugard then wrote to the Catholic Bishop, Monsignor Jean-Joseph Hirth, asking for a conference to discuss the situation, but the Bishop replied that he was quite satisfied with the Kabaka's ruling and warned Lugard not to take sides with the supporters of the Protestant victim.

Lugard was still trying to find a solution to the problem, when the Wa-Fransi's war drums began to beat and as a sensible precaution, he issued arms and ammunition to his troops, but his actions were misinterpreted by the Wa-Fransi who decided that he was about to declare war against them!

The situation was rapidly getting out of hand so Lugard sent messages to the European Catholic and Protestant missionaries, offering all of them sanctuary in his fort at Kampala until he could find some way of calming down the excited Bugandan natives of both factions. Mgr. Hirth declined the invitation outright and the Protestant missionaries said that they would only come if Lugard provided them with sufficient porters to evacuate their Mission station. They claimed, probably with every justification, that if they abandoned their station and took refuge in the fort at Kampala, it would certainly be ransacked by the Wa-Fransi. Lugard duly sent them porters whilst he continued to try to get the Kabaka to hand over the murderer for trial and execution.

He felt that he was actually making a little progress when the Wa-Fransi opened fire on some Wa-Ingereza supporters, and the long expected civil war began.

There was a large open space between the opposing 'armies', and Lugard decided that his two Maxim guns should fire bursts into this space, to keep the two factions apart. However, Williams' gun jammed and Lugard's own gun - the one which he had 'inherited' from Henry Stanley - failed to fire properly so this ploy failed, and the Wa-Fransi mob broke into the neutral space and advanced on the Wa-Ingereza. Lugard managed to fire a few rounds from Stanley's old Maxim gun into the crowd before it too jammed, and he ordered his troops to charge and clear the space of all warriors. This action came to be called the 'Battle of Mengo'.

The native advance was temporarily stopped and the open space cleared. There had been casualties on both sides when Lugard sent his troops to rescue the Catholic Fathers from a Wa-Ingereza mob which was setting fire to the huts in the Catholic Mission compound.

Despite this, the French Fathers still refused to evacuate, so Lugard mounted a pony and personally intervened, giving his pony to Mgr. Hirth, and finally persuading him and his priests to retire to the relative safety of the Kampala Fort.

But the killing continued, and each 'Christian' faction plundered the others' property with enthusiasm. Lugard tried to get the Kabaka to take command, but he refused, and the army was forced yet again to fire its Maxim guns to prevent a further escalation of the troubles. The Kabaka eventually agreed to co-operate, and between them, he and Lugard managed to arrange a temporary cease-fire. The Kabaka, who by now seemed to be grateful to Lugard for his efforts to bring about peace, worked with him to try to find a solution to the problems of

the two opposing Christian factions. Eventually they came up with the answer which has since been used with such awful results elsewhere from India to Ireland and Bosnia – partition! Land to the south and west of Mengo was to be given exclusively to the Wa-Fransi, with the Wa-Ingerizi located some way apart. This was agreed by all parties, and signed on 5th April 1892, but, having signed it, the Protestant and Catholics began to argue about the partition, the Catholic Fathers claiming that the area allocated to them was too small, and the Protestants protesting that the area given to the Catholics straddled the route into Buganda from the outside world and thereby discouraged potential Protestant converts. It was a 'no-win' situation.

Between them the Kabaka and Lugard worked out another treaty with the IBEA, which was signed on 11th April 1892 confirming the Company's suzerainity over Buganda in exchange for protection which was to be provided by the Company, and an undertaking that the Kabaka would not trade with any other European Power without the Company's consent. The treaty provided for freedom of religion and trade, and ruled that no European could carry arms or own land in Buganda without Company consent, but as Lugard drafted this fresh treaty he was, of course, privately aware that it would only last until December 31st of that year, unless he could get the ruling changed. For this reason, he very much wanted to go to England to try to persuade the British Government to declare a Protectorate over Buganda and its neighbouring territories, but this was not possible, and he knew that he had to stay in Kampala to keep the lid on a pot which continued to threaten to boil over again at any time.

Moreover, there remained the problem of the Muslims who were still gathered together to the north west of Buganda, and who considerably outnumbered the combined Catholic and Protestant supporters - even supposing that the Christians could be persuaded to stop fighting each other long enough to unite against them. To solve this problem, Lugard decided to go and talk to the Muslims, and assure them of the new spirit of religious tolerance in Buganda.

He set out in mid-May with a force of only four hundred and fifty men. The Muslims, numbering over ten thousand came to meet him and on May 22nd the two 'armies' confronted each other but Lugard had a shelter built and invited Muslim leaders to come and talk - which, surprisingly, they did! After two days of intensive pleading by Lugard, the Muslims agreed to come in peace and live in the vicinity of Kampala. Their leaders added their names to the latest treaty, and peace appeared to have come to Buganda - at last. This was not the way that the French saw it, but Lugard was unaware of the storm that his actions were causing in Europe.

Mgr. Hirth's version of the Bugandan civil war first reached Paris via the French Consul in Zanzibar. It spoke of Catholic missions being 'wiped out' by Protes-

tants, of Catholic priests being 'imprisoned' by the British authorities, and of Catholic converts being killed or enslaved by their Protestant rivals. When the news reached the French press, *Le Temps* reported that French Catholic missionaries had been fired upon by British Troops using Maxim machine guns, and when the German press took up the story, it did nothing to lessen the tension.

The French Foreign Minister protested to the British Ambassador in Paris claiming that a 'cathedral', sixty 'chapels', and twelve 'schools' had been destroyed - failing to explain that these buildings were mud huts with grass roofs, thereby conjuring up horrific pictures in the imagination of the Ambassador. He further claimed that fifty thousand Catholics had been sold into slavery. When a garbled account of the war then appeared in a French newspaper published in London, claiming that the *"Catholics in Uganda"*[1], who had *'long been persecuted'* had been driven out by the Protestants, supported by agents of the English Company', the news was pounced upon by Irish Members in the House of Commons, who as always glad of anything to embarrass the Government, pressed for an explanation. The Government couldn't offer an explanation even had it wanted to because it had received no news whatsoever from Lugard. However, instructions were telegraphed to a Captain James Macdonald of the Royal Engineers who was in East Africa conducting the promised survey on the feasibility of building a railway to Uganda from the coast, telling him to go to Buganda as quickly as possible, and find out and report on exactly what had happened.

Macdonald didn't immediately receive these instructions since he was already on his way to Kampala bringing with him letters which confirmed what Lugard called the 'death sentence' on all that he, and Williams had tried to do. To make matters worse Macdonald was unable to give Lugard much encouragement when he told of his views on the feasibility of a railway.

Lugard was more than ever determined to return to England to plead his cause, so he trekked back to Mombassa with Macdonald, but their personalities clashed and they fell out on the way. They reached the coast in early September 1892 where Macdonald's instructions from London caught up with him only after Lugard had sailed for England. Lugard was carrying with him a letter from the Kabaka to Queen Victoria (which cynics suggest that Lugard had himself drafted), asking Her Majesty to allow the IBEA to stay in Uganda and spread its influence throughout the territory. The letter also praised Lugard for his efforts

---

[1] The outside world had come to use the name 'Uganda' for the territory covered by the three nations of Buganda, Karagwe and Bunyoro. This was because the British Company Officials, not to mention British politicians and Civil Servants, knew little and cared less for 'native' kingdoms or their boundaries, and used Swahili (the lingua franca of the East African coast) to describe the area in which they had an interest. In Swahili, the prefix 'U' is used to form the name of countries - as an example the Swahili 'root' for English people, matters and things English, is 'ingereza'. The English, as a nation are the Wa-ingereza, the English language is Ki-ingereza, and the country of England is U-ingereza. Thus, the 'land of the Ganda people, became U-ganda and has remained so. It will be referred to as 'Uganda' from now onwards.

to bring peace to the country.

On his way home, Lugard was able to read, with amazement, the French accusations against him and he wrote, and later published a thirty one page memorandum in reply to the charges. He also addressed a letter to the French Ambassador, which he sent to the Foreign Office and wrote an article which was to be published in the *Fortnightly Review* in which he openly accused the French priests of trying to gain political supremacy in Uganda in order to hand the territory over to France.

Despite this, when he arrived in England, his main purpose was not to defend himself - for he had a clear conscience - but to mount a campaign to persuade Britain to retain a hold on Uganda after the December 31st 'deadline'.

Meanwhile, events in Uganda were being discussed in the House of Commons, with the Opposition getting as much political advantage as it could out of the French accusations. The Duke of Norfolk, as a Catholic, raised the matter in the House of Lords, and although Lugard wrote to the Duke seeking to explain the situation, the Duke refused to meet him.

Macdonald, who seems to have disliked Lugard as much as Lugard disliked him, went back to Uganda to carry out his instructions, and finally sent his report on the Uganda affair to the Foreign Office. In it he criticised Lugard on a number of counts - for his handling of the murder of the Protestant supporter, for trying to go against Ugandan law and custom, and for leaving Kampala for six months whilst taking most of his troops with him. He further accused Lugard of failing to give the Catholic priests adequate protection during the civil war, and of having 'leaked' his confidential report to a German journalist. Two articles appeared in a German newspaper giving details of matters which the British Cabinet was intending to keep secret, and this did little to help the situation and Lugard made matters worse by defending himself with vigour, but not always with tact.

A Cabinet committee was appointed to examine the facts, but at last, Bishop Tucker, by then the Church of England's Bishop in Buganda, together with Captain Williams, Lugard's erstwhile second-in-command, returned home, and both gave evidence in favour of Lugard. The Bishop claimed that Macdonald had failed to hear evidence from leading Chiefs in Uganda, or from representatives of the Church Missionary Society, and suggested that his report was biased, and therefore invalid.

This claim was being digested when news arrived in England that Macdonald, having assumed 'command' in Uganda, had himself taken action against the Muslims and had partitioned their territory amongst tribesmen who supported Christian factions. The pro-Lugard lobby used this as evidence that the 'man-on-the-spot', whoever he might be, had a very different view of matters than an outsider considering events after they had occurred, and that Macdonald, now in a similar position to that which Lugard had occupied, was now singing a very different tune.

In November 1893, whilst all the debate and argument was going on, Lugard published a book in two volumes, called *'The Rise of our East African Empire'*. He was, of course, anxious that the book should get good reviews, not only for his own sake as an author but for the good of his campaign to keep Uganda under British control, so he went to see the *London Times* reviewer, who surprisingly turned out to be a Miss Flora Shaw.

Miss Shaw was five years younger than Lugard, and was a remarkable and very handsome young woman. She was the daughter of General Shaw, a distinguished soldier. Her mother had been Marie de Fontaine, the daughter of the last, very aristocratic French Governor of the Ile de France before it was ceded to Britain in 1814 and renamed 'Mauritius'. As a very young woman this highly intelligent, though largely self-educated, girl had taken an interest in poverty amongst the labouring classes in and around Woolwich on the outskirts of London where her father was serving at the time. In an attempt to help them she bought basic supplies in bulk and opened a shop from which she sold them cheaply to the poor and needy. In 1877 she published a novel, and in 1880 set about studying the problems of prostitution and poverty in the East End of London. At a time when most young women of good birth stayed at home and waited to get married, she became a journalist and worked for the *Pall Mall Gazette* and the *Manchester Guardian*, astonishing prominent men by competently conducting interviews with them, before writing articles about their activities. She visited Morocco and Egypt, and became an authority on Mediterranean affairs. She met Cecil Rhodes and was one of his many admirers, and was sent by the Manchester Guardian to cover a conference in Brussels on the continuing problem of slavery in Africa, where amongst others, she met Sir John Kirk.

In 1890 Flora began to work for the *London Times* covering 'Foreign and Colonial' news, but she soon had the title of the column altered to 'Colonial and Foreign', reflecting her views on Britain's role in the world.

Flora Shaw

After their initial meeting, Flora gave Lugard's book a good review, and they began to meet socially. His efforts were favourably received by most critics and reviewers, and the Queen, the Prince of Wales and Leopold, King of the Belgians, all graciously agreed to accept specially bound volumes. But the Uganda affair rumbled on.

The Government refused to publish Macdonald's report because it was 'not in the public interest' so to do, but the Opposition screamed 'Whitewash!', and the Duke of Norfolk in the House of Lords, representing the country's Roman Catholics, accused the Government of 'bottling up' the report. However, by the time Macdonald returned to England, his own reputation was sadly blemished by reports of his activities in Uganda, and in the end, the Government issued a statement which avoided attaching blame to Lugard, but which indicated Britain's willingness to compensate the French Roman Catholic missions in Uganda. Then the haggling began with offers from Britain as low as five thousand pounds, and claims from France of one million francs [1]

.

Lugard was never officially 'cleared' of the charges made against him by the French, but the Foreign Office showed its faith in him by sending him on an important mission to France to meet Major Monteil, a French explorer who was contemplating an expedition to the upper Nile, to claim the area for France. This, if successful, would cut off Uganda from the Sudan, and thereby threaten the security of Egypt - and, of course, Britain's precious route to India.

The two men met, liked each other immediately, and Lugard sent a very satisfactory report back to the Foreign Office where his reputation was restored, but he could never be allowed to go back to Uganda!

---

[1] The sum finally paid in 1898 was ten thousand pounds.

CHAPTER THIRTY

By comparison with what was happening in Africa in the 1890's, the 'wind of change' about which Harold Macmillan spoke in 1958, was a gentle zephyr, a mere riffling of sun-burnt grasses on the open veldt!

The startling events in Uganda were by no means the only changes taking place in Africa, indeed the whole continent was in a state of turmoil! The French had not been at all happy about the Anglo-German treaty of 1890 because, although she had been involved in a treaty in 1862 which regulated the status of Zanzibar, neither Britain nor Germany had bothered to consult her about their latest arrangements. In the end, France agreed to raise no objection to Britain's protectorates in East Africa, if Britain would support her claim to the 'hinterland' of Algeria and Tunisia which she had annexed in 1881 and 1883 respectively; (i.e. before the 'Berlin' agreement of 1884 at which the 'hinterland' rule had been agreed). Although this meant that France acquired a vast area of Africa stretching from the Mediterranean coast to the borders of present day Nigeria, Britain agreed with her demands but Lord Salisbury, announcing this to the House of Commons on the 11th August 1890 said;

".........Anyone who looks at the map and merely measures the degrees will perhaps be of the opinion that France has laid claim to a very considerable stretch of country. But it is necessary to judge land not merely by its extent but also by its value. This land is what agriculturists would call "very light land"; that is to say, it is the desert of Sahara"

This taunt could not have pleased the French, who were still very concerned about Britain's occupation of Egypt, even if things were not going too well there! Ever since Arabi's revolt in 1879, the *fellahin* (peasantry) had been unsettled, and British guidance of Egypt's rulers had failed to produce either a more contented peasantry, or - for that matter - a more enlightened ruling class. Indeed, the Egyptians showed no sign of being able to govern themselves, and so, however much she wanted to, Britain could not withdraw from Egypt for fear of an uprising which would overthrow the Khedive, and so threaten the Suez Canal, and the route to India.

The French knew that Britain also had potential problems in the Sudan. The Khalifa Abdullah had proved to be a fanatical despot who had carried on from where the Mahdi had been stopped by his death in 1885. By 1887, all remaining Egyptian garrisons in the Sudan - except Emin's garrison in Equatoria - had been starved into submission or annihilated, and the Khalifa was now ruling a territory half as big as Europe. Ten thousand of his troops crossed the borders into Egypt and they occupied all Red Sea ports, except Suakin, which was still held by the British on behalf of the Khedive.

The Khalifa sent a letter to Queen Victoria, the Sultan of Turkey and the Khedive of Egypt demanding that they should come to Omdurman to pay him homage (on the strict understanding that the Queen should first embrace Islam!) All three declined his invitation, but his attention was soon occupied when famine struck the Sudan in 1889. In Omdurman, starving people were said to have turned to cannibalism, eating young children in order to keep themselves alive. Gradually the Khalifa's grip on his territory began to weaken, the Egyptian army drove him back across the border, and the British reclaimed most of the Red Sea ports.

In Britain, there had long been a popular demand for Gordon's death to be avenged, and, it was claimed, a well organised force could now take back the Sudan and deal, once and for all with the troublesome Khalifa. This popular view was not shared by the British Government because Egypt hadn't sufficient money to mount such a huge campaign and Britain didn't intend to finance it on her behalf. Anyway, it was argued, so long as the upper Nile was in the hands of the Dervishes, no other European power was likely to be able to take over and Britain was content to leave it that way, at least for the time being. However, the British - and the French - knew that a weakened Egypt might well encourage the Russians to march on Constantinople, and thereby threaten India and French territory in the Mediterranean. The situation was potentially dangerous for both countries.

Nevertheless, the longer British troops remained in Egypt, the more hostile the French became. Britain held Gibraltar, Malta and Cyprus, and her grip on Egypt gave her control of both entrances to - and exits from - the Mediterranean Sea, which France had come to regard as her own 'sphere of influence', and where,

early in 1888, she had increased her Naval presence.

To make matters worse for Britain, France had started to woo Russia. Her fleet had already visited Russian ports, and when the Russian fleet paid a courtesy visit to Toulon, alarm bells began to ring in the British Admiralty!

In 1889, Italy's government had made a treaty with Ethiopia which gave Rome influence over the Blue Nile, and this also alarmed the British Government, so much so that in 1890 it was clear to Italy - and later to Germany and France - that Britain would oppose any nation which sought to gain control over the headwaters of the Nile. When Khedive Tewfik died in 1892, Abbas II became the new Khedive of Egypt, and in January 1893 openly rebelled against British control and there were sinister signs that the French - and the Russians - were backing him. Lord Cromer, the British Consul General in Egypt, called for and received additional British troops and relations with France worsened. The French then began to consider plans to force Britain into negotiations about her presence in Egypt and her control of the Mediterranean, and decided that if she could somehow take control of the upper Nile, and thereby threaten the life-blood of Egypt, Britain would be *made* to talk. In May 1893, the French President produced a plan to get a French force established at the confluence of the Nile and the River Sobat (which flows into the Nile near the present day town of Malakal), and he chose the town of Fashoda as the site for French occupation. The general plan was for one French force to move westwards through Ethiopia towards Fashoda whilst another was to approach Fashoda from the west coast of Africa where, thanks to the activities of the Count de Brazza, France had gained a foothold on the north bank of the Congo.

On the west coast of Africa there was even more Anglo-French rivalry. European merchants, having been denied the trans-Atlantic slave trade, had started to trade in palm oil and rubber and as long ago as 1849 a British Consul had been appointed to look after the traders' interests. In 1852, another consulate had been established in Lagos and an anti-slaving treaty had been signed with the local chiefs. Although Lagos was not yet British Territory, the Consul, backed by ships of the Royal Navy which carried out anti-slaving patrols from Lagos, effectively ruled the place. In 1854 Britain had encouraged another expedition to explore the Niger River and in 1861 with hopes of more trade in the interior, Lagos had been annexed by Britain.

These moves were said to be in the interests of trade and not of imperialism, and indeed the British Government had tried hard to disentangle itself from official involvement on the west coast of Africa. In 1865 a Select Committee of the House of Commons had even recommended ultimate withdrawal from western African territories, with the possible exception of Sierra Leone, and Britain had even tried to 'give' the Gambia to France, but France was not interested. Britain began to realise that she was not going to rid herself of responsibility on the west coast after all and, after the Ashanti campaign in 1874, Britain had had no real option but to take over the 'so-called' Gold Coast. To complicate matters further, whether their Governments liked it or not, British traders and their French rivals continued to infiltrate the hinterland of the west coast of Africa.

In 1877 an extraordinary man, George Taubman Goldie, had appeared on the scene. Goldie, a former officer in the British Royal Engineers, who proudly claimed that he had taken his final army examination whilst he was blind drunk, had gone to the Niger with his brother to find out why certain family interests there were not paying dividends. The brother fell ill and returned to England but Goldie decided to stay and sort out the source of family revenue. He soon discovered that many of the smaller trading enterprises were inefficient, so he set about amalgamating a number of the smaller concerns into what he proudly called the 'National African Company'. In 1881 he had applied for a Royal Charter, but his request had been denied.

Goldie:
A remarkable man

Until the British occupation of Egypt in 1882 Anglo-French relationships in west Africa had been fairly amicable, and both governments had been happy to allow their traders to operate without interference from London or Paris. However in 1879 when the French colony of Senegal began to extend its borders towards the River Niger, and showed signs of wanting to encircle the British run territories on the Gambia river and in Sierra Leone, the British Government had proposed, and the French had agreed, a 'stand-still' pending a Commission of Demarcation. This Commission met in 1881 and, as a result, Britain had agreed not to interfere with French aspirations on the coast between the Gold Coast and the Gambia, and the French had similarly agreed not to interfere with those of Britain, between Senegal and Liberia. But then came Britain's invasion of Egypt.

France, anxious to compensate for what she saw as a blow to her national pride, began sending her agents up the Niger River to make treaties with native chieftains, and these activities soon clashed with those of George Goldie. The British Government began to have second thoughts about granting him a Royal Charter.

By the end of 1884, French traders were operating four hundred miles up the River Niger and five hundred miles up the River Benue, but Goldie soon bought out two of the French firms involved, and thus regained a British trading monopoly in the region. In December 1884, Goldie had sent a representative to make treaties with the Muslim Emirs far to the north, and in 1885 he had made a second application for a Royal Charter. After a great deal of debate, a Charter had been granted in 1886, and the new company, soon to be called the 'Royal Niger Company' was empowered to administer justice, enforce treaty rights, and to collect taxes to cover administrative expenses. This grant, whilst recognising a British sphere of influence, did not establish national boundaries, and the French, as keen as ever, continued to press forwards carving out a colonial empire with the help of her army, whilst Britain was still content to leave everything to her traders as represented by Goldie and his Royal Niger Company.

It was not only the French who had territorial designs on the west African coast and in 1884 the Germans had declared a protectorate over Togoland, which lay on the eastern border of the British colony of the Gold Coast, and over the Cameroons, which lay to the east of the mouth of the Niger.

In southern Africa, after the defeat of British Forces at Majuba Hill in 1881 the British army, backed by the Conservative Opposition, wanted to go and teach the Boers a lesson, but the Liberal Government then in power didn't agree and wanted to smooth matters over in the hope that, sooner or later, the Boers would see the error of their ways, and return to the fold of the growing British Empire.

With this in mind, the Transvaal had once again become an independent republic, but this did not satisfy the Boers in the rest of South Africa, and they became increasingly restless and anti-British. They still had territorial ambitions and continued to encroach on native lands, particularly in Bechuanaland (now Botswana). Britain's Liberal Government was not concerned with what happened to Bechuanaland and, fearing another confrontation with the Boers, rejected the suggestion that Britain should protect native interests by declaring a protectorate over the territory. This view of matters had not been shared by traders and merchants in the Cape Colony who had pressed Britain to protect Bechuanaland, pointing out that it provided the only remaining free access to the interior of Africa, which, if occupied by the Boers would effectively put a stop to further expansion of British interests in southern Africa. The Liberals sought a compromise, and at first had managed to persuade Kruger - their 'leader' - to agree to leave a road open through the native territory through which traders and

explorers alike from the south could penetrate further into the heart of the continent. In 1884, when Germany had established a protectorate over Angra Pequina (now Namibia), Kruger had granted a monopoly over railways in the Transvaal to a German-Dutch syndicate which planned a rail link between Pretoria and the German Protectorate, thus threatening the Cape's monopoly of trade in the area. So, in 1885, yielding to pressure from Cape Colony traders and to try to combat increasing German encroachment, Britain was forced to take Bechuanaland under her protection.

In 1886 gold had been discovered in the heart of the Transvaal, and expertise, money, and miners, mostly from Britain, had poured into the Republic making it tremendously wealthy. All the Transvaal's rail links with the coast still had to go through the British owned Cape Colony or Natal, and the British colonies took advantage of this pushing their railways further and further northward. The railway mileage and the white population in southern Africa doubled at about the same pace, but Kruger forbade the extension of British South African railways into the Transvaal and decided instead to build his own railway from Johannesburg to Delagoa Bay in Portuguese Mozambique, to make the Transvaal truly independent of the British at last.

Paul Kruger

British colonists in the Cape wanted to expand northwards into Bechuanaland and through Matabeleland to the Zambesi and beyond, whilst colonists in Natal looked upon Zululand and Swaziland as their natural hinterland. Then the peoples of the Transvaal, having won their independence from the hated British, decided to make treaties with the native chieftains in Swaziland and to set up a new republic in Zululand. In 1886, the Governor of Natal had urged the British Government to check the advances of the Transvaalers, and pressed for the remainder of Zululand to be placed under British 'protection', but the Liberal Government, still anxious to placate the Boers, yielded a quarter of Zululand to the Transvaal, thus cutting off Natal from Swaziland. In 1886 the Marquis of Salisbury's Conservatives won a General Election, and in 1887, Britain annexed eastern Zululand to Natal, but did nothing about Swaziland for fear of offending the Portuguese and the Boers. South African colonial leaders, largely inspired by Cecil Rhodes, had tried to spoil Kruger's plans by attempting to buy the Portuguese end of the proposed railway line to Delagoa Bay, but the British Government, whilst stating that it would be happy to see the railway in the hands of the

South African colonists, declined to participate in the negotiations, and would not risk going to war with either Portugal or the Transvaal to achieve this!

Meanwhile, white men from both the British South African Colonies and from the Transvaal were stirring up trouble for themselves - and for others - as they tried to buy 'trading' rights and mineral concessions in Matabeleland and Mashonaland where they hoped to find gold in similar quantities to that which had been found in the Transvaal.

Speculators of all nationalities, German and Portuguese, Transvaalers, and British, arrived at the court of King Lobengula (Mzilikazi's successor), but by the end of 1888, Rhodes' company alone had somehow persuaded Lobengula to grant it a monopoly on all minerals in his kingdom.

Cape Colonists, urged on by Rhodes, had tried to persuade Britain to extend her protectorate over Bechuanaland northward to the Zambesi - Livingstone's 'God's Highway' - to protect the tribesmen in the area from exploitation by the Transvaal and by adventurers from other European nations. This time Salisbury's Conservatives obliged, and claimed that the whole of the area south of the Zambesi was within the 'British sphere of influence'. This was disputed by Germany and Portugal.

It was at about this time that Lugard had taken arms against Arab slavers on Lake Nyassa, and had backed British traders and missionaries in their bid for a British protectorate over that area. Rhodes had come to London in 1889 seeking a Royal Charter for his 'South African Company',and had offered to colonise and administer Matabeleland on behalf of Cape Colony. He offered to take over the Bechuanaland Protectorate and extend its railway and telegraph system northwards to the banks of the Zambesi river, and - in October 1891 - he had been granted his Royal Charter, which gave his Company full financial and administrative responsibilities for the landslying to the north of Bechuanaland, to the north and west of the Transvaal, and to the west of Portuguese Mozambique.

CHAPTER THIRTY ONE

In the summer of 1894, Frederick Lugard was unemployed, but although he was still a serving soldier he seems to have been surprised when he was ordered to return to his regiment in India! He had no wish to return to regimental life and he applied to the Liberal Prime Minister, Lord Roseberry, who obtained a further secondment to the Foreign Office for him. However, the secondment was illusory since he occupied no post and received no salary. Furthermore, although he was on extended leave, he still received no Army pay, and once again, Lugard was penniless, and was forced to find some means of earning his living.

In April 1894, he had received an invitation from Goldie to go to the Niger, but he wasn't in the least interested in west Africa and only wanted to return to Uganda. However, in June, when the British Government was still debating the Ugandan issue, Goldie wrote again, urging Lugard to join him and go to a place called 'Borgu' - of which Lugard had never heard. This, he discovered was an Emirate to the west of the Niger and to the north of French-held Dahomey (This country is now called Benin, but it should not be confused with the historical kingdom of Benin, which lay in modern Nigeria). Goldie added that if Lugard was going to go to west Africa, he had better make his mind up quickly and sail within a month, because it was vital to get a treaty signed by the Emir of Borgu before the French did.

Reluctantly, Lugard agreed, and he sailed for Lagos towards the end of July 1894. During the southbound voyage, he read all that he could about west Africa

Lord Lugard

and also started to learn 'Hausa', the *lingua franca* of much of the hinterland. Like Livingstone, some forty years earlier, he persuaded the Captain to teach him how to use a sextant so that he could accurately fix his position when deep in uncharted bush.

The ship stopped briefly at Freetown in Sierra Leone, where Lugard went ashore to stretch his legs and was appalled by what he saw of the British officials there, who in his opinion, appeared to drink too much, and take far too little exercise. The next stop was at Accra on the Gold Coast, where Lugard again went ashore to see for himself some of the 'dungeons' where, during slave trading days, human cargoes were held, pending shipment across the Atlantic. Again, he was appalled!

By the 19th August 1894, his ship was anchored off Lagos where he went ashore and met a party of Royal Naval Officers who invited him to join them on a reconnaissance of a position held by a native chief, who, despite the embargo on slave trading, was reported to have some five thousand slaves in his stronghold, awaiting sale to the highest bidder.

Lugard, who was suffering much from the humid heat, and from a bout of malaria, declined the invitation, so the launch went up river without him. It returned a few days later, its decks stained with the blood of a number of dead and wounded sailors, the slaver having repelled the launch with a battery of twenty three heavy cannon. It is perhaps hard to appreciate that only one hundred years ago the war against slavery in Africa was far from over.

Lugard left his ship at the port of Brass where he embarked on a river boat to travel up-stream accompanied by two young white officers. They reached Lokoja at the junction of the Niger and the Benue rivers on September 5th, where Lugard was given thirty Hausa and ten Yoruba soldiers who were to accompany him on his journey to Borgu. The riverboat steamed up the broad muddy brown river to Jebba, where he and his 'army' were to disembark and march overland to Nikki, the capital town of Borgu Emirate. At Jebba he recruited a large number of porters and purchased thirty four donkeys to carry his loads and equipment across the bush. The expedition set out at the end of September - 1894, despite heavy tropical rain, which made the crossing of the many rivers and rivulets difficult and dangerous. Nevertheless, they reached Kishi, a town on the borders of Borgu, by mid-October where Lugard signed a treaty with the local Chief on behalf of the Royal Niger Company before marching onwards towards Nikki.

As he neared his destination, he was met by a messenger from Borgu who told him that a local 'medicine man' had told the Emir that if he looked upon a white man, he would die within three months and that therefore Lugard should proceed no further. Undeterred, Lugard told the messenger that he was the bearer of many gifts for the Emir, but, of course, if the Emir didn't want them, he would find someone who did! This had the desired effect. The messenger left and returned within days, saying that the Emir would receive Lugard - and his gifts - after all.

Early in November, the march towards Nikki recommenced but many men were ill with fever and only fourteen out of the thirty four donkeys were still alive - and most of these were in poor condition.

On November 5th, not perhaps an auspicious date - they reached the walls of Nikki and, there being no sign of the French having arrived first, Lugard sent a message to the Emir, requesting an audience. The Emir replied demanding his gifts, but Lugard told the messenger that the Emir would not get his gifts until after he had signed the treaty with the `Royal Niger Company`.

The bargaining continued but in the end, the chief Imam (the Muslim religious leader) of Nikki came by night and asked Lugard what would happen if the medicine man was right after all and the Emir die within three months. Lugard was unable to think of a suitable answer, and the Imam went back into the town and wasn't seen again for three days.

Then, because they were short of food and water, Lugard's men began to steal from the locals and one of them was caught red-handed. Lugard had him publicly flogged for his sins, and this impressed the Emir, who immediately provided Lugard and his 'army' with food and water - but still wouldn't meet him face to face.

Lugard never did meet the Emir, but, using the Imam as a go-between, he obtained the Emir's 'signature' to a treaty dated 10th November 1894, in which the Emir agreed to recognise the Royal Niger Company as being the sole representative of the great white Queen of England, agreed to accept British protection against attacks from neighbouring tribes and agreed not to have any dealings with any other foreign power - meaning, of course, the French.

Having achieved his object, Lugard left Nikki on the 12th November to return to Jebba. The French reached Nikki only sixteen days after he had left, and, despite having signed the treaty with Lugard, the Emir signed another one with the

French! This was to have interesting repercussions.

On November 16th, Lugard's small force was attacked by hostile natives, who shot many poisoned arrows at his troops, before he eventually gave the order to open fire. The attack was beaten off, and thirty or so natives were killed. Lugard was hit by a poisoned arrow which penetrated his pith helmet and stuck in his head. One of his troops wrenched it out, removing a piece of skull with it, and he was then treated with some mysterious substance which acted as an antidote to the poison on the arrow. Miraculously, he survived and they marched on, reaching the Niger River opposite Jebba by mid-January 1895. When the news of the treaty reached Goldie, he sent a telegram saying:

`Bravo Lugard'

The French Government soon got to hear of Lugard's Treaty of Borgu, and, still smarting over his activities in Buganda, accused him of lying, claiming that he had never reached Nikki at all, and had fled when he heard that the French expedition was on its way. Goldie wrote to the London *Times* claiming that the British treaty was in proper form and confirming that it had been signed by the Emir. The French then counter-claimed that Lugard had never even seen the Emir (which, of course, was true), whilst the leader of the French party had seen him, face to face (again, true), and, they added, Lugard had failed to leave any troops at Nikki, whilst the French, having achieved their treaty, had! They claimed therefore that Lugard's treaty was invalid under the terms of the Berlin agreement of 1884 (which required the 'hinterland' to be physically occupied by the representatives of the European Power).

Goldie bore the brunt of the French fury and since the French continued their incursions into what Goldie regarded as his (i.e. British) territory, he told the Foreign Office that he could not hope to fight all the Company's enemies with the revenue which he was allowed to retain under the terms of the Royal Charter. The British Government was unwilling to do more than complain to the French Ambassador in London about his country's activities on the Niger river, and a statement was made in the House of Commons to the effect that French activities in west Africa were placing a great strain on the relations between Britain and France. If the French entered the valley of the Nile (which, of course, was what they were about to do), this would be regarded as an 'unfriendly' act!

Lugard, having left the Niger, arrived back in London in May 1895 to find himself, once again, at the centre of an Anglo-French crisis! Nevertheless, this time he was not regarded by Britain as the 'villain of the piece', and indeed was made a Companion of the Most Honourable Order of the Bath. Both the London *Times* and the *Spectator* complained that this was insufficient honour for some-

one who had achieved so much for the Empire.

By the end of August, Lugard was again asked by the Army when he proposed to return to regimental duty! He didn't reply, but went straight to the Foreign Office to try to clarify his position, and was immediately offered command of troops in Uganda. He refused and said that he would only return there as Governor. He was then offered a post on a Boundary Commission in Northern Rhodesia, but he refused this also. Then Goldie asked him to return to work with him on the Niger. Again Lugard refused.

He was then offered a post with the newly formed 'British West Charterland Company' which had been formed to discover whether or not there were diamonds in the Kalahari desert in the region of Lake Ngami, 'discovered' by Livingstone forty six years previously. This post carried with it a salary of six thousand pounds a year, which the penniless Lugard could not refuse, and he was appointed as the Company's Managing Director. He took with him as his second-in-command, his younger brother, Lieutenant Edward Lugard, also on leave from his regiment in India, and was given a free hand to run the expedition as he saw fit, but he insisted that he would immediately be released from his contract should he be offered a better appointment elsewhere by the British Government.

The territory to which he was going was, by now, a British Protectorate held under the High Commissioner for South Africa. Cecil Rhodes had wanted these lands for a railway to Bulawayo in Rhodesia, and had claimed that when the South Africa Company had been granted its Royal Charter it had been understood that this area was to be included. Local native chieftains did not agree with Rhodes and much disliked being transferred from direct British protection to the somewhat doubtful protection offered by Rhodes and his Company, and some of them had gone to London to protest - an incredible journey for people who had never before left their kraals and never even dreamed of seeing the sea!

The Colonial Secretary had listened sympathetically to their plea and decided to grant Rhodes only a 'corridor' for his railway; the rest of the area to remain a British Protectorate. Rhodes was furious and Lugard - who had cordially disliked Rhodes ever since the Nyasaland Lakes Company incident - was told that he would have to deal directly with him on matters arising from this decision. Before any such confrontation could take place, however, Rhodes was discredited.

Having achieved his Royal Charter, and become Prime Minister of the Cape Colony Parliament, Rhodes had set about trying to persuade Kruger of the Transvaal Republic to enter into some kind of commercial union with the Cape, but Kruger wasn't interested. Even though the Cape Government lent money to the Transvaal's Railway Company to enable it to extend the railway to the ridge of hills to the west of Johannesburg which the Boers called 'Witwatersrand' (The ridge of white waters) and which English speakers had come to call the 'Rand'. At first, the Transvaal Railway Company gave the Cape Government control of freight rates, but in June 1892, it borrowed monies from the financier Rothschild in London to enable it to complete the railway to Delegoa Bay, which would make them independent of the Cape railway system.

Both Rhodes and the British Government had continued to try to come to terms with Kruger, and offered the Transvaal control of Swaziland in exchange for some form of franchise for what the Boers called 'Uitlanders' (aliens) working in the Transvaal. These Uitlanders were mostly British nationals, and were responsible for producing much of the wealth of the Transvaal Republic, but they had no say in matters of taxation or laws which affected them and the Boers, knowing that they were outnumbered by the Uitlanders, realised that, if given the vote, the British would effectively take control of the Transvaal. This of course was unthinkable to the Boers!

Many people - including Rhodes - thought that the re-occupation of the Transvaal was the only answer, and there was talk of an 'Uitlander' rebellion which would give the British an excuse to enter the Transvaal to 'protect' her nationals, but the British Government was uneasy about this proposal, because there were indications that Germany was ready to take sides with the Boers, and the last thing that Britain wanted was a war with Germany!

Oddly enough, not many of the Uitlanders wanted the Transvaal to come back into the Empire, because the British Government had unwelcome ideas about how native labour should be treated. They wanted the Transvaal to remain a separate republic, but run on British lines, similar to those obtaining in the United States of America, but this didn't suit the Empire-building Rhodes, who badly wanted the Transvaal back in the Empire, so he decided to take the matter into his own hands.

Although many of the Uitlanders disliked Rhodes and his policies, they needed his money, and between them they began to plot a 'bloodless' revolution against the lawful Government of the Transvaal, arranging secretly with Rhodes that when the revolution started, he and his South African Company Police would come to the 'rescue' to protect them from the Boers. But Rhodes' right hand man, Doctor Leander Starr Jameson, did not wait for the rebellion to start - he started it!

In 1895, with four hundred and seventy mounted Police, he made a dash from Bechuanaland into the Transvaal, but he and his companions were captured. The British Government denied all knowledge of the raid and might have calmed things down, had not the German Kaiser exacerbated the matters by sending a

telegram to Kruger, congratulating him for 're-establishing peace and maintaining the independence' of his country! In a continued attempt to calm the situation, Jameson was sent back to England, tried, found guilty and put in jail, and Rhodes was forced to resign his premiership of British South Africa.

Lugard - no longer under threat from Rhodes - was able to proceed with his work in the Kalahari Desert. His team included a medical doctor, a sergeant surveyor of the British Royal Engineers and an American mining engineer with the unlikely name of `Colorado Browne`. They sailed for Capetown at the end of February 1896 arriving to find that the `Jameson Raid` had affected everything in South Africa and that there was even talk of war with the Transvaal.

Far to the north, Kitchener, as 'Sirdar' (Military Chief) of the Egyptian army, but acting under orders of the British Government, had marched across the border into the Sudan with the intention of re-claiming it for Egypt. This was to have a considerable 'knock-on' effect throughout the continent.

CHAPTER THIRTY TWO

In 1896 Britain had invaded the Sudan to oust the Khalifa and his supporters, to restore the upper waters of the Nile to Egypt (and therefore in practice, to British control), and to avenge Gordon's death, but for international and diplomatic reasons she needed an excuse for her actions. Had it not been for an Italian bid for a protectorate over Tunisia, the excuse Britain used would not have been forthcoming. It is a strange, involved and complicated story, but worth the telling.

Tunisia in North Africa is only some ninety miles south of the Italian island of Sicily, and the Italians had always seen it as their God-given right to use it as their foothold on the North African coast. However, the French also wanted Tunisia as a naval base to counter British activities in the Mediterranean. After much diplomatic - and not so diplomatic - activity, Germany backed France to Italy's disadvantage, and Tunisia became a French protectorate in 1883.

Italy's national pride was deeply hurt, and she set about trying to find somewhere else in northern Africa from which she could make advances into the continent, to create a protectorate or a colony, which would compensate for the loss of Tunisia. She eventually looked towards the Red Sea for a solution.

During Napier's punitive expedition to Ethiopia in 1867, through which Stanley achieved his first journalistic coup, Prince Kassa of Tigray, a 'province' of Ethiopia, had co-operated with the British invaders, and had taken arms against the Emperor Theodore. After mad Theodore's suicide, the British, having achieved their object, handed over to the Prince all of Napier's surplus armaments before withdrawing. With this military hardware to support him, the

Prince soon became the new Emperor of Ethiopia styling himself 'Yohannes'.

Yohannes set about trying to unify the warring Christian tribes in Ethiopia, who had been fighting one another on and off for centuries. He badly wanted to obtain an outlet to the sea through which he could import arms and ammunition with which to fight the Egyptian armies, which were hoping to extend the Egyptian Empire by capturing Ethiopian territory.

Yohannes beat off numerous attacks, and slaughtered thousands of Egyptians until the situation changed in 1882, when the British virtually took control of Egyptian affairs. In 1884 Yohannes entered into a treaty with the British, and agreed with them to take action against the common enemy - the Mahdi. By this treaty, Yohannes promised to stop all slave trading in his territory and, in exchange, was assured of free transit of arms and equipment through the port of Massawa on the Red Sea. It seems that the agreement did not envisage a change of ownership of Massawa which was, in any case, technically still part of the crumbling Ottoman Empire - as was Egypt itself, but in 1885 in the face of a Mahdist attack, Britain made Egypt abandon Massawa.

Emperor Yohannes

Yohannes saw this as his chance to occupy Massawa and gain his much longed-for access to the Red Sea, but he didn't know that Britain had done a secret deal with the Italians offering them Massawa rather than leaving it unoccupied with the danger of it falling into the hands of the French who were already active in the area.

The Italians were either unaware of the arrangement with Yohannes, or ignored it, and Yohannes' precious Red Sea access was closed to him. In 1885 the Italians occupied the port hoping to use it as a bridgehead for an advance into the horn of Africa. (It was during this campaign in 1888 that Lugard had attempted to find employment as a soldier with the Italian armies).

The Italian invasion was fiercely resisted by the Emperor of Ethiopia who wanted to retain what he saw as his "right" to the port of Massawa, and the Italians would certainly have been driven into the sea by the Ethiopians had not Emperor Yohannes been killed by the Mahdists who had invaded Ethiopia from the west. The Italians stayed, and in 1889, Italy entered into a treaty with Menelik, the new Ethiopian Emperor. Menelik agreed to give the Italians a small area of his country in return for a supply of modern rifles with which to fight the invading Mahdist armies, but Italy, believing that Menelik was now totally dependent upon them, soon claimed a protectorate over the whole of Ethiopia and not just over the area given to them under the treaty of 1889. They also laid claim to the town of Kassala which commanded one of the main tributaries of the Nile. Britain was not happy with this, still fearing the presence of another European power in the Nile basin, and she tried to get Italy to agree to limit her sphere of influence in this region, but failed.

Menelik disputed the Italian protectorate, and was backed in his opposition by the French and the Russians who supplied the Ethiopians with arms and ammunition to use against the Italians who had decided to fight for their right to control Ethiopia. The Italians were soundly beaten on many fronts and the Mahdists formed a temporary alliance with Menelik and attacked Italian positions from the west.

Italy then asked for - but was refused - British help, and in January 1896, Kassala which had been occupied by the Italians in 1894, was under attack by the Mahdists. Again Italy asked for Britain to help, but again Britain was not inclined to come to the rescue. Italy had occupied Kassala without consulting Britain and rather against British interests and it did not much matter to Britain if Kassala fell to the Mahdists. As and when Britain and Egypt regained the Sudan, they would soon recapture the place. In the meantime the Mahdists were conveniently keeping Italy occupied, and preventing her from making further advances into the Nile basin.

However In 1896 after the Italians had suffered a humiliating defeat by the Ethiopians at a place called Adua, where over seven thousand Italians died, the German Kaiser played his hand. He told Britain that he detected a Franco/ Russian plot to undermine the British Empire, and suggested that Britain would be well advised to go to Italy's help after all.

At first Britain still resisted, but then realised that this was an ideal opportunity to be seen by the rest of Europe to be helping Italy - whilst in fact re-invading the Sudan for her own ends. In the spring of 1896, British and Egyptian forces marched on Dongola (now Dunqulah) - a small town on the Nile to the north of Khartoum - to create a diversion; designed to relieve pressure on Kassala by the Mahdist forces.

In March 1897, a French mission was sent to the Emperor of Ethiopia urging him to push forward his boundaries to the right bank of the Nile at Fashoda. The French encouraged the Emperor by telling him that they recognised his authority as far as a point one hundred miles up stream (south) of Khartoum, and an Ethiopian force together with some French Nationals set out for Fashoda to establish a bridgehead on the Nile. Because France was busy wooing Russia at the time, the expedition included a Russian from the Legation in Ethiopia.

In anticipation of this expedition, a French Officer, Captain Marchand, had sailed from France for the French Congo in July 1896, where - with eight other Frenchmen, and one hundred and twenty French West African troops - he boarded a steamer (supplied by King Leopold of Belgium). He steamed up the River Congo, intending to go as far as he could by river, and then to cut across land towards Fashoda to meet up with the Ethiopian expedition, and help establish a French bridgehead which would make the British get out of Egypt.

As General Kitchener was requisitioning Mr. Thomas Cook's pleasure steamers at Cairo, to help him get his troops up the Nile, Lugard, at the other end of the continent was getting ready to trek towards David Livingstone's Lake Ngami. He was anxious to make a start, but a rinderpest outbreak which was sweeping through southern Africa, reached Bechuanaland and spoiled his plans by killing off all available trek oxen. The alternatives to oxen were horses, mules or donkeys, but tstse fly affected both horses and mules and donkeys were pitifully slow and Lugard's experiences with donkeys as pack animals on the way to Nikki were still very fresh in his mind. Furthermore, because oxen were the main draught animals in southern Africa, few men had any experience in trekking with donkeys.

He travelled first to Kimberley to get as close as possible to a starting point for his long trek, but here he learned that huge swarms of locusts were destroying all plant life, which would mean that grazing for his donkeys would be minimal. He also learned that the Matabele were doing their best to wipe out the white settlers in the territory which Cecil Rhodes had named 'Rhodesia'. Understandably, poor Lugard was depressed.

The authorities in Mafeking advised him to pack up and go home, but despite his depression, Lugard disregarded them and went ahead buying stores and collecting donkeys. He found it hard to get on with the American Colorado Browne, who accused him, (probably with some justification) of trying to deal with everything himself however trivial, even if it didn't concern him, but despite this clash of personalities, his expedition of ten Europeans, one American, twenty seven Africans, together with twelve horses, one hundred and thirty five donkeys and sixty six mules, marched out of Mafeking towards Ngami on 4th May 1896.

After ten days, four mules, two horses, and three donkeys had died, Colorado Browne overloaded his wagon, and had broken an axle. His driver, fearing retribution, deserted and Lugard could find nobody to take his place. Then Browne himself decided to 'go sick', leaving the exploratory mining expedition without a mining engineer! Lugard cabled his Directors from Gaberone asking for a replacement, but pressed onwards towards Ngami. By mid-June, twenty of the mules and nearly all the horses were dead, but still they trekked onwards and

reached the extraordinary river system surrounding the lake by mid-September.

Lugard surveyed his progress. They had covered six hundred and seventy miles since leaving Mafeking, at first averaging eleven miles a day but of late, not much more than four! Of the sixty six mules, only forty four had survived; thirty three of the donkeys and all but four of the horses had died. (Lugard made an interesting note in his diary observing that he had heard that there was a 'movement' in England for the adoption of 'motor cars' - vehicles which were self-propelled. If such vehicles could be obtained, preferably burning wood as fuel, he said, they would be invaluable in the African Bush!).

General Kitchener

A messenger then arrived bearing a note saying that a replacement mining engineer - this time a German national - had been recruited, and was on his way with another European overseer. Lugard was delighted, so he made a base camp and set off with one companion, a man called Hicks, who had originally obtained a concession from the native chiefs to search for minerals in the Ngami area, but who had sold his concession to the new Company. Hicks fell ill, but Lugard put him in a cart and rode alongside on one of the few remaining horses. By the time they reached the lake, Hicks was clearly seriously ill, and they moved northeastwards to a village where Herr Muller a German trader and his young English companion had set up camp. The Englishman, although without medical qualifications of any kind, was acting as 'doctor' to the local population and Lugard thankfully handed Hicks over to him for care. The next day Lugard tried to meet the local Chief, but he was a Christian convert and he refused to do any work on a Sunday and Lugard simply had to wait until Monday! Then, using Muller as an interpreter, he discussed his problems with the Chief, stressing that his company had come to search for wealth and not to rule. After a great deal of procrastination, the Chief signed a treaty with Lugard - it was dated 26th September 1896 - and promised to keep in touch with him by sending regular messengers to his camp. Lugard, "considerably relieved", set off again, eventually found a site for his headquarters and waited impatiently for the arrival of the German Mining Engineer, without whom he could achieve nothing.

The rinderpest plague reached Ngami in November, and soon pools and dry river beds were full of rotting animal corpses. Two days later the locusts arrived and Lugard's few remaining animals were threatened with starvation since every living green thing for miles was stripped and eaten by the swarm. Lugard's men began to get restless and when one man died, many of the others wanted to go home. It was all horribly reminiscent of Lugard's 'army' at Karonga on Lake Nyassa! By mid-November the rains broke and the wilderness became a garden of wild flowers, but the rains also brought more sickness and death. All the native servants seemed to fall ill at the same time and some of the remaining horses and mules died. Lugard was about to send his brother off to Capetown to buy additional stores, when the long-awaited German engineer and the new overseer arrived. However, the overseer was in a highly nervous state and committed suicide two days later by cutting his own throat!

Despite these misfortunes, the German engineer began prospecting, but then the promised flow of messengers from the friendly Chief stopped. It was just too dangerous. Six had died on the way to Lugard's camp, and one had been eaten by a lion but Lugard managed to maintain contact by sending his own people back to 'civilisation' to collect mail and copies of the *London Times*. These he and his brother read avidly, following the progress of Kitchener in the Sudan, and no doubt wishing that they were there with him instead of being miles from nowhere in the African bush. Meanwhile work continued and Lugard's team built roads and dug wells, but after a while the German engineer declared that most of the rock in the area being of volcanic origin, was not gold-bearing. There was no sign of diamonds.

In August 1897, Lugard and his brother were sitting outside their dining tent waiting for their Sunday lunch, when a white police sergeant arrived bearing a large envelope addressed to Lugard and marked 'SECRET'. It contained a copy of a cable dated 30th July from the Colonial Office to the High Commissioner in Capetown stating that the British Government had decided to raise a force of three thousand men to occupy the hinterland of the Gold Coast and the Niger Territories to stop them falling into the hands of the French. Lugard was offered command of this force at a salary of fifteen hundred pounds a year, the title of Commissioner and Commandant of the Force and the local rank of Lieutenant Colonel. If he accepted the offer, Lugard was to return to England immediately. He required no prompting and soon set out for Capetown with one horse, a mule and two of his 'boys'. When he reached Palapye he cabled his directors for permission to leave the company and - without waiting for a reply - sent another cable to the Colonial Office, accepting the appointment.

He sailed from Capetown on October 6th 1897, and had his first meeting in London on 12th November, when he was instructed to get to West Africa 'at once' because Kitchener's advance into the Sudan, which amongst other things would threaten French ambitions on the Nile seemed to make the British Government now determined to protect their ambitions on the Niger also.

IN MEMORY OF
LORD KITCHENER OF KHARTOUM
SOLDIER STATESMAN AND ADMINISTRATOR

Who answered the call of LORD KITCHENER
FOR HIS KING & COUNTRY

Early in 1897, Goldie's forces had occupied Nupe and Ilorin, but he had been ordered by the Prime Minister in person not to proceed north of Jebba because Britain did not, at that stage want to risk war with France. So long as things were going well in the Sudan, French incursions on the Niger were seen by the Prime Minister as being of secondary importance. However, Chamberlain - the Colonial Secretary - didn't see eye to eye with the Prime Minister, and argued that Britain should make a stand for Imperial Expansion and said that it was 'now, or never'. If France would not negotiate on west Africa, she must yield to strength. Chamberlain won his point, and prepared for a 'counter-offensive' against French incursions into what he regarded as 'British' territory. He was also of the opinion that the Royal Niger Company had had its day, and that Britain should declare a protectorate over the Company's sphere of influence. Cabinet colleagues agreed, and allowed him to establish a military unit which would defend 'British' territory against the French. It was to be called the 'West African Frontier Force' (WAFF) and this was the force which Lugard was to command.

Lugard was delighted, and, with typical energy, set about recruiting men, indenting for stores and arms and ammunition, and, on 27th November 1897, twenty British Officers and forty NCOs sailed for west Africa bound for Lokoja, where they would recruit and train native troops. Lugard selected, and was given as his second-in-command, Colonel Willcocks, under whom he had trained as a transport officer in India in the early 1880s, and on March 12th 1898 (as the Franco/Ethiopian expedition was on its way to the Nile), Lugard and Willcocks boarded the *S.S. Benin* in Liverpool bound for Lagos.

CHAPTER THIRTY THREE

A nglo-French problems in Africa on the Niger, and on the Nile, were having extraordinary repercussions elsewhere. The strength of Russian influence in China was increasingly worrying to Britain, and - after the defeat of the Chinese by the Japanese in the war of 1894/5 Russia had been instrumental in persuading Japan to give back some Chinese territory captured during that war. France also was gaining in strength in China, and both nations looked as if they could - and might - close the "Chinese Door" to British trade.

Early in 1898, the British Prime Minister, fearful that Russia might push Britain out of China altogether, tried to bargain with the Tsar, and said that if Russia would recognise the British position in China and in Egypt, Britain would respect Russian ambitions in Northern China and elsewhere, but the Tsar rejected the suggestion.

As a result, Britain decided that she must strengthen the position of Hong Kong, her main toe-hold on the South China coast, and in June 1898, a convention was signed in Peking, leasing an area from the north of Kowloon to the banks of the Shum Chun river, together with two hundred and thirty five outlying islands for a period of ninety nine years. This move was directed against Russia and France, and not against China, whose warships were still permitted by the terms of the convention to use the wharf at British owned Kowloon. The newly leased land was known as the 'New Territories'.

Lugard and Willcocks reached Lokoja on 16th April 1898, where the men of the 1st Battalion West African Frontier Force, by now one thousand and seventy strong, were paraded for Lugard's inspection. Lugard immediately began to occupy as much territory as possible without actually going to war against France, but a number of highly dangerous confrontations took place.

On the 5th May 1898, troops under the command of Colonel Willcocks had occupied a village and had raised the Union Flag, when a French NCO with twelve Senegalese soldiers appeared on the scene carrying the French tricolor. The NCO politely saluted the British Flag and Willcocks and his men duly returned the compliment and saluted the tricolor, after which exchange of courtesies, the French NCO told Willcocks that he was in 'French' territory and invited him to leave at once. Willcocks politely declined and told the French NCO, that, he was mistaken, and that he and his men were in British territory.

Neither side would budge, and Willcocks was preparing to prove his point by force, when he received a very civil letter from the French Commandant of the area asking for a week's grace to allow him to seek instructions from his HQ. Willcocks welcomed the suggestion, and took the opportunity of seeking instructions from Lugard, who was at that time, in Jebba.

The French used the week to bring up reinforcements, and the British used it to prepare for a fight, digging trenches, and throwing up a palisade around their camp, but before matters could develop further, a message reached the French saying that a convention had been signed by Britain and France and that no further action should be taken against the British forces. A major war between Britain and France had narrowly been averted.

Lugard was soon to discover that the British had decided to come to terms with France over the Niger before Khartoum on the Nile was recaptured - after which negotiations would become impossible - so a 'Niger Convention' was signed on 14th June 1898, whereby the French gained access to the navigable part of the river Niger, and retained the disputed area around Nikki, whilst Borgu was equally divided between Britain and France (without, of course, any consultation with the peoples of the area). Finally, France reluctantly agreed to Britain's claim to the Sultanate of Sokoto, far to the north. The treaty had not immediately been ratified however, because the French still hoped that events on the Nile would tip the balance in their favour.

The Franco/Ethiopian expedition reached the junction of the Nile and the Sawba rivers by the end of June 1898, fully expecting to meet Marchand there, but he had not arrived. (They were not to know it, of course, but Marchand and his men had experienced great difficulty, dragging a collapsible boat across the land to the Bahr-el-Ghazal, where they had re-assembled it, and were still sailing downstream towards Fashoda.) The expedition from Ethiopia was exhausted by the intense heat and weakened by fever, and only the Russian representative had enough strength to wade to a small island in mid-stream to plant a tricolor on the

Nile, and claim it for France. Having done this, the expedition retreated, and returned to Addis Ababa.

Marchard and his men eventually reached Fashoda in July, after a hair-raising journey of two thousand five hundred miles, and awaited the arrival of the expedition from Ethiopia, not knowing, of course, that it had come and gone!

Meanwhile, Kitchener's forces were driving forwards and, by 1st September 1898, were close enough to Khartoum for them to open fire on the eighty foot high dome of the Mahdi's tomb which the Khalifa had built at Omdurman. On 2nd September, the Dervish forces advanced on British positions and fought with fanatical bravery with sword and lance against artillery, machine guns and repeating rifles. Some eleven thousand Dervishes were killed at the Battle of Omdurman and Kitchener's forces lost three hundred and eighty six. Winston Churchill, who took part in a cavalry charge said later that this was the *"most signal triumph ever gained by the arms of science over barbarians"*.

Almost immediately after the battle, Kitchener was told that Marchand and his men had reached Fashoda and he steamed upstream to meet them. They met with great courtesy on 19th September but both leaders knew that - once again - their meeting could precipitate a full scale European war between France and Britain.

The Battle of Omdurman

When news of the encounter reached London, Britain immediately demanded that the French should withdraw, but the French refused and for about six weeks, the British, French, and Egyptian flags flew over Fashoda. There was furious negotiation between London and Paris as outright war drew nearer, but then Marchand - who had no means of knowing what was going on in Paris - decided that the situation was hopeless, and at the end of October voluntarily left Fashoda, whereupon the French case collapsed.

Bickering continued between London and Paris, but at last, on 21st March 1899, an Anglo/French Declaration spelled out the agreed spheres of influence of the two powers in Africa. France was to keep the central Sudan - from Darfur in the east, to Lake Chad in the west - but she would finally and entirely be excluded from the Nile basin. The Niger Convention was ratified on June 13th 1899, and arguments over the Nile and the Niger finally ended. But although peace had 'broken out' on the Niger and Nile, there was more trouble brewing for Great Britain at the southern end of the continent.

For the three years after the abortive 'Jameson Raid', bitter negotiations had taken place between Britain and the Transvaal but to no avail, and in April 1899 a petition, signed by twenty thousand 'Uitlanders' arrived at No.10, Downing Street. This was followed by a dispatch from the High Commissioner in Cape-town, claiming that the treatment of British Citizens by the Boers in the Trans-vaal was undermining the influence and reputation of British peoples in the rest of Africa.

The British Government was in a dilemma. It did not want to go to war against Kruger and his Boers, but saw little alternative, and an ultimatum was drafted demanding the repeal of all legislation in the Transvaal which imposed disabili-ties on aliens living and working in the Republic, insisting that all Uitlanders be given the rights and privileges which were open to them in 1881 and demanding equality for all white races in the Transvaal. The ultimatum was never sent, be-cause Kruger sent his own ultimatum to Britain on October 9th demanding the withdrawal of all British troops from the borders of the Republic.

This ultimatum was rejected by Britain, and - three days later - British troops moved across the borders into the Transvaal, and the second Boer war had be-gun.

CHAPTER THIRTY FOUR

After the signing of the Niger Convention, Lugard left Willcocks temporarily in command and went to London to recruit additional officers for the Frontier Force. When he got home he was told that, when the treaty was ratified, Britain intended to buy out the Royal Niger Company from Goldie, and to turn the areas controlled by the Company into 'Protectorates'. Lugard was offered - and immediately accepted the post of Governor or High Commissioner of this new Protectorate.

Lugard learned that it was proposed that the remaining 'British Niger' territories would be divided into three administrative areas, each under the control of the Colonial Office instead of the Foreign Office. (The Niger Coast Protectorate had alredy been transferred from Foreign Office to Colonial Office control in April 1899). This Protectorate was to be amalgamated with former Royal Niger Company territory as far North as Idah, and made into an entirely new Protectorate. Lagos was to remain as a Crown Colony, and another new Protectorate would be formed to absorb all the remaining territory bounded by the Anglo-French Convention of 1898.

There was much debate about a suitable name for the new territoty, which Lugard wanted to call 'Niger Sudan'. Somebody proposed that it should be called 'Goldesia' in honour and recognition of Goldie's role in developing the area, but this didn't suit Goldie who regarded Rhodes - and Rhodesia - as being somewhat 'vulgar'. In the end it was Flora Shaw of the *London Times* who proposed the name of 'Nigeria'. The two new territories would be called the Protectorates of Northern and Southern Nigeria respectively.

After the Fashoda incident and the ratification of the Niger Convention, and after the necessary legislation in the House of Commons, Lugard's name was submitted to the Queen on December 1st 1899 seeking her approval for his appointment as 'High Commissioner for Northern Nigeria' and he sailed for Lagos on 4th December, 1899, arriving at Lokoja on the 31st December, formally taking over the new Protectorate on January 1st 1900.

He set about the administration of his territory with his usual verve and enthusiasm and attention to detail, but faced many problems, including the fact that many young British officers in the Frontier Force wanted to leave and go and join in what they saw as the 'fun' in South Africa, where the opening battles of the Boer war were being fought. Some indeed went, but others were persuaded to stay and help Lugard settle his new territory by means of 'Indirect Rule', whereby existing native rulers were, in effect, used as 'agents' of the British Administration.

In 1901, Lugard was made a Knight Commander of the Most Distinguished Order of St Michael and St George (KCMG), but his work in Northern Nigeria continued. One of his major problems concerned slavery, because slave trading between the various Emirates seemed to be endemic, and played an important part in the economics of the region. Lugard discovered that the majority of slaves were not badly treated, and he realised that to abolish slavery by the stroke of a pen would bring about chaos. However, Sir Frederick - as we must now call him - was determined eventually to stamp out the evil trade, and he ruled that, after 1st April, 1901 no new slaves could be taken, and that slave-owners could no longer force slaves to remain in their service against their will. His ruling did not meet with widespread approval, and one Emir is reported as having said that Lugard might just as well try to stop a cat from catching mice and, he added, he would 'die with a slave in his mouth'. It is noteworthy that many slaves, occupying positions of high authority, chose to stay with their 'masters', and that Lugard was clearly fighting an uphill battle by attempting to apply European standards to an African culture.

The emblems of British Northern Nigeria

Having established a new 'Capital' of the Protectorate at Zungeru, Lugard went on leave to England, where he proposed marriage to and was accepted by Flora Shaw, who, after having been questioned by Parliament about an alleged pre-knowledge of the Jameson Raid (she was a staunch supporter of Rhodes and his ideals of Empire), had been to the Klondike to report for her newspaper on the gold rush.

Miss Shaw, who always travelled in the dress of an English lady of the period, had spent much of her intervening time in the `Klondike`, sleeping rough on the floors of log cabins, travelling on the river on rafts, and in canoes and, as a result, her health began to suffer. By 1900 she could no longer work full time for her newspaper, and in 1902, Sir Frederick took special leave and they went to Madeira, where they were married. After their honeymoon they went back together to Northern Nigeria, where Lady Lugard soon became bored. Instead of being a busy newspaper reporter in her own right, the role of wife of a busy Government Official who spent most of his time away from her side did not suit her. The hot and humid climate of Zungeru didn't suit her either and her health and spirits began to suffer. When she contracted malaria, the Government doctor finally ordered her to go home to England, and by 1903, Sir Frederick was once again alone in Africa, busily conducting and directing campaigns to pacify and control the two most northerly Emirates of Kano and Sokoto.

Lugard had never liked what he saw as 'interference' from others and he was almost always at odds with the Colonial Office back in London. In 1904 he proposed a system whereby a new department of the Colonial office should be created, under the control of an experienced Permanent Secretary, in which he, Lugard, and presumably, other Colonial Governors would work for six months of the year, whilst spending the other six months in 'their' territory. There was, of course, much self-interest in this proposal since, if approved, it would allow him to spend some of his time with Flora, without subjecting her to the climate of West Africa, but his scheme was finally rejected in March 1906.

In May 1906, Lady Lugard was staying as a guest of the Duke of Marlborough at Blenheim Palace, where she met Winston Churchill, who, having resigned his commission in the Army to become a 'War Correspondent' for the *Morning Post*, had been captured by the Boers, had escaped, and returned to England to enter politics. When Lady Lugard met him, he was Under Secretary of State for the Colonies in the Liberal Government, then in power.

Together, Flora and Winston discussed Nigeria, and Churchill although expressing admiration for her remarkable husband told Flora that he thought that Sir Frederick had gone too far, too fast. Churchill was opposed to the sort of punitive expeditions which Lugard was sending to various trouble spots, and said that, in his opinion, the Frontier Force should now be disbanded and that the

greater part of Northern Nigeria be abandoned because it was too large a territory to be governable.

It is recorded that Lady Lugard and Churchill argued 'furiously', and, exposed to the fury of a woman whose dear husband was being scorned, Churchill retreated and promised to talk things over with Sir Frederick when next he was on leave in England.

Churchill went to stay with the Lugards at their home in Abinger when Sir Frederick was next in England, but although the meeting was marginally successful, Lugard realised that he would never get his own way. If he continued to serve in Northern Nigeria he would inevitably be almost permantently separated from his beloved wife Flora, so after much thought, in July 1906, he tendered his resignation.

The Lugards languished at home in England, and were unemployed for some time. They endured this enforced idleness with impatience, but it at least gave them time for reflection.

In March 1906 - just before Lugard's resignation - the British Government had published a 'Blue Book' which proudly showed that the British Empire, its colonies, Protectorates and Dependencies, now occupied one fifth of the world's land surface and that no less then four hundred million people lived in comparative peace and prosperity, under the British Flag. Sir Frederick must have read these statistics with some personal satisfaction. Nyasaland (now Malawi) was now a Crown Colony. (It will be remembered, that in 1859, after the failure of the Zambesi expedition, Livingstone had proposed that the area be 'colonised'. In 1887, after his private 'war' against the Arab Slave Traders, Lugard had himself urged that the region be made a British Protectorate. It was in fact given this status in 1891, and was only declared to be a British Colony in 1895.)

Kenya, where Lugard's adventures on behalf of the `Imperial British East African Company` started, was now firmly under British control (although it did not become a Crown Colony until 1920), and Uganda where he had fought against fearful odds in 1892, was declared to be a British Protectorate in 1896.

In 1907, Sir Frederick was offered the post of Governor to Hong Kong, and in mid 1907 the ship carrying the new Governor and his lady, steamed slowly through the Tathong Channel, through the Lei Yue Mun gap into Hong Kong harbour, which had become British Territory as a result of the Opium Wars.

His Excellency the Governor, wearing his richly plumed hat and his Colonial Service Uniform (which he called his 'armour'), was greeted by a salute of seventeen guns. All the ships in the harbour were dressed overall, and it was a

scene of Colonial splendour at its best, but as the new Governor stepped ashore, it is unlikely that anyone gave a thought to the extraordinary chain of events which had brought him to Hong Kong.

Few people present, almost certainly including Sir Frederick, had ever heard of the Reverend Doctor Karl Gutzlaff, but even if some had, it is doubtful if they realised that, without Gutzlaff's influence and example, David Livingstone might never have become a medical missionary in Africa and that had Livingstone not seen the Zambesi as 'God's Highway', Lugard might never have gone to Africa at all.

And so this strange 'circular' story of African adventure almost ends as it started, in China, but we must complete the 'African' side of the tale. Lugard's Governorship of Hong Kong was not a success, and he found his suave Colonial Civil Servants difficult to deal with, having previously only experienced the more rugged attitudes of fellow Army officers. He tended to despise them, privately calling them 'The Twice Born' and he continuously fell out with them and with the Colonial Office in London.

In August 1911, he received a private letter from London telling him that for economic reasons, the British Government was anxious to amalgamate the two West African Protectorates of Southern and Northern Nigeria and to place them

Lugard lays the foundation stone for a
Hong Kong University

under one Administration. The Governor of the unified 'Nigeria' would have three Deputies, one in the Region to the east of the Niger, one to the west of the Niger and one in Lugard's own 'Northern Region'. Sir Frederick was told that he was the only man for the job and, although he knew that Flora could not come back to Africa with him, he accepted the appointment and thankfully left Hong Kong in April 1912.

The two protectorates were amalgamated on 1st January 1914, and although Lugard was only carrying out the orders of the British Government, he is usually blamed for what has come to be called 'the mistake of 1914' which, many claim, is directly responsible for Nigeria's current problems.

Sir Frederick who retired from Nigeria in 1918, was raised to the Peerage on 1st January 1928. Flora, his much loved wife and companion did not long enjoy this new status, and died a year later, but Lord Lugard, first Baron Abinger, lived on until just before the end of the Second World War and died on April 11th 1945 at the age of 87.

With his death, one might be forgiven for supposing that the final curtain fell on this remarkable story, but in history, there are no final curtains. The drama in Africa and China 'bideford to s will continue long after the roles played by the original characters have been forgotten.

◙ END ◙

BIBLIOGRAPHY

BROWNE, G. History of the British & Foreign Bible Society.

BURTON, Charles. An Anecdotal History of Old Times in Singapore 1819 -1867. University of Malaya Press 1965.

CAMERON, V. L. Across Africa, 1877.

CANTON, W. History of the British & Foreign Bible Society.

COLLIS, Maurice. Foreign Mud. Faber&Faber, 1946.

CROWDER, Michael. The Story of Nigeria, Faber & Faber Ltd., 1962

GRIFFITHS, Sir Percival. A Licence to Trade - A History of the English Chartered Companies. Ernest Benn Limited, London 1974.

HALL, Richard. Stanley, An Adventurer Explored. Collins, 1974.

HARMAN, Nicholas. Bwana Stokesi. Jonathan Cape, London, 1986.

HUXLEY, Elspeth. Livingstone and his African Journeys.

JEAL, Tim Livingstone. Heinemann Ltd., 1973.

LIEBOWITZ, Daniel The Physician and the Trade. 1998, W. H. Freeman and Company

MILLER, Charles. The Lunatic Express. 1972, Macdonald, London.

MOORHEAD, Alan. The White Nile. Hamish Hamilton, 1962. The Blue Nile. Hamish Hamilton, 1962.

PAKENHAM, Thomas. The Scramble for Africa. George Weidenfeld & Nicholson, 1991.

PERHAM, M. Lugard, The Years of Adventure 1886 -1898, ????, 1956. Lugard, The Years of Authority 1898 -1945,????, 1960.

ROBINSON, CALLAGHER & DENNY. Africa and the Victorians. St Martin's Press, 1961. Anchor Books edition: 1968.

WALLIS, J.P.P. (edited) The Zambesi Expedition of David Livingstone, Chatto & Windos Ltd, London. 1956.

- INDEX -

-A-

-B-

-C-

-D-

-E-

-F-

Faloro - 100
Fanti - 127,
Farida (Emins Daughter) - 176
Fashoda - 207, 223, 224, 230-232, 234
Federal Arsenal (Harper's Ferry) - 79
Foreign Office (British Government) - 87, 98, 101, 110, 111, 166, 171, 176, 177, 201, 203, 213, 216, 217, 233
Fort Edward - 193, 194
Fort George - 193
Fort Jesus - 36
Fort St. George - 18
Fort Sumter - 80
Fountains of the Nile - 124
France - 12, 13, 14, 33, 36, 53, 118, 120, 140, 145, 147, 149, 150-152, 157, 201, 203, 205-209, 216, 221, 223, 224, 227, 229, 230, 231, 232
Franco-Ethiopian Expedition - 227, 230
Franco-Prussian War - 120, 157
Frere, Sir Bartle (Governor of Bombay) - 94, 159,172
Futabangi - 188

-G-

Gardner (porter) - 116
Gedge, Ernest – 190
'Geographical Conference' on Central Africa - 146
Gibraltar - 146, 206
Gladstone, William, Prime Minister - 150, 151, 155
God's Highway - 50, 56, 82, 89, 211, 237
Gold Coast (Ghana) - 34, 127, 208, 209, 214, 226
Goldie, George - 208, 209, 213, 216, 217, 227, 233
Gondokoro - 100, 133
Gordon, General. Sir Charles – 131, 133, 147, 149, 153-155, 175, 206, 221
Grant, James Augustus - 99, 100, 114, 130, 132
Great Exhibition, (Crystal Palace) 1861 - 59, 92
Gutzlaff, Karl - 19, 21, 22, 28, 29, 30, 237

-H-

-I-

-J-

-K-

-N-

-O-

-P-

-Q-

-R-

-S-

ABOUT THE AUTHOR

John Downes was born in Plymouth in 1925. His family left Devonshire in 1930, and he was not to return until after the war in 1947 when, having completed a training course in practical agriculture, he worked briefly for the Ministry of Agriculture in North Devon.

He married Mary in 1947, and in 1953 they moved to Northern Nigeria where he worked in a post designed to bring modern agricultural techniques to the region's farmers, before being transferred to an administrative position and posted to Hong Kong. He returned to Devonshire in 1971, where he rekindled his interest in Devonshire culture and rural pursuits, and in 1998 his book *'The Dictionary of Devon Dialect'* was published.

His other books include `*Granfer's Bible Stories*` (2005).

He was widowed in 2002, and has two children: Jonathan (born 1959) and Richard (born 1963), and four grandchildren.

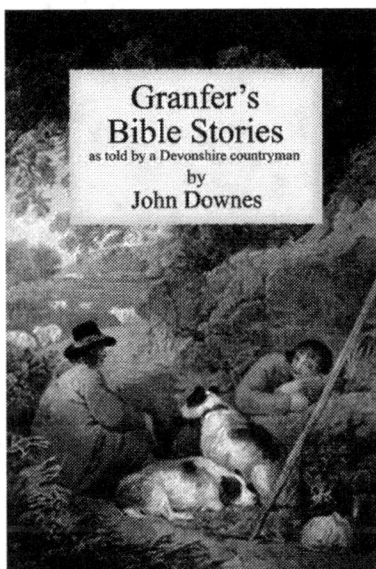